ice bird

By the same author
The Ship Would Not Travel Due West
Dreamers of the Day
Daughters of the Wind
Children of Three Oceans
We, The Navigators
From Maui to Cook
The Voyaging Stars
Voyage to the Ice
The Maori
Icebound in Antarctica
Shapes on the Wind

ice bird

**The classic story of the first
single-handed voyage to Antarctica**

DAVID LEWIS

Adlard Coles Nautical
London

This edition published 2002 by Adlard Coles Nautical
An imprint of A&C Black Publishers Ltd.
37 Soho Square, London W1D 3QZ
www.adlardcoles.co.uk

First published in Great Britain 1975
By William Collins Sons & Co Ltd
This edition published 2002 by Adlard Coles Nautical in the UK
And by Sheridan House Inc. in the USA

ISBN 0–7136–6411–8

A CIP catalog record for this book is available from the British Library.

Printed in Australia.

Contents

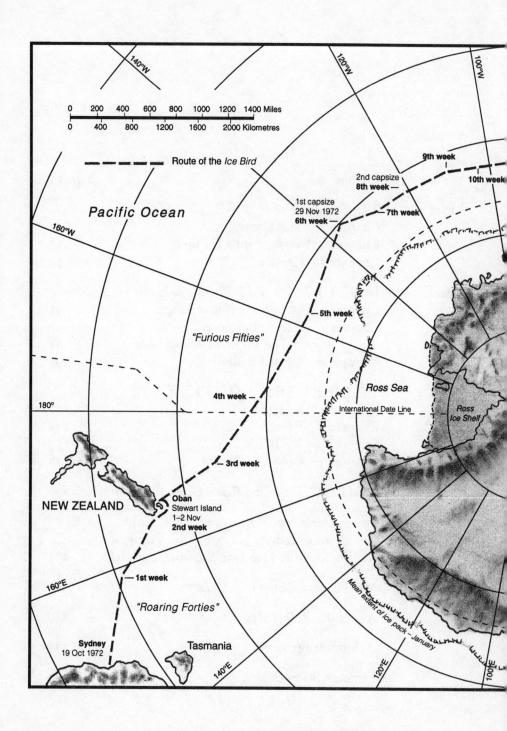

0 200 400 600 800 1000 1200 1400 Miles

0 400 800 1200 1600 2000 Kilometres

140°W

120°W

100°W

160°W

Route of the *Ice Bird*

Pacific Ocean

9th week

10th week

2nd capsize
8th week —

1st capsize
29 Nov 1972
6th week —

7th week —

— 5th week

"Furious Fifties"

Ross Sea

180°

4th week —

International Date Line

Ross
Ice Shelf

— 3rd week

NEW ZEALAND

Oban
Stewart Island
1–2 Nov
2nd week

160°E

— 1st week

"Roaring Forties"

Mean extent of ice pack – January

Sydney
19 Oct 1972

Tasmania

140°E

120°E

100°E

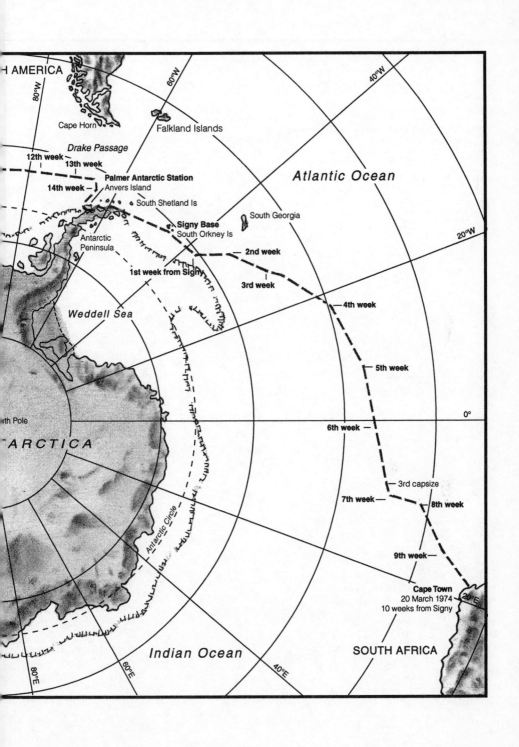

To Barry, my son, who took over
the adventure

My grateful acknowledgements to those
who so kindly helped me in this
venture will be found on page 221.

Parts of Yacht Shown in Diagram

1 Complicated mechanism of self-steering gear
2 Under-water lever of self steering gear
3 Stern railing
4 Main sheet
5 Tiller (inside cockpit)
6 Cockpit (cutaway view)
7 Headsail sheet winch
8 Washboards reinforced with steel partially closing entrance to cabin
9 Pram hood frame
10 Perspex dome incorporated in hatch
11 Companionway hatch (main hatch)
12 Headsail sheet passing from sail through fairlead on deck to sheet winch
13 Rigging screws (bottle screws; turnbuckles)
14 Pulpit or forward railing
15 Fore hatch
16 Gooseneck fitting, the swivelling attachment of boom to mast
17 Steel shutters covering windows
18 Stanchions and wire rails
19 Companion ladder down into cabin (cutaway view)
20 Engine (cutaway view)
21 Propeller
22 Rudder

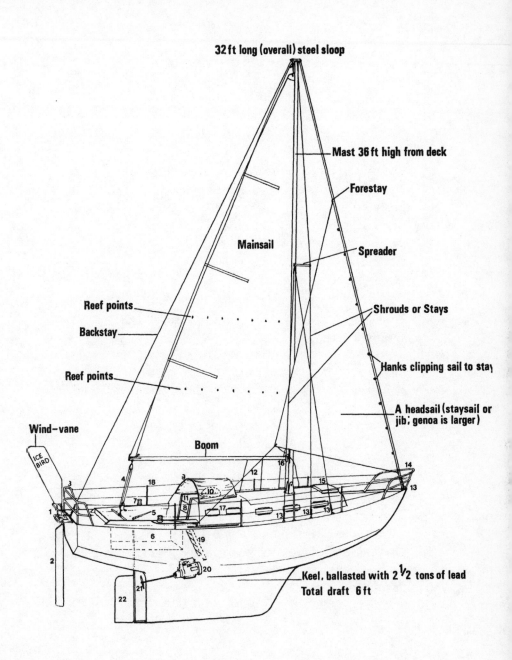

32 ft long (overall) steel sloop

Mast 36 ft high from deck

Forestay

Mainsail

Spreader

Reef points

Backstay

Shrouds or Stays

Reef points

Hanks clipping sail to stay

A headsail (staysail or jib; genoa is larger)

Wind–vane

Boom

ICE BIRD

Keel, ballasted with 2 ½ tons of lead
Total draft 6 ft

Preface

I should introduce myself. The other main protagonists in this story, the yacht *Ice Bird* and my son Barry, come into it a little later. I am a fifty-four-year-old New Zealander of Welsh and Irish descent (I did claim only to be forty-nine until the *Sydney Morning Herald* looked up my birth date). I practised medicine in East Ham in London for eighteen years. How did I come to be outward bound upon such a voyage as this?

As a boy and young man I was painfully shy but I was also adventurous in the sense of needing to come to grips with nature. I cared little for organized games, which I found oppressive and restricting in a land full of forests, mountains and wild rivers. At seventeen I celebrated my last days at boarding school by building a canoe and informing the headmaster that I was going home in it at the end of term – 450 miles across New Zealand by river, portage, lake and sea coast. His prompt veto was undermined by my parents' written permission. At what cost to their peace of mind, since I was an only child, I only realized after becoming a parent myself. Since no one else would come with me I set out alone.

It was on this trip that I first experienced the fulfilment of enforced self-reliance in struggling towards a goal. There were times, like a capsize in the icy Tongariro River – that had only once before been shot – when I came close to losing heart. To haul the light craft on long portages I constructed a trailer with bicycle wheels. Anticipating frequent wettings, I carried no blankets and slept wrapped in a ground sheet. But when I did reach my home in Auckland I had an empty feeling, as if an essential ingredient of endeavour were missing – left behind somewhere in the rapids of the Tongariro.

I rediscovered it while taking part in the ascent of nineteen unclimbed peaks in the South Island, where I went to medical school. (One of these mountains I called Mt Carinna, after my mother.) But then followed a period at Leeds Medical School in England and, after qualification, the tail end of World War II and adventure, as a parachute medical officer, of a much less pleasant sort. Indeed, the war convinced me of the need for socially useful activities; so, after a period in the West Indies, I settled down to a practice in East Ham, where I did my best to put aside thoughts of free winds and open spaces.

Yet even here restlessness intruded from time to time; lying in bed on foggy nights I could not sleep for the hooting of ships' sirens that came clear across two miles of sooty roof tops, through the frosty air. I tried to ignore the message that the sea was there waiting, still untamed and free and aloof as it had always been; still beautiful and terrible in its impersonal anger. I made tentative approaches to the sea – like sailing a dinghy that I built myself, and a twenty-seven-foot, sixty-year-old barge yacht in which I became acquainted with most of the sandbanks of the Thames Estuary. In general, however, I did succeed in overcoming these irresponsible longings.

Then the breakup of my first marriage and the unhappy consequences for my children, Anna and Barry, forced me into critical self-examination and, among the conclusions I could not but accept, was the belated realization that the link connecting that first canoe, through mountain and forest to the old barge, was in fact the very essence of my character. I thereupon bought a pair of climbing boots and a ship's lifeboat. I had become embroiled in a love affair – with the sea. (Women and the sea have much in common, of course: both are subject to unpredictable change – and would be boring if they were not.) The particular challenge that fascinated but also appalled me with its difficulty was the first single-handed transatlantic race of 1960.

Ultimately I sold the lifeboat, bought the twenty-five-foot *Cardinal Vertue* with the aid of a bank loan, and made New York in fifty-four solitary days to come third behind Francis Chichester and Hasler. The story is told in my first book, *The Ship Would Not*

Travel Due West. I had begun to realize another cherished ambition, to write.

After this it was inevitable, I suppose, that the call of distant seas should become irresistible. *Rehu Moana*, probably the most seaworthy catamaran ever designed, was built at the cost of all my savings. A trip to the Arctic Circle north-east of Iceland tested her well. Then my new wife and I sold our home and set out with Susie, aged two, and one-year-old Vicky to sail around the world, free from all encumbrances, including a regular income. After the difficult passage of Magellan Strait it became clear that another adult was needed aboard and Priscilla Cairns joined us for the rest of the circumnavigation, which lasted, all told, from 1964 to 1967.

Now a new element entered the equation. Ever since my schooldays in New Zealand and on the Pacific Island of Rarotonga I had been fascinated by the voyages and migrations of the Polynesians who, in mankind's greatest sea epic, colonized the remotest specks of land dotting the Pacific – an ocean so vast that it covers a third of the earth. In an attempt to test how accurate were the old navigator-priests' methods we tried using them on *Rehu Moana* between Tahiti and New Zealand with surprisingly successful results. (See *Daughters of the Wind.*) Some time later on Tonga and on other islands I encountered sailing canoe and cutter captains who still guided their vessels by the traditional star paths, the complex ocean swells and the birds that signpost the way to land. These encounters led ultimately to a four-year Research Fellowship at the Australian National University in Canberra, which involved going to sea as the pupil of the last great pre-instrumental navigators of the world; to be instructed in the secrets that conferred upon them the freedom of the ocean. I was reluctantly forced to replace the faithful *Rehu Moana* with the thirty-nine-foot gaff ketch, *Isbjorn*, because the latter's fifteen-hundred-mile range under power was indispensable for the job in hand. With my son, Barry, added to the ship's company we set out again in 1968 from England for the Pacific.

After the oceanic 'fieldwork' had been completed I retired to Canberra for library research and to write up the results in a book entitled *We, The Navigators.* Unfortunately, my wife and I had separated; and I had the major responsibility for bringing up Susie and Vicky. Meanwhile Barry sailed *Isbjorn* to Tarawa in the Gilbert Islands, where he traded for nearly three years. The sequel we will soon come to, for my story has now caught up with the present.

Part 1

The Last Sea Frontier

Chapter 1

The Dreaming

The personal dreaming of an Australian Aboriginal may be defined as doing that which is nearest to his heart – as fulfilling his own destiny.

> All men dream: but not equally. Those who dream by night in the dusty recesses of their minds wake in the day to find that it was vanity: but the dreamers of the day are dangerous men, for they may act their dreams with open eyes, to make it possible.
>
> T. E. Lawrence, *Seven Pillars of Wisdom*

No one had sailed alone to Antarctica; nor had any relatively small yacht, even with a crew, made the passage. That whole white continent lay virgin, entrenched behind pack and berg and the furious storms of the 'screaming sixties'. I had long been obsessed with the fascination of the frozen Southern continent; to reach it, relying entirely upon my own resources, was to accept the ultimate challenge of the sea.

Certainly others would follow who would make much faster voyages or command smaller or perhaps more efficient vessels. But for me, the chosen role would be that of a trail blazer. There was an aspect of internal discovery, too. In confronting Antarctica alone, I should learn to know myself as I really was, for I would be deprived of all outside support; there would be nobody to lean upon. I would find out what manner of man remained after the familiar supports of society had been stripped away – would there be a worthwhile man there at all? Such was my personal dreaming.

When I heard that my thirty-nine-foot yacht *Isbjorn*, long prepared for this voyage at the cost of years of skimping and saving and heavy labour, had been lost, I was glad. Such an anomalous reaction seems odd indeed. This is the explanation: my son, Barry, had been making *Isbjorn* ready for the Antarctic voyage. In Tarawa,

Gilbert Islands (an atoll no more than sixty miles from the equator) where he had been operating her as a trading ketch. Ice guards had been fitted round the propellor, collision bulkheads constructed, the rudder strengthened and old spars replaced. There still remained some very important structural alterations that I decided would best be done in Australia.

Now, *Isbjorn* was on her way towards Sydney under Barry's command. By 7 September I was seriously concerned because the ketch was overdue. The telephone rang: a long distance call from Villa, New Hebrides. With enormous relief I recognized Barry's voice over the wire.

'Are you all right, Barry?'

'Yes, everyone is okay, but the *Isbjorn* has sunk. I'm so sorry, David.' All I could feel was thankfulness that he and his companion were safe. Compared with this, the loss of our ketch was nothing.

The story that emerged was one of structural failure in heavy gales. (Why had I decided to postpone those vital alterations until Sydney?) Only by superb seamanship had the young skipper kept *Isbjorn* afloat until he and his companion could be taken off in a freighter.

'For goodness sake, stop blaming yourself,' I told him. The yacht had only been abandoned at the last possible moment. And it had been *my* (mistaken) decision to put off strengthening a bulkhead and the mast supports. 'It would not have helped, to throw away your lives.'

'What will you do now?' Barry asked. A pause, with the silence broken only by the static of the intercontinental radio link . . .

'I'm getting a smaller yacht. A steel one if I can. The trip is still on.'

I hadn't stopped to think. It was as if the decision had been made for me. Now the hugeness of the difficulties to be overcome suddenly became apparent.

'Was *Isbjorn* still insured?' I asked, without much hope.

'The insurance lapsed last week, when we delivered our cargo from the Gilberts. What will you do for money?'

'God knows. I'm negotiating a largish book advance, and – well – I will just have to try to borrow, I guess.'

'See you then; good luck, David.' Barry rang off.

The spring snows had melted from the Brindabella ranges behind the Australian capital city of Canberra and spring blossoms were already breaking out along the streets. In Sydney the first surfers were catching their waves at Bondi, but far to the southward the Antarctic continent remained in the iron grip of winter. The icy fields under the grey half-light were only now attaining their maximum winter limits. The seventh of September. One-and-a-half months to go until I must sail, if I were to be off to the Antarctic Peninsula, six thousand miles east of Australia, in time to take advantage of the December breakup of the pack ice. And I had no boat.

A word about the project and its background will not come amiss here. The plan to visit Antarctica had long been maturing. In fact, I had consulted Sir Vivian Fuchs, head of the British Antarctic Survey, in England, as far back as 1964. I had met him first at an exploration medical conference in London. 'Experts' were talking learnedly about snow glare and protective goggles. Fuchs, fresh from his transantarctic crossing, was asked for his opinion by the chairman.

'Well, actually,' he replied diffidently, 'I went into Woolworths and bought a pair of dark glasses.' I had liked him ever since.

The Antarctic plans that I was considering at that time came to nothing. But I now found myself in Canberra completing a Polynesian navigation study and with six months to spare before starting an investigation into how Aborigines find their way in the central Australian deserts. The moment was, therefore, opportune.

Australia, however, was about the most unsuitable point of departure for the Antarctic that could have been found. The only portion of the Southern continent readily accessible to small craft is the Antarctic Peninsula, from whose western coastline the pack ice recedes during three summer months, close pack ice being quite impenetrable to a yacht. Yet this peninsula projects northwards from the Antarctic Circle opposite South America; so the shortest logical route to Antarctica is from the tip of South America, which involves no more than 450 miles at the most, in unsheltered waters. Australia, on the contrary, is a third of the earth's circumference away from the Antarctic Peninsula and the voyage thither involves traversing six thousand miles of the fearsome Southern Ocean.

The difficulties were formidable indeed. However, certain preparations for the venture were already far advanced. Nautical almanacs, pilot books, British and Chilean charts, the latter by courtesy of the Chilean Embassy, had been acquired.

I had spent some time in Melbourne collecting ice and weather data under the kindly guidance of the Commonwealth Bureau of Meteorology there. Here it became apparent that in working out a preferred course there must be compromise, a juggling of the risks of ice against the dangers of storms. To reach the Antarctic Peninsula at the best time would necessitate leaving Sydney in the latter part of October. The plan that in the event I followed was to head south-east to 60°S., then run my easting down along the 60th parallel, where, according to the pilot charts, there was a good chance of *relatively* weaker but consistent westerlies and minimal ice risks. When north of the Antarctic Peninsula at about 65°W. I would turn due south. Unfortunately this would place me south-east of New Zealand around 60°S. over the Pacific-Antarctic submerged mid-ocean ridge, a notorious zone of converging storm tracks in November, the time of the spring equinoctial gales.

Poring over the Soviet Atlas of Antarctica (*Soviet Geography. Atlas of Antarctica.* 1966, Moscow; 1967, New York, American Geographical Society, 102.) in the Melbourne office, I had noticed that waves over thirty-five feet high were occasionally encountered in this area. Big waves, I thought. But how odd that Russians measured in feet. I looked closer. The wave heights were not in feet at all, they were in metres. Waves *over 105 feet high*. These were monstrous, unthinkable. Small comfort that they were only very rarely encountered. For the next two nights I hardly slept, so vivid and horrifying were the pictures that persistently haunted my mind.

The better part of the clothing and some of the equipment I needed had been amassed before the *Isbjorn* debacle. But gloves were needed and suitable ones were not easy to come by in

Australia – a lack I was later to rue bitterly. The Royal Australian Navy had been doing their best to arrange radio schedules and generally to give me all the help in their power. This was rather limited, through no lack of good will on their part, but because they had no Antarctic facility. They even went to the length of creating a special post for me, that of 'Honorary Liaison Officer', so they could more readily assist me.

Leading experts had recently gathered in Canberra to attend the Scientific Conference on Antarctic Resources and I had been able to renew my acquaintance with Sir Vivian Fuchs and other Polar leaders, notably Phil Smith from Washington. Fuchs generously offered me the hospitality of the British Antarctic Survey bases and it was agreed that my first objective should be the one at Argentine Islands. His parting words were to prove more than a little prophetic.

'If I spot you from *John Biscoe* waving your shirt from an ice floe, I'll assume that your trip isn't going so well,' he laughed. When I next encountered him many months later at an American base forty miles from Argentine Islands his first words were, 'Well, what did I tell you?'

These preparations were on the credit side. The debit was rather more formidable. My sextant, life raft, Avon inflatable boat, navigation tables, the thousand dollar Marconi transmitter and much else besides had gone down with *Isbjorn*.

As well as having no boat, I had no money.

The book contract was not yet signed, and even when it was, the advance would be insufficient to buy a boat, let alone equip it. Moreover, I had grave doubts whether any sane publisher (I so classified Collins) would consider it reasonable to make a substantial advance to an author without a yacht for a book about a yacht expedition to the Antarctic!

To make matters worse, the newspapers and radio commentators had heard of my plans, though they were unaware that *Isbjorn* had sunk. Where was my yacht? How big was it? If the truth be known, I was downright dishonest in some of the things I told those concerned people from the media, and I am ashamed. I would like to take this opportunity of tendering them my apologies. But what else could I have done? I dared not let the fact leak out that at this late stage I had no boat at all. Why, I would be laughed out of Australia.

One of my lies rebounded against me as, indeed, I deserved. When reporters asked me the length of my yacht (which I did not yet possess) I answered according to impulse 'forty feet', 'thirty-five feet', and once, in a moment of aberration, 'twenty feet'. The then Minister of Transport made a statement (perfectly correctly) that such a voyage in a twenty-foot boat would be extremely unwise. Thanking him for his concern I suggested that if he did want to make my trip safer he would induce the Air Force to part with some de-icing fluid. To his credit he complied. The laugh was on me in the end, for by the time the large can of de-icer – and the bill – arrived I had decided to dispense with the fluid and to chip away with an ice axe any ice that should accumulate dangerously on deck and rigging.

Clearly a yacht had to be procured and quickly. I had no idea how to go about finding one but obviously Canberra, a hundred miles from the sea, was no place to try. My possessions, packed in cardboard boxes, were soon distributed among the attics, cellars and cupboards of my long-suffering friends. My daughters, Susie, eleven and Vicky, ten, went to live with their mother.

Into my battered old Morris van went all my worn skivvies and jerseys, my sleeping bag, a sack of paperback books, the charts, my Puma knife, a fork and spoon, a billy, a non-stick saucepan and frying pan and two box files full of photostats of works on ancient voyaging and navigation. Four years of academic life had ended. Now for the future, splendid in hope but deficient in promise. What was in store? The most monumental anticlimax of all time I suspected. I set out, forlorn after an emotional fare-well dinner, and after driving the 180 miles to Sydney, pulled into the yard of my friend Jos Doel's ship's chandlery at Rushcutters Bay at about 2 a.m., where I crawled miserably into the back of the van and went to sleep.

First had come the dream, the imagined goal, the compelling urge that was to lure a very ordinary middle-aged man un-wittingly into a rendezvous with peril in the lonely wastes of the Southern Ocean. But for the moment I had no time to fear icebergs or nightmare waves such as I had read about in Melbourne, for the decision to go, once made, was irrevocable. It was how to translate this particular dream into reality that occupied all my thoughts.

There could be no half measures; the enterprise was going to demand all I had in the way of persistence, courage and skill. I must draw on every last reserve of financial credit too. Everything without stint must be thrown into this venture, else it were better abandoned once and for all. Half measures, like an ill-equipped boat, would be a sure passport to disaster.

The morality of leaving loved and dependent small children or, for that matter, my grown-up son and daughter, Barry and Anna, weighed heavily on my mind. But the decision had already been taken in that split second on the telephone to the New Hebrides. Doubts were firmly pushed into the background to emerge only in the black moods of midnight wakefulness that disrupted every night's exhausted sleep. In the daytime all my powers were bent towards surmounting practical problems.

Singularly unrewarding was the search through Sydney's boatyards and marinas; and beyond, up remote creeks where bellbirds called in the surrounding bush. Stock glass fibre yachts were far too fragile for the job in hand. Nor could I find anything in wood within a possible price range – bearing in mind the need to make major structural modifications to the vulnerable cabin coach roofs that would never withstand a knock down or a capsize. The one steel boat I was cynically offered was a sea-going coffin that had already, Jos's researches revealed, nearly drowned three men. Each succeeding night that I unrolled my sleeping bag in the van found me more tired and depressed.

The search was complicated by doubts as to my ability to pay for the boat when I did find it. My friends racked their brains. Yachting correspondent Sheila Patrick's delightful children, for instance, were full of ideas. Their first suggestions, which might be summed up as 'wealthy widow, rich sponsor', were rejected regretfully on the grounds that we knew none. All their other projects, elaborated enthusiastically, involved midnight raids and disguising the stolen yacht's identity. Sad though it was to dampen such ardour, I had to veto these attractive plans, too.

Then, after nearly a week of fruitless searching, when I was ready to give up, I discovered the ideal ship – *Ice Bird*. She had been lying at the marina right behind Jos's ship's chandlery all along.

Ice Bird was not her name then, but I had decided to call her that before ever I encountered her. The ice bird (Antarctic prion or whale bird) is a small petrel, grey-blue above with white markings and silvery below. It ranges throughout the whole Southern Ocean, skimming the sea surface where it feeds on tiny squid and krill. What more appropriate name for a very small yacht that was also to brave the Southern Ocean (more than that, it was similar enough in sound to be mistaken for *Isbjorn* of unhappy memory: another ambiguity to confuse the media).

Of course, once *Ice Bird* had been found and the deposit paid, all need for secrecy was past and the pressure was taken off the loyal Jos Doel, whose shop was my headquarters. Instead of having to answer an enquirer with, 'He went up the Hawkesbury today', or 'I think he is in Botany Bay', he could admit that I was available. So on the morrow of *Ice Bird*'s discovery no less than four television crews and five reporters had gathered on the marina.

'Aren't you,' Jos said wickedly, as he directed one interviewer to the marina, 'going to take pictures of him with his parrot on his shoulder? He's left it over there.' I have never owned a parrot in my life but Jos possesses a raucous and evil-tempered cockatoo that lives in a cage suspended among festoons of yacht equipment. Nothing could convince the media that the bird was not mine.

'But it isn't mine.'

'Just one loving shot of your shipmate on your shoulder, Doctor Lewis,' the misguided man pleaded.

'Think I want my bloody ear bitten off by that devil!'

'I'll go and get it.' Quite unmoved. He soon returned, to my inexpressible joy wiping blood off his finger.

'Decided it wouldn't photograph all that well,' he muttered.

Ice Bird was designed by Dick Taylor of Sydney and built in 1962 of $\frac{1}{8}$-inch steel throughout – hull, deck, cockpit and cabin coach roof. She is of hard chine (vee bottom) design with a six-foot fin keel, which is ballasted with two and a half tons of lead.

Length overall is 32 feet; beam is 9 feet 6 inches; draft is 6 feet. *Ice Bird* is sloop rigged, implying in England or Australia that she sets a mainsail and but a single headsail (genoa, staysail or jib) at one time – smaller or larger headsails being substituted depending on the strength of the wind. There are two ways of reducing the mainsail's area, or reefing. One is by threading a reefing line through the eyelets in the sail and tying down a reef. The other, quicker but less neat, is by rolling the lower part of the sail around the boom.

The aluminium mast was thirty-six feet high from the deck on which it was stepped. Mast and stainless steel rigging were only one season old at the start of the voyage and both were far stouter than is usual in an ocean racer of this size.

A new 12 h.p. Dolphin petrol motor provides auxiliary power and charges the batteries. Cooking is by a three-burner Primus kerosene pressure stove suspended on gymballs. Electric light is supplemented by a Tilley pressure lantern and a simple wick hurricane lamp. Both burn kerosene. Heating – there is none.

The saloon table can be raised or lowered flush with the bunks. These are on either side and are fitted with canvas lee-boards to hold the occupant in place. I was to find it, as a rule, most comfortable to use the leeward, or down-wind (downhill) one.

Tim Curnow, my literary agent, now announced the good news that the publishers' advance was in. He also made gallant attempts to obtain newspaper sponsorship. In this he was unsuccessful until the very last moment, when Australian rights were taken up for a modest, but welcome, sum. This would be doled out, the newspaper rather cold-bloodedly insisted, in instalments – in case I went missing. My one-time lawyer in England and shipmate to Iceland, Merton Naydler, stepped into the breach by volunteering to lend me the balance of the money I needed: a most generous action since I could give no security at all. My friend, Sue Brierley from Canberra, undertook to sell, after I had sailed, the trusty van in which we had so often taken the children skiing or camping. She actually got $250 for it – a welcome sum that enabled Tim to reduce my overdraft.

The sheer decency of *Ice Bird*'s owner was hard to match, yet typical of the Australians I was beginning to meet.

'I will pay you $8,000 for the yacht if you insist, but I would find it much easier to pay $7,500,' I told him frankly.

He would obviously have preferred the larger sum. 'I'll take the $7,500,' he said.

Innumerable matters had to be seen to: the hull thoroughly inspected on the slipway, the rudder suspension strengthened by an extension from the keel, every dubious wire and rope replaced. An 18-inch diameter clear Perspex dome (rather too small, I found), in turn sheltered by a canvas and celluloid 'pram hood', was fitted over the main hatchway to allow me to see out and steer, from inside the cabin, by lines leading from the tiller round blocks and through holes drilled in the washboards. A canvas dodger was laced round the back and sides of the cockpit. Steel plates ⅛-inch thick were bolted over all the windows, leaving only tiny rims of Perspex showing round the edges. The result was perpetual gloom below and the eventual saving of *Ice Bird* from foundering. Similar steel plates welded over the lower two washboards in the companionway rendered access to the cabin awkward and further accentuated the semi-darkness within. By the same token, they would deny access to a sea sweeping us from astern.

Strong new 11-ounce Terylene sails had to be made. Wires to which I could clip my safety belt were strung along the deck. Battery boxes, floorboards and locker tops were fitted with battens or catches to prevent their coming adrift no matter what buffeting the ship might receive. The very modern Racal SSB radio transmitter, lent to me by its makers, was mounted, tuned, inspected and licensed. I already had a separate transistor receiver and a new-found friend constructed an invaluable small set pre-tuned to WWV, a station that broadcasts the time signals a navigator needs.

The friends who took time off work to help me made up a kind of international team. The young South African yachtsman, Graham Cox, was with me seven days a week, doing everything from welding (I am the most unmechanical of men) to shopping. While a tall American from the Australian National University was fitting a tiller, the long-suffering Tim, considerably exceeding his literary agent's terms of reference, was collecting motor car

tyre fenders and filling cans with petrol and kerosene. Dick
Taylor, the designer, was constantly on board advising on neces-
sary alterations. One morning when the yacht was on the slipway
I emerged from the cabin to find that Graham and an Australian
Antarctic medical researcher had been painting the hull since
5 a.m.

There were so many jobs to be done. I counted eighty-six items
to be bought or attended to on one scribbled list. These ranged
from unshipping the mast, through renewing sea cocks, to buying
a sextant and swinging the compass. Every fitting had to be of the
finest quality, no job could be skimped, for *Ice Bird* must be
watertight above and below. Her deep ballasted keel insured that
she would right herself even in the dreaded event of capsize, but
only provided that her deck, hatches and windows remained intact
to prevent swamping. The little yacht must be able to take a
battering from the sea and ice that no vessel of her size had ever
been asked to withstand before.

Some memories of this period are particularly vivid. The firm
of Marlin were providing me with waterproof clothing, parka and
overtrousers. I had to choose sizes large enough to cover bulky
cold weather gear, so there I was, in a sweltering 33°C. temperature, streaming with sweat and purple in the face, dressed in
sheepskin trousers and a fur coat that a girl had presented me with
in Canberra, trying on oilskins. The amused comments of the
tailoresses did nothing to relieve my incipient heat stroke.

Marlin's also donated a safety harness, perhaps the most important item of equipment for a single-hander. The lone sailor
who goes overboard without clipping himself on is liable to be in a
similar predicament to a man falling from an aircraft without a
parachute. He has more time to contemplate his fate – that is all.
I normally wear my harness day and night, especially in my bunk
at night; for, when wakened by some flogging sail, there is no
inclination to fumble with straps before rushing on deck. And
half asleep, hurried and off balance, a man can readily make that
fatal mis-step, trip and go over the side. Hence my rule. The time
was to come, however, when other dangers loomed so menacingly
that I forgot it entirely.

A telephone call from New Zealand; an old friend was offering me more storm clothing. There really was no end to people's identification with the adventure, so much so that, to avoid boring the reader, I must refer him to the acknowledgements.

Naturally, no enterprise goes altogether smoothly. The local PRO of an emergency raft firm that I had long had dealings with in England had never heard of me and made it abundantly clear that he did not want to either. Nor were some of the yachting bodies, unlike individual members, much concerned since their interests lay in organizing coastal racing in respectable home waters rather than voyages of exploration into the unknown.

The continual necessity of approaching strangers, asking them for favours, explaining what my trip was all about, was rendered more difficult by reason of my shyness. Nor was it easy for me, when asked the purposes of the voyage, to reveal my inner motives, for I find this only possible with specially sympathetic personalities, or on paper to anonymous readers.

The requirement that transoceanic adventurers be morally and physically self-reliant is, to my mind, paramount. When we voluntarily step off the pavements we have no right to expect others to pull us back: we ought to be well enough equipped with know-how, tools and spares to be wholly self-sufficient. Once embarked, we are on our own. In the past I have requested that no search or rescue operations be launched on my behalf and would reiterate the sentiment. (Naturally, once a yachtsman is in mid-ocean, well beyond radio range, he could be anywhere at all; so looking for him would be pointless.)

Rare were the people I met who did not share some of the spirit of this adventure. Time pressed ever more relentlessly. During the last week I was at my wits' end; money had run out and I had as yet no life raft, no provisions at all and our home-made self-steering gear was proving a failure.

Jos called me to the telephone. 'You don't know me. Name of Fox. I'm a racing man and I admire a good sport,' drawled an Australian voice. 'How are you off for food?'

'Got none yet,' I replied wearily.

'Cheer up, she'll come good. I know what, you order up to say $400 worth and charge it to me. Will that be enough?'

'More than enough,' I got out when I had recovered my breath. I stammered my thanks.

Soon, another racehorse owner presented me with a $500 Beaufort life raft (which is now blowing around the world along the sixtieth parallel; its serial number, should any reader happen to come across it, is 3534 and I should be glad to have it back).

By now I was beginning to suspect that it had been one Jack Muir, yachtsman, bookmaker and old friend, who had told these racing people about me in the first place. Sure enough, his modest disclaimers could not long be sustained. I had begun to realize that Australians were sportsmen in the fullest sense of that over-worked word.

One present from the manufacturers I owed to Tim's happily broad interpretation of the job of literary agent. It was to stand me in good stead in dark days to come – two dozen bottles of Red Mill overproof rum.

I chose my provisions with an eye to the realities of single-handed sailing in stormy waters where cooking might often be impossible. The main items were 120 cans of corned beef, 90 pounds of ships biscuits, 25 pounds of margarine, a variety of canned vegetables, fruit and fruit juices, 48 tubes of condensed milk, 28 packets of potato powder, 24 boxes of muesli, 20 pounds of brown sugar, 12 pounds of instant coffee, 13 dozen eggs, 12 pounds of smoked bacon and a like weight of salami, 25 pounds of cheese. There were sultanas, chocolate, peanuts, sweets and so on. Vitamin requirements were adequately catered for by Marmite and a supply of 50 mgm tablets of Vitamin C, one to be taken daily. A fair proportion of my matches were Greenlights, which will strike when wet.

Graham and I were faced with this impressive pile on the marina one evening at dusk.

'It will never stow away,' I exclaimed, appalled.

'You just wait, we will get it in,' Graham assured me.

And stow the lot under the floorboards and in lockers we did – all in two hours. Furthermore, not one hurriedly packed glass jar (as for coffee or pickles) was broken at sea, though I was to regret that we had not replaced cardboard containers, so vulnerable to damp, with wooden boxes. The more perishable items and

a general assortment of foodstuffs designed to last a month were
stowed away in special boxes underneath the saloon table. Before
leaving the yacht that night, I made out a list of where everything
was stored.

The following essentials were also on board by the time I sailed.
Fresh water: 17 gallons in the tank, 17 gallons in plastic containers – 34 gallons in all. Petrol for the motor: 7 gallons in the
tank, 23 gallons in plastic cans in the cockpit or lashed to the
rail – 30 gallons in all. Kerosene for cooking and lighting: 10
gallons.

A wind-operated self-steering arrangement is virtually a must
for a single-hander, for it takes over most of the chore of steering
day and night, without ever tiring, leaving him free for other
tasks. Every type works on the same general principle. A wind-
operated vane is linked indirectly to the rudder (or to a trim tab
on its trailing edge, or to a lever in the water – refinements designed to increase mechanical advantage). The description below
is over-simplified.

The yacht is put on course and the vane allowed to trail freely
with the wind. When it has lined itself up with the wind the vane
and rudder systems are locked together. If the yacht veers off
course the wind impinges on one side of the vane, rotating it.
The connecting mechanism causes the rudder to rotate in the
opposite direction until it has steered the vessel back on course
and the wind pressure on both sides of the vane has equalized.

Only days to go before the time set for departure it became
obvious that our home-made, self-steering system was not going
to work at all and would have to be scrapped. Enquiries revealed
that there was only one solitary suitable commercially manufactured unit in Sydney, a Hasler-Gibbs gear. This is a very efficient
type that gains added power through a lever that is swung over
by water pressure whenever the vane turns. A wild dash across
Sydney in Tim's Mini Moke secured it minutes before the im-
porter closed for the long weekend. Unfortunately the model was
designed for smaller yachts than the *Ice Bird* so its strength was
limited. Never mind: it would do. Graham, sawing away with a
hacksaw and drilling the tough steel by hand, spent all that Friday
mounting it securely on the transom.

Just to prove that sportsmanship is not an Australian monopoly, an American lady, a total stranger but one who loved the Antarctic, came shyly aboard one afternoon and gave me a cheque for this Hasler apparatus.

Susie and Vicky flew down from Canberra for a trial sail and a family weekend. They scuttled about, nosing like terrier puppies into every corner of the yacht. The mooring ropes were slacked away. We were ready to go. The motor kicked once, then stopped. The process was repeated. What could be the matter? For a solid hour and a half I tried everything fruitlessly. Then suddenly I saw what was wrong. Idiot! I had forgotten to remove the protective cap from the exhaust pipe.

My properly chastened mood gradually lifted as we beat up the harbour in sunshine and spray towards the Sydney Heads. Graham was fiddling with the self-steering unit; the girls tended the sheets. Passing out into the Pacific the chop became so steep that we roped the two younger crew members in for safety. Further out it was calmer and Susie wedged herself in the pulpit at the bow, a position she refused to abandon, even when the afternoon grew colder on the homeward leg. Dusk was falling as *Ice Bird* stole silently before the dying breeze into a sandy, bush-fringed cove under the shelter of North Head. Here we anchored. The cabin lights flicked on and soon the smell of frying bacon heralded the close of a very happy day. The trial had gone well with *Ice Bird* handling beautifully.

There was more than enough to be done in getting ready for sea without outside distractions, but there were some things that had to be attended to. For instance, a paper on ancient Polynesian astronomy, that was to be read on my behalf at a Royal Society symposium in London, came back for correction. I did the best I could, huddled in the seclusion of the van, but eventually I had to send it off with apologies, still incomplete.

Regrettably, I was not always so patient. A particularly irritating communication from an armchair critic of my findings on Polynesian navigation was more than I could stand. Shamefully throwing aside all academic restraint, I scrawled 'Bullshit' across the letter and posted it back to its author.

I.B.—C

Drafting a will was another chore that could not be postponed. At first I was unable to take the exercise seriously and left *Ice Bird* to the University 'for navigational experiments on Lake Eyre' (the lake is a vast salt pan – it contains no water). Then more sober second thoughts prevailed: I tore up the paper and wrote a more serious document.

Being so busy, I had ignored a stream of somewhat irrelevant messages from a government department in Melbourne; however, at length, I phoned them collect. Was I acquainted with the provisions of the Antarctic treaty? Yes. A long explanation followed. Blue whales were strictly protected – very strictly, I was informed.

'Do you think,' I asked hesitantly, my mind boggling at the picture of tiny *Ice Bird* at grips with the largest creature the world has ever seen, 'that blue whales would really be in danger from *me*?' A pause, then a grudging admission.

'Well, no, perhaps not.'

Chapter 2
Voyage into Danger

At last came the day of departure. 'Thursday, 19th October, 1972, – Port Jackson towards the Antarctic Peninsula', the log-book opens. 'Towards', never 'to'. No sailor would ever dream of so tempting providence.

Personal goodbyes were submerged in the demands of the public send-off. Sylvia Cook and John Fairfax were there to wish me well. They had recently rowed across the entire Pacific (and borrowed a pilot book from Barry in Tarawa en route). John looked tough enough to have swum the ocean, I thought. There was no one at the marina who was unwelcome: there were too many of them, that was all.

Nor was there any relief when I cast off from the dock and hoisted sail. Two hours were spent tacking down the reaches of Port Jackson – Sydney Harbour – and what with adjusting a self-steering apparatus I did not as yet fully understand, dodging criss-crossing ferry boats and being interviewed by a television crew that was on board, I scarcely had time to draw breath. So great was the effort of trying to attend to a half dozen things at once that I was more than glad to be rid of my perfectly amiable passengers when the time came to transfer them to Jack Muir's yacht. The unworthy hope even crossed my mind that their overloaded dinghy might sink; though I immediately relented at the sight of the ubiquitous Tim at the oars.

3.30 p.m. 'Took departure from South Head.' Now *Ice Bird* was pitching into the long swells of the open Pacific. The cabin thermometer read a comfortable 21°C., giving no hint of what was to come. Accompanying vessels were taking their leave. The barquentine *New Endeavour* wore round and squared her yards. Jack's auxiliary that was carrying Susie and Vicky, circled *Ice Bird* for the last time, everyone calling and waving. Then I was alone, bound towards an unknown destiny.

At first I had no real concern beyond sailing details, the innumerable small jobs that I did not seem able to catch up on. I was preoccupied more by the intricacies of the Hasler self-steering gear than with having said goodbye for so long to women and children. I was very tired; tired and a little sick, too exhausted by the strains of the past months to do anything but try to relax.

Then painful thoughts began intruding. I squirmed at the facile, shallow answers I had given to the TV interviewer that morning. I had altogether failed to explain my adventure-born motives for making the voyage. I do not think I was trying to 'prove' something, any more than a runner attempting a record. Competitive sport is generally accepted; the kind of competition in which one pits oneself against natural forces is surely equally valid, though the idea may be less familiar. Nor was I trying to 'conquer' – the Antarctic, the Southern Ocean or whatever. This concept is the stock in trade of publicists, not adventurers. We have too much respect for the seas, mountains, glaciers, deserts and forests to seek to subdue them – rather we would learn their ways and adapt to them. 'Conquest' has more in common with destroying forests and causing erosion or polluting air and water in the name of progress.

I do not, myself, fully understand the power that drives me, but I will try to analyse it as best I can. There seems to be a restless spirit inherent in the very nature of mankind that impels us across new frontiers. Without it, indeed *homo sapiens* could hardly have developed his technology and thinking powers. The basic character of this exploring urge would appear to be always the same, regardless of the particular way in which it is manifested. Thus it may equally be expressed in searching for truer forms of artistic expression; in seeking insight into the workings of the soul and mind of man; in the search for scientific truth; or in coming to grips with untamed nature. Thus each of us has his own dreaming – possesses the potential for his own personal kind of adventure.

There is a sense of wonder at the world around us that gives rise to a compulsion to question and explore and to refuse to be satisfied with accepted explanations or assumed limitations placed upon endeavour. The imperative is present in individual men and women – in varying degrees, of course. The chosen, or cursed, ones are devil-driven; the call comes to them and they must answer.

For myself, as is obvious from this narrative, the need is to venture physically beyond familiar horizons or to enlarge by a little the accustomed limits of our vision – as in helping to rescue from oblivion fragments of the ancient Polynesians' (and humanity's) maritime heritage. Brave words, but I was full of doubts and uncertainties all the same.

A TV interviewer had asked Susie that morning whether she was worried about her father's safety. 'No,' replied the eleven-year-old stoutly. 'Vicky and I have spent half our lives at sea in yachts (see *Daughters of the Wind*, 1967, London, Gollancz; *Children of Three Oceans*, 1969, London, Collins). A storm at sea is safer than crossing roads on land, and Daddy knows what to do,' my young champion finished. I only hoped she was right about me. Certainly her own claim was true enough. When the two veterans arrived in Australia after sailing one and a half times round the world, their ages had been six and seven. But I, myself, was plagued by doubts. I recalled how Vicky had kept touching me before my departure, as if for reassurance that I would return. I was worried about Barry in the New Hebrides, his self-confidence impaired by the loss of *Isbjorn*.

However, immediate consideration soon demanded my attention. The wind fell light and the waves, deprived of its flattening effect, reared up lumpy and pyramidal. I unrolled a reef in the mainsail without incident, but rigged a downhaul for the boom so clumsily that a canvas sling was lost overboard: first casualty. Already the plastic petrol cans in the cockpit were beginning to come adrift. I re-lashed them, then stumbled down the companionway into the cabin and, despite the nauseating smell of petrol, ate some rolls and butter and stretched out on the bunk for relief from the unaccustomed motion.

I awoke two hours later, feeling better. The glow-worms of Sydney's lights astern were alternately revealed and hidden as *Ice Bird* climbed and dipped over the waves in the now freshening breeze. As the wind hardened further I rolled down two reefs in the mainsail. Midnight found me tethered by my safety line on the reeling foredeck, changing down to a smaller headsail. I could barely keep my balance even sitting, for *Ice Bird*'s swoops and plunges were breathtaking. I had forgotten how violent was the motion of a yacht standing to windward. A ship's lights showed to port – the only vessel I was to encounter at sea during the entire voyage to Antarctica.

Snugged down to the smaller headsail, the sloop rode easier. Even so, the as yet unfamiliar whine of the wind in the rigging was unsettling. So unused to the motion had I become that I kept tumbling over and crashing into things; my balance was non-existent. It was a relief when, warmed by a cup of coffee, I could place a mattress on the floor of the cabin and gratefully lie down.

I awoke on the 20th, tired as ever, to a sunny, white-flecked sea, marred only by the black triangular fin of a cruising shark. My mind was still too occupied with practical problems to have room for the excitement of the adventure itself. Indeed, there was more than enough to do. I had decided to type the log from the start – a page of navigational data, such as course and wind strength, and, opposite, a page of miscellaneous notes. With *Ice Bird* jumping so that my fingers repeatedly missed the keys this proved easier in the planning than in the execution. Cameras needed loading; the motor must be run to charge the batteries. Before the battery acid could be tested, two thoughtlessly placed four-gallon drums of kerosene had to be moved out of the cramped space underneath the self-draining cockpit.

One of the two wrist watches aboard had already given up the ghost. Accurate time is essential for navigation, so it was rather unhappily that I put it to soak in kerosene. Perhaps it would have been better to have boiled it in oil after the manner of Captain Slocum (the first man to sail alone round the world, who had so treated the alarm clock that was his only chronometer) for my treatment was ineffective. I only hoped that the second watch, an Omega, would keep going.

Almost equally disconcerting was the realization that I had forgotten how to navigate. Clumsy sextant work was compounded by repeated mistakes in the working out of sights. Had this figure to be added or subtracted? I could not remember. Where did you look in the tables for this particular correction? But by degrees the methods began to come back. I was at least able to confirm that we had covered a hundred miles in the twenty or so hours since departing from Sydney Heads – not bad going.

The log for those first few days, 19th, 20th and 21st, is full of references to strain, tiredness, re-stowing gear, sail changing and reefing. My greatest concern was to prevent the sails and sheets from chafing against the rails or the rigging. This is the cruising man's nightmare and needs constant watchfulness to forestall. Thus a new Terylene sheet sawing unnoticed against a wire or stanchion will chafe itself through in a single night. Soon the guardrails and shrouds were decorated with strips of sheepskin and unsightly but effective rags. This vigilance must continue throughout the entire voyage.

It was the radio, however, that caused the most worry. Contact had been established with Sydney when about a hundred miles offshore but thereafter my signals had been too weak for the operator to read.

'Victor Juliet 43 43, calling Sydney Radio, yacht *Ice Bird* calling Sydney. Can you read me? Come in please. Over,' I repeated endlessly and fruitlessly.

The truth of the matter was that the engine generator was incapable of keeping up a full twelve volt charge – this despite the installation of a pair of brand new heavy duty batteries, my forgoing electric light altogether, and even running the motor for a full two hours. All to no avail. No more than an ineffective flickering tuning light could be produced in the $800 Racal SSB set.

A decision to call at New Zealand was inescapable if I were to re-establish communication and forestall any unnecessary anxiety about my safety. I had also to report progress to the *Sydney Morning Herald*, with whom we were under contract. (The royal 'we' is not intended. Increasingly I was writing we in the log, meaning *Ice Bird* and me.) Half Moon Bay, Stewart Island, the southernmost port in New Zealand, being directly en route, was the obvious choice for a stopping place.

By 22 October my mood was changing. The wind had been
blowing hard from ahead, the south-east, but now its howl was
generally in a lower key, further deadened inside the protective
cabin. The little sloop, not over pressed but carrying all the
canvas she needed, stood to windward powerfully enough to
burst through the head seas. Without plunging she was easily
driven.

'*Ice Bird*,' I wrote, 'is fast becoming a tested companion for this
venture.'

The day started badly enough by my being flung right across
the cabin before I realized how violent was the motion. For the
second night running I had slept in oilskin jacket and trousers in
deference to the rough weather though most of the time I was
still in jeans, shirt and bare feet. Now, as the wind eased, I was
able to wash the jeans in hot salt water with liquid detergent.
Over the waves astern danced Wilson's storm petrels, flicking the
water on tiptoe as they sought tiny crustaceae and minute squid
in the stirred up surface foam. A pair of paint-splotched Cape
pigeons, their white markings justifying their other name of
pintado (painted) swept down the valley between long, crested
waves.

The unromantic subject of toilet facilities was to loom rather
large in my life later on, so a brief digression is perhaps in order.
I had never enough time in Sydney to unblock a corroded valve;
and in any case the lavatory compartment, or head, was so convenient for stowage that it was soon stacked high with stores.
From the first, therefore, I fell back on a plastic bucket that, even
at this early stage, was hard to balance in choppy weather. Goodness knows what it was going to be like in the south, when I
would encounter real gales and be further encumbered by layer
upon layer of clothing encasing me like a mummy.

Evening, 22 October: the rhythm of the sea had at last become
established. I ate my first cooked meal – masses of bacon with
bread and butter, followed by canned fruit salad. I sat wedged on
the floor, eating and reading and drinking from a flagon of
Burgundy, musing happily on the sea, with which I was now in
tune. Despite pleasurable anticipation at the prospect of seeing

land and people, I resented the need to call at New Zealand with all the tedious telegrams, telephoning and formalities involved. These extraneous demands would destroy my self-sufficiency, my newly forged bond with the sea. And the ocean was especially beautiful now. As the sun sank, a full moon rose. Albatrosses and sheerwaters weaved a dance in the glowing dusk astern.

Next morning, after the first really quiet and dry night out of Sydney, I felt too lazy to start at once the routine daily tasks: winding the watch; checking the tightness of the grub screws in the tiller head; examining the rigging for chafe; charging batteries; taking the morning sight and typing the log. Instead I lay snug in my bunk for an hour, skimming from one book to another. There was *Lord of the Rings*, I remember – surely the greatest adventure story ever written – a spy thriller and Arian's *Campaigns of Alexander*. I was enjoying life now, my appreciation only slightly marred by apprehension at the storms to come.

Only now did I have leisure to grieve for the lost *Isbjorn*. Hitherto the pressures of making ready for sea had overshadowed all else. Was Barry all right? He had certainly inherited my sea fever. I remembered our traversing the North Sea together, from Norway to the Thames. He must have been about twelve then.

'I do want to be in a gale, Daddy.'

His wish was granted all too soon by a force nine north-wester that had him lying in his bunk for two days, pale green, with bilge water surging over him.

'For a little while in the gale, Daddy,' he admitted shamefacedly as we drew into the Thames Estuary a week later, 'I *almost didn't like* sailing.'

Calmer weather provided an opportunity to check the errors of the two sextants, my own hurriedly purchased plastic one whose index arm was liable to slip and invalidate the sight, and the standard brass instrument Jack Muir had lent me. The wind was light and the albatrosses abandoned the air currents. Extending their webbed feet and tilting back into stall position, they would skid to a halt like water skiers, to rock majestic in their bulk. 'Cape sheep' the old sailors had called them, and the name seemed apt enough.

Experience had by now indicated a good deal of rearrangement.

It was good that I was developing the old-maidishness so very necessary for seagoing – a meticulous fussiness. There must be a set place for everything. The reefing handle, for instance: in darkness or in storm I must be able to lay my hands on it instantly, nor must it be so stowed as to be flung into some inaccessible corner.

The first week at sea ended on 26 October: 640 miles had been covered since Sydney, mostly against strong blustery head winds. The night before we had crossed the 40th parallel. I had been anxiously attuned to the wind note as we tore and crashed along but in spite of my tenseness I could not fail to be stirred by the magnificence of that wild night ride. That same day the first ice bird circled us. A good omen, I wondered? Two days later a whole flock appeared and faithfully kept us company for three whole months.

Rough weather began again, this time a force eight head-on gale from the south-west. From time to time, the ship would wince to the crash of a bursting sea but there was more noise than punch to their blows. I had the uneasy feeling that this was only an introduction, an overture, to what waited below New Zealand. Now the happy little ice birds came back again in still greater numbers: twenty or more. Beating to windward in gale and near-gale conditions was slow work and uncomfortable, but there was no way to speed our progress. Fortunately I had long learned the uselessness of fretting at the sea's moods. Instead I fell to musing about being alone.

I was not in the least lonely. This solitude was a different thing altogether from the lonely emptiness you suffer in a strange city where, knowing no one, you are surrounded by uncaring men and women, all supported by their own human ties. I for one am not particularly self-sufficient – I am peculiarly susceptible to loneliness among crowds. The sea or, for that matter, the desert or the mountains are companionable – or at least they are neutral once you have learned to respect their ways.

'And in the fellowship of peak and sky enrol the cold and lonely mind of man,' as the Everest climber Wilfred Noyce expressed it. His vision of unity with untamed nature is equally applicable to the ocean.

Knowledge of the number of people whose unselfish support had made this venture possible would, in any case, have prevented my ever feeling isolated. I was very conscious of this when I wrote, 'I don't want to let people down, the very many people who are part of this enterprise; so many that I doubt if I can even list them all systematically later. I'm just the driver for this company of venturers. This is why I don't feel alone. But I do feel responsible.'

The gales subsided but the weather continued unpleasant: overcast and squally. Driven spray rattled against the pram hood and now and again a wave crest slopped aboard (once while I was on 'bucket manœuvres'; the bucket slid disconcertingly to and fro and the wave soaked both me and the toilet paper). The sun was generally obscured: accurate sights were difficult to obtain. My boots kept slipping on the gyrating bridge deck, only the safety line holding me as I waited to glimpse the elusive sun whenever the yacht lifted on a wave crest and the horizon became visible. Under this leaden sky the longer seas became steel-grey rolling pastures. Once, clutching the sextant as *Ice Bird* pitched to windward, I watched a lonely albatross gliding along a grey valley that seemed an impossible distance below. All at once I was startled to see what looked like an earless dog poke its head up from the sea. The seal regarded us curiously, turning to follow us with his great brown eyes as we passed by.

The complex depression through which we had been sailing moved away towards the south-east, leaving indelibly, if temporarily, written on the sea's face a record of every recent wind in the shape of a complex pattern of interlocking swells. Patches of sunlight relieved the habitual grey but visibility remained consistently poor, less than ideal for landfall. By the evening of 30 October I estimated that the South Island of New Zealand was near enough to make it prudent for me to lay-to for the night for fear of coming on the coast without warning in darkness and murk.

Sail was hoisted again at first light and, sure enough, high land loomed up ahead two hours later. It was the hill country flanking Breaksea Sound. I turned south along the coast, past the bush clad entrance to beautiful Dusky Sound, tacking so close in that we once had to thread our way among crayfish pot buoys. Night found *Ice Bird* running before a rising gale while I anxiously calculated exactly the right moment to turn sharp left in the unrelieved blackness; hopefully down the middle of the strait that separates South Island to the north from Stewart Island to the south.

When day dawned a wild snow-peak panorama on the left and gentler wooded slopes to starboard showed that I had been correct in my estimate. The yacht drove along the Stewart Island coast, the land sheltering her from the seas, though the wind was strong enough to blow the tops off the waves. Half Moon Bay: the wind funnelling out between the hills overpowered the motor. I quickly winched up the mainsail and tacked in anxiously between underwater rocks, whose position was betrayed by streams of kelp. Penguins popped up and dived again and Cape pigeons circled. A small amphibian aircraft landed in a cloud of spray, taxied up on to the beach in front of the hotel to disgorge a handful of passengers. I threaded through the anchored fishing vessels to bring up alongside one that was tied up in the quay. Throttle closed, a rush along the deck to lower the mainsail, warps hastily thrown, and *Ice Bird* was made fast.

Thirteen days out from Sydney, 1,260 nautical miles to the north-west. The date was 1 November.

A figure in overalls jumped aboard. 'I'm the cop. Where are you from? Sydney. Good on you mate.' He clambered down the steps into the cabin. 'My God, what's that?' He pointed to a painting on the bulkhead.

Its story was this: a friend in Sydney had painted a picture of a kiwi, our New Zealand national emblem, but so much had Australians contributed to the venture, that I had asked him to add a kangaroo. It did in truth seem to loom rather menacingly behind the little bird.

My new friend regarded the mural intently before making up his mind. 'Typifies the Australian-New Zealand relationship, doesn't it? Kangaroo screwing the kiwi. Come along to the pub.'

'It's good to be drinking Kiwi beer again,' I said politely, raising my glass.

'You don't need to be all that patriotic, mate. You know that compared to the Aussie stuff it's piss.'

These were the essential formalities of entry. How good it was to be back in my homeland, New Zealand again, even for so short a time.

That night the Aurora Australis flooded the whole southern sky with searchlights and curtains of pale greenish fire. Beautiful it was with an unearthly beauty, but cold and remote, so that it chilled your heart.

Michael Gomes, the part-Maori descendant of a Portuguese whaler, helped me replenish water and petrol and arranged a radio telephone link with Sydney. To my dismay I learned from Tim Curnow that two substantial cheques of mine had 'bounced' (due to my having forgotten to make overdraft arrangements in the last-minute rush). This was doubly regrettable, since one cheque was to the most helpful of all my friends, Jos Doel; the other was to a yachting body that had been convinced all along that cruising people were bums: the last thing I wanted was to confirm their view. Fortunately, with the help of Merton Naydler and my bank manager, the matter was soon put right.

Next I was dragged along to the school to answer the children's eager questions. There was time for only one evening ashore with Michael's hospitable family, for I dared not linger. Nevertheless I found this place of hardy crayfish catchers – it lies in 47°S. – about as congenial as any I had ever visited, and very hard indeed to leave.

Next day, 2 November, having lunched with the Island Chairman, I tied down a reef I didn't expect to have to shake out again now that we were entering high latitudes, and motored out into a dank mist. That evening, with land still close, we were unexpectedly becalmed, a calm that lasted sporadically well into the following day.

At last a low moan announced the advent of wind and the four albatrosses and twelve Cape pigeons that had been paddling round *Ice Bird* were reduced all of a sudden to white dots far astern, like distant sheep. A radio schedule that I had arranged with Avarua, a station on the southern New Zealand mainland, again failed through the inadequacy of the batteries. 'Why

don't they respond to this continual charging?' I wrote plain-
tively. There was little hope, I realized, of making contact with
Australia direct three weeks hence, as had over-optimistically been
arranged.

I went to my bunk, depressed at this failure. Awaking at 4 a.m.,
I saw aft through the cabin hatchway the new moon riding a pale
yellow dawn, with the Southern Cross to its right. Beautiful, but
all wrong. We had turned round and were sailing *back in our tracks*.
I swore, then pulled on my rubber yachting boots (the steel deck
was beginning to strike very cold against my bare toes) and spent
the next hour bringing *Ice Bird* on to the opposite tack and changing
the headsail. Then, bad tempered and grumbling, I returned to
my sleeping bag.

All boats take in some water. *Ice Bird*, for example, leaked a little
from the stern gland (where the propeller shaft pierces the hull)
and a surprising amount of spray entered the main hatchway. In
my hurry in Sydney I had inexcusably failed to test the bilge
pump properly after mounting it, with the result I was now faced
with the unpalatable conclusion that it was altogether useless. At
this time both portable plastic pumps also took the opportunity
to give up the ghost. The situation was compounded by the wells
beneath the floorboards being so crammed with cans of corned
beef, butter, tomatoes and fruit juice that there was no space for
bilge water to accumulate; the slightest excess and the cabin
floorboards were awash. The only solution was laboriously to
remove every one of the hundreds of cans (they amounted to
eleven bucketfuls) that occupied the central and deepest bilge well
and re-stow them in the forepeak lockers, packing them in with
rags.

The arrangement left this deepest well available for bailing
with a bucket, from now on my only method of emptying out the
bilge water. The procedure went as follows: first undo the bolts
locking the floorboard battens in place (since the wood had
swollen, a punch and hammer were required for this); lift the
floorboards and drag them forward out of the way; fill bucket;
stagger to companionway and rest bucket on lowest step; timing
the ship's roll, step up and grasp the hatch coaming; then up with

the bucket and empty its contents into the cockpit, whose drain holes channel it into the sea; finally, replace and bolt down the floorboards.

November 5, a day of calms and light airs, was largely taken up with this re-stowage, made no easier by the yacht's violent, rhythmic rolling, when deprived of the steadying effect of the wind. After the work was finished, in the late afternoon, I dined rather un-conventionally on rum, fried ham and the last of the bread, reading the while a James Bond novel and a book of more immediate moment – by the veteran Cape Horner Bernard Moitessier, whom I had met in Tahiti. His experiences in severe gales round the Horn in his steel sloop *Joshua* were salutary and well worth digesting.

That night fog closed in. What a strange and unreal feeling fog at sea always gives me. Provided no land or traffic is near there is a sense of cosiness. 'Stealing along silently through the dank mist with only the ripple of the bow wave; the cabin an oasis of light; the whole ship a little world protected from the forces outside by the fog.' This was how it seemed to me then.

But those light airs irked me. I was anxious to be across the notoriously stormy fifties and to be able to turn eastward parallel to the ice fringe. Then I would have begun to achieve something at last.

Next day we crossed the fiftieth parallel and I felt as if we were entering a wild animal's preserve. At any moment from now on the Southern Ocean might pounce with overwhelming fury.

I had reason for apprehension, for we were approaching the area of intense frontal activity south-east of New Zealand and centred in about 55°S., that I had read about in Melbourne. It was far from certain, for that matter, that there would be any improve-ment south of 60°S. either, for the Antarctic Pilot had this to say: 'The indicated decrease in velocity south of Lat. 55°S. is not so much a real decrease in speed, as an increase in variability. Thus ... an increasing number of easterlies, in these higher latitudes, has the effect of reducing the resultant speed.'

The wind circulation in the Southern Ocean is made up of two systems. In the 40s and 50s strong westerlies, compounded of an endless series of low pressure systems or cyclonic depressions, sweep round the world, virtually unhindered by land. The 'roaring forties', 'screaming fifties', 'howling sixties': the names coined by the old Cape Horn sailors speak for themselves. But from about 62° to 63°S. and then on southward, Antarctic easterlies prevail. My aim was to run my easting down in about 60°S. in the southernmost fringe of the westerlies, avoiding the head winds that would be met with further south and taking advantage of the steady 1/2 knot eastflowing current that is a feature of the west wind belt.

Ice was the other consideration in planning my route. The types that concerned me were icebergs, pack ice and the formation of ice on the ship – spray freezing on the superstructure and rigging into such massive accumulations as to endanger the vessel's stability.

Icebergs might be encountered anywhere, but in significant numbers only within fifty miles of the Antarctic Peninsula itself. Until I closed the coast, therefore, their possible presence would call for vigilance during the increasingly long daylight hours – and for nervousness in fog and snowstorm. Icebergs are, of course, carved off from ice cap that covers land and flows down to the sea as glaciers or those enormous ice shelves so characteristic of the Antarctic. The latter may produce bergs more than a hundred miles long. As treacherous to the seaman as icebergs themselves are growlers, worn lumps of hard ice as big as houses, rolling just awash and practically invisible.

Pack ice is sea water that has frozen. Usually about three to five feet of ice is added each winter. It guards the southern continent in a belt hundreds of miles across, forever cracking apart or else squeezing so close that it buckles into pressure ridges or rafts like a monstrous pack of shuffled cards producing sheets up to a hundred feet thick. Again, my route was planned to lead clear of ice, though loose pack might well be encountered close to the Peninsula in December. The most up-to-date information on pack ice limits was provided by satellite observations embodied in a publication with the unlikely title of *The Life Cycle of Antarctic Krill* that Sir Vivian Fuchs had recommended. One other factor is germane to this story. Pack ice more than two seasons old loses its salinity. When melted it yields fresh water.

Serious accumulation of ice on ships does not occur in summer north of the Antarctic Convergence. This is the line, the same in all seasons, along which cold north-moving Antarctic water encounters and sinks beneath warmer and therefore lighter sea water from temperate latitudes. In the Pacific it is nowhere very far north of 60°S., though in the Atlantic and Indian Oceans, it lies up to seven hundred miles farther north. Thus I had few anxieties on this score, at least up to the Peninsula. The heavy New Zealand alpine guide's ice axe aboard should be fully capable of chipping away any spray that might freeze on deck. It was an historic axe in a way, having been lent to me by Colin Putt, the New Zealand mountaineer, who had used it in such disparate places as Big Ben on Heard Island in the sub-Antarctic and the Star Mountains of West Iran.

Just over a week out from Stewart Island and three weeks from Sydney, on 9 November, I had my first taste of what was in store. The south-west wind was gusting up to gale force but the weather was in no way alarming. The log speaks for itself. 'I have been running undercanvassed, being awed by the latitude – but not too overawed, I now know. I was reading, the moan of the wind muted in the cabin. It rises to a shriek; we are pushed gradually but firmly over as if by a hand and race ahead, luffing (storm trisail and storm jib only). I put the helm up from the cabin with the tiller lines, gasping in the spray showers even here. *Ice Bird* tore crashing along until the squall was past. Then I shook with reaction.'

Two days later we crossed the International Date Line in 55°S. and the Southern Ocean had really begun to show its teeth.

Time zones and the date line are important in determination of longitude (one's distance east or west). Since the earth revolves through 360° every twenty-four hours, it must turn 15° each hour, giving twenty-four zones with a one-hour difference between them. The date line, except where altered for administrative convenience, is the 180th meridian, directly opposite the Greenwich Prime Meridian. Places east of Greenwich are in east longitude and vice versa. Thus eastern Australia is in eastern time zone ten, or Z—10, meaning that zone time —10 gives Greenwich Mean time. On 11 November, we were nearing the boundary of

I.B.—D

zone —12. Then we crossed the Date Line from west to east and gained a day, so that the following day was *also* 11 November, but in zone Z+12.

It was on this second Saturday of 11 November that a severe gale of force nine and ten, that had been heralded by mare's tails and a mackerel sky, burst upon *Ice Bird*. It was much colder now, down to 5°C., and I was wearing two skivvies, two woollen jerseys, corduroys, woollen socks and my tattered ski anorak, a quilted one. Great smoking seas out of the south-west pounded the little yacht, periodically breaking completely over her in a confusion of thundering sound and violent shock.

The following evening we passed south of all continental land (except Antarctica. Cape Horn is in latitude 55° 50'; *Ice Bird* was now below 56°) and I felt at once unprotected and alone, past that frontier beyond which small ships durst venture only at their peril. Fear and the possibilities of danger began looming very large.

The notes for 7 November contain just one entry. 'All that I need for this trip is courage – and that I possess only in very small measure.' This sums up the relationship between adventure and possible risk, I think. It is the enterprise itself that fires the imagination, driving you to go further than man has ever gone before. Naturally if you venture into the unknown you must be prepared to encounter unforseeable dangers and, especially where these are not fully known, the sensible man is fearful and wary.

None but the psychologically unbalanced are attracted to danger for its own sake. Risk is a disadvantage unfortunately often inherent in too many worthwhile ventures. Awareness of it may at best help promote that wild animal alertness upon which man's survival may depend when he steps off the pavements. The call comes to the adventurer and he must by his nature answer it. But he reduces any element of risk to an absolute minimum, acting out his destiny *in spite of* anxiety and fear.

There was certainly enough reason to be afraid of the Southern Ocean and its Antarctic shores and I made no secret of my own forebodings, yet now that the struggle was joined, the very magnitude of this self-imposed task–and perhaps my impertinence at having attempted it – fired my imagination more and more. All my perceptions were increasingly heightened; while art is a distillation and refinement of life at secondhand, here was I living the actual raw material of poetry.

Cause for anxiety was now occasioned by the barometer. It fell so rapidly and remained at such a low level, especially when nothing very alarming seemed to be happening, as to raise doubts as whether it was broken. Could the barometer be faulty, over-sensitive (like me), deranged? I could not quite forget the sailor's rhyme: *'With a low and falling glass, Soundly sleeps the careless ass.'* So I remained uneasy. After some days, however, the barometer gradually rose again to near normal, leaving unsolved the mystery of its behaviour. Its fluctuations would not always have such innocent import, as I was soon to find out.

Repeated snow showers all day on the 14th seemed to mark our sudden arrival in the southern world. 'The rattle of wind-driven snow in the short night – complete darkness now only lasted from about 9 p.m. until 2 a.m. – showed that we were really getting somewhere,' I wrote, adding 'Come now. Relax and put aside those fears a bit!' We had by the 14th been at sea four weeks from Sydney and had at length reached the long-sought latitude of 60°S. During the past week the wind had reached gale force on six days out of seven.

The preferred course from now on would no longer be south-east, but east. A degree of longitude, because of the earth's spherical shape, measures only thirty sea miles in latitude 60° as against sixty miles on the equator; so, other things being equal, following the 60th parallel eastwards would be a quick route to my objective nearly half-way round the world. I would not abandon the eastward course until we were north of the Peninsula, when I would turn southward towards either the British base at Argentine Islands or the more conveniently situated American one at Palmer. These were only about forty miles apart, in roughly 65°S., both being on the west side of the Antarctic Peninsula.

I have spoken about going into the unknown but *Ice Bird* was not the first yacht to brave these latitudes. She was very much a pioneer, however, by virtue of her small size and by the fact of her being sailed single-handed.

My friend Bill Tilman, the veteran British Everest mountaineer, was the first to cross Drake Passage from South America and reach the south Shetland Islands off the tip of the Antarctic Peninsula. This was in 1967. His ship was the 45-foot Bristol Channel Pilot cutter *Mischief* and he carried an extremely dubious scratch crew recruited in Montevideo, one of whom later robbed him.

In 1970 Bob Griffith's 53-foot ferro-cement *Awahnee*, American with a New Zealand ship's company of five, circumnavigated Antarctica along much the same route I was now following. At Palmer she encountered the Italian lateen-rigged *San Giuseppe* which had come across Drake Passage. She was also a 53-footer. Her skipper, Angione Cat, had had her steel-sheathed and she was exceptionally well appointed.

Down on the 60th parallel the temperature inside the cabin was $-1\frac{1}{2}$°C. and the ubiquitous drips, which had formerly left runnels down the walls, froze. I was now bundled up in two skivvies, three woollen jerseys, a Dacron quilted flying suit and my quilted anorak. This was indoor rig. For excursions outside the cabin, waterproof Marlin smock and overtrousers, safety belt and sheath knife were necessary additions. Truth to tell, it was rare for me to remove any of these even when below during the seemingly endless succession of gales and bad weather we were now experiencing.

My insulated boots, again often worn day and night, had been borrowed from Warwick Deacock, leader of the successful expedition that had climbed Mt Big Ben on desolate Heard Island. Their expedition ship *Patanella* had, incidentally, been skippered by the redoubtable Bill Tilman of *Mischief* and Everest fame. My own pair, made to my measurements free of charge by the Milwaukee Rubber Company, had not arrived in Australia by the time I sailed, so I was grateful to Warwick for stepping into the breach. However, since I am short and Warwick is over six feet tall, the fit of his boots was anything but snug!

These foam rubber or Neoprene insulated boots work on the wet suit principle. Your feet quickly become wet with sweat but remain (reasonably) warm because the heat generated by the body's metabolism cannot dissipate itself through the thick insulation. For that matter, the rest of my clothing and the cabin itself functioned in the same way. My clothes were always damp, the sleeping bag clammy and the PVC covered mattresses sodden. Everything was wet from condensation (except where frozen) and from what spray and snow managed to penetrate the cabin; but the hull and deck enclosed me, cutting down heat loss and shielding me from the chilling effect of the wind.

The phenomenon of wind chill was particularly menacing. Strong winds, through their evaporating effect, accentuate dramatically the effects of cold on the human body. Thus a wind of only 25 m.p.h., merely a stiff breeze at 10°C., produces the same heat loss from unprotected skin as would be lost in windless conditions at −30°C. My temperatures were always lower and winds often very much stronger than this. In the sub-Antarctic ocean the constant dampness compounds the effects of cold and wind chill from gales. Thoroughly wind-and-water-proof clothing that can shield one from wind-cooling and wetting, with sufficient layers beneath to prevent heat loss, is the key to survival. Since I was often on deck in gales (securing sails, lashing down anything loose, making steering adjustments) for one or two hours at a stretch, adequate protection against wind chill was obviously vital.

All this sounds detached and physiological. In more human terms I was damp, dirty and generally uncomfortable. My clothes smelled unpleasantly of stale urine. I was rarely warm enough. Some form of heating in the cabin, I thought, would have been more than welcome.

16 November. Another gale. It was too rough to attempt to cook. Wedged in a corner of the cabin, I breakfasted on ships biscuits, salami and chocolate, washed down with rum. The main sheet and the back stay radio antennae were sheathed in ice and the Perspex dome was thickly covered with snow. How eerie it was to watch the whirling snow driving across watery hills that themselves were sweeping by with frothing crests. I was not yet accustomed to snow at sea. A flock of ice birds went drifting by, perfectly at ease with the gale, like large snow flakes . . . ghostly.

Chapter 3

Capsize

Ice Bird continued to make steady, if unspectacular, progress eastward, keeping generally about 61°S. A progression of gales – north-west with heavy snow and falling glass, as the warm front of the depression rolled over us – would be succeeded abruptly after eight to twelve hours by the cold front, with its falling temperatures, clearing sky and rising glass – and intensified south-west gale. The resulting jumble of cross seas kept the ocean's face in a state of furious confusion even without the rogue seas which, every now and then, reared up and dashed right across the line of the prevailing swells. I kept the yacht running with the wind on one or other quarter, nearly down-wind. Usually she carried only the storm jib, sometimes the storm tri-sail as well. The mainsail had been put to bed somewhere in the mid-fifties and had remained furled ever since.

One of the most awkward operations that had to be carried out in the brief intervals between gales was filling the petrol tank. Balancing a four-gallon plastic can on a deck rolling at a 30° angle was not easy, but at least it had the advantage that the considerable spillage was soon washed overboard. This was more than could be said when I performed the chore of topping up lamps and stove with kerosene. Inevitably a good deal of kerosene spilled over as the yacht lurched and wallowed and this made of the cabin floor a skating rink on which I slithered helplessly.

The fresh water in the tank let into the keel froze. Fortunately I had a supply of plastic cans to fall back upon. The drop in sea temperature was because we were now south of the Antarctic Convergence. Fogs, due to relatively warm north-west winds blowing over a colder sea, became more frequent and persistent than ever. Heavy snow showers became the norm.

Navigation was far from easy. A quick sight of the sun emerging from cloud cover; a dubious horizon as the sloop, rolling her gunwales under, lifted on a crest; numb fingers feverishly manipulating the sextant. To balance things a little, radio time signals were being received very clearly. Not so radio transmissions. An attempt to keep a schedule with Sydney on the 22nd, not unexpectedly, failed.

Evening, 26 November, the worst gale so far, a raging 50 knot, force ten north-wester that drove long lines of foam scudding down the faces of enormous waves and literally whipped away their crests. Each time a breaker burst against *Ice Bird* everything loose in the cabin went flying and I was forever thankful for the steel plates protecting her windows. The bilge water appeared to defy gravity by distributing itself everywhere. It surged violently uphill and whizzed round the hull.

I kept *Ice Bird*, under snow-plastered storm jib, running off before the seas at about 20° from a dead down-wind run, so that she moved diagonally across the faces of those huge waves at a slight angle. During the night the gale backed to the south-west and the glass began to rise. It must eventually blow itself out, but when? I was shocked with the scene that full daylight revealed; scared, then gradually fascinated; though still terrified on looking out through the dome. It seemed as if the yacht's stern could never lift to each wave that reared up behind us. But rise it did; each time with a sensation like being whisked up in a lift. The yacht was being steered by the wind vane, assisted from inside the cabin by occasional tugs at the tiller lines. 'She's bloody near airborne,' I wrote, and added that she was running incredibly smoothly. But was this in spite of, or because of, my tactics? Were they the right ones?

This last is a perennial query in storms. Vito Dumas, the heroic Argentine farmer who in 1944 circumnavigated alone through the roaring forties in a yacht the same size as *Ice Bird*, never took in his jib. He did the same as I was doing now. Bernard Moitessier, after his memorable non-stop voyage from Tahiti to Spain, had also suggested the tactics I was adopting – running before gales at an angle under headsail, the sail being necessary to give control and manœuvrability.

Dumas and Moitessier had been two of the successful ones, but so many had come to grief in the Southern Ocean. I recalled reading in Captain W. H. S. Jones's book, *The Cape Horn Breed*, that out of 130 commercial sailing vessels leaving European ports for the Pacific coast of America in May, June and July 1905, four were known to have been wrecked and *fifty-three* were still missing in Cape Horn waters in November – four to six months later.

The 37-foot Australian ketch *Pandora*, the very first yacht ever to round Cape Horn – this was in 1911 – was capsized and dismasted off the Falkland Islands. She was towed into port by a whaler. The Smeaton's big British *Tzu Hang* was pitchpoled and dismasted on her first attempt to round the formidable Cape; on her second gallant try she was rolled and lost both masts. She succeeded the third time. Only the previous year the 34-foot *Damien*, crewed by two young Frenchmen, was thrice capsized off South Georgia, the first time righting herself only after a considerable interval. Again the mast was a casualty.

Yet here I was, traversing even stormier waters than they. No wonder I was scared. The gale seemed to be bearing out what I had somewhat wryly termed Lewis's law – for every point the wind increases your boat shrinks and becomes one foot shorter. This great truth has been my own discovery. I was brought back from my musings about other voyagers by bilge water surging up over the 'permafrost' that coated the inside of the hull these days, as an exploding crest threw the yacht over on her beam ends. She righted herself, water streaming off her decks. So far there had been no damage. But there was very little respite. This 26–27 November gale was barely over before, on the night of the 27th, the barometer started dropping again.

These repeated gales were at last seriously beginning to get me down. Gradually my morale was being sapped and increasing physical exhaustion was taking its toll. My whole body was battered and bruised and I was suffering from lack of sleep. Increasingly I dwelt on my in many ways disastrous personal life; what a mess I had made of things. I could hardly remember when my storm clothes had last been removed; standing in squelching boots had become habitual but was hardly comfortable. To make matters worse, my left hip, damaged in a skiing accident the previous winter, ached intolerably. I no longer day-dreamed about the voyage and its outcome – I had already dreamed and was now living it.

Instead, present reality became illusory. In my exhausted state the wild irregular seas that were tossing us around like a cork were only half apprehended. I jotted down in the log that everything was an effort; there were constant mistakes of every kind in my sight workings; I could no longer grasp simple concepts. Twice, I recorded with scientific detachment that I heard ill-defined imaginary shouts. I drifted out of reality altogether . . .

A girl companion and I are ploughing through the long fragrant grass of autumn towards the Ginandera Falls. Green scarlet lorikeets flash by in streaks of vivid colour. We push our way through some heavy scrub, then go stumbling thigh-deep over slippery stones across the icy Murimbidgee. A tangle of deadfall, tall gums and casuarinas, then a grassy glade under lichen-covered rock walls and ahead the leaping cascade. Imperceptibly the scene changes to the coast. A water-lily covered secret lake behind the sandhills. The same girl, Susie and Vicky, naked and laughing in the hot sunshine, splashing up into the shallows.

Such are my memories, false and nostalgic though they be, of 27 November, the last day of my great adventure; such was my mental condition on the eve of disaster.

On the 28th the bottom fell out of the glass. How true, even if unintended, were the words of the poet MacNiece.

The glass is falling hour by hour, the glass will fall for ever,
But if you break the bloody glass you won't hold up the weather.

Nothing I or any other man might do could control the barometer. The pointer moved right off the scale and continued downwards to about twenty-eight inches or 950mb during the night. This time it was for real. Long before the barometer had reached this point it was apparent that something altogether new had burst upon us – a storm of hurricane intensity. This was the home of the unthinkable 105-foot waves the Russians had recorded, I recalled with dread. A breaker half as tall, falling upon *Ice Bird*, would pound her flat and burst her asunder.

The waves increased in height with unbelievable rapidity. Nothing in my previous experience had prepared me for this.

Yet I had known the full fury of North Atlantic autumn gales when homeward bound in 25-foot *Cardinal Vertue* from Newfoundland to the Shetlands in 1960 (coincidentally, the Shetlands straddle the 60th *north* parallel).

Barry and I had weathered Coral Sea cyclone 'Becky' in *Isbjorn*, only partially sheltered by an inadequate island. Severe gales off Iceland, Magellan Strait and the Cape of Good Hope had been ridden out by *Rehu Moana* – the most seaworthy catamaran built so far – in the course of her Iceland voyage and her circumnavigation.

But this storm was something altogether new. By evening the estimated wind speed was over sixty knots; the seas were conservatively forty feet high and growing taller – great hollow rollers, whose wind-torn crests thundered over and broke with awful violence. The air was thick with driving spray.

Ice Bird was running down wind on the starboard gybe (the wind on the starboard quarter), with storm jib sheeted flat as before. Once again I adjusted the wind-vane to hold the yacht steering at a small angle to a dead run, and laid out the tiller lines where they could be grasped instantaneously to assist the vane. This strategy had served me well in the gale just past, as it had Dumas and Moitessier. But would it be effective against this fearful storm? Had any other precautions been neglected? The Beaufort inflatable life raft's retaining strops had been reinforced by a criss-cross of extra lashings across the cockpit. Everything movable, I thought, was securely battened down; the washboards were snugly in place in the companionway; the hatches were all secured. No, I could not think of anything else that could usefully be done.

Came a roar, as of an approaching express train. Higher yet tilted the stern; *Ice Bird* picked up speed and hurtled forward surfing on her nose, then slewed violently to starboard, totally unresponsive to my hauling at the tiller lines with all my strength. A moment later the tottering breaker exploded right over us, smashing the yacht down on to her port side. The galley shelves tore loose from their fastenings and crashed down in a cascade of jars, mugs, frying pan and splintered wood. I have no recollection of where I myself was flung – presumably backwards on to the port bunk. I only recall clawing my way up the companionway and staring aft through the dome.

The invaluable self-steering vane had disappeared and I found, when I scrambled out on deck, that its vital gearing was shattered beyond repair – stainless steel shafts twisted and cog wheels and worm gear gone altogether. The stout canvas dodger round the cockpit was hanging in tatters. The jib was torn, though I am not sure whether it had split right across from luff to clew then or later. My recollections are too confused and most of that day's log entries were subsequently destroyed.

I do know that I lowered the sail, slackening the halyard, hauling down the jib and securing it, repeatedly unseated from the jerking foredeck, half blinded by stinging spray and sleet, having to turn away my head to gulp for the air being sucked past me by the screaming wind. Then lying on my stomach and grasping handholds like a rock climber, I inched my way back to the companionway and thankfully pulled the hatch to after me.

I crouched forward on the edge of the starboard bunk doing my best to persuade *Ice Bird* to run off before the wind under bare poles. She answered the helm, at best erratically, possibly because she was virtually becalmed in the deep canyons between the waves; so that more often than not the little yacht wallowed broadside on, port beam to the sea, while I struggled with the tiller lines, trying vainly to achieve steerage way and control.

And still the wind kept on increasing. It rose until, for the first time in all my years of seagoing, I heard the awful high scream of force thirteen hurricane winds rising beyond 70 knots.

The remains of the already-shredded canvas dodger streamed out horizontally, flogging with so intense a vibration that the outlines blurred. Then the two stainless steel wires supporting the dodger parted and in a flash it was gone. The whole sea was white now. Sheets of foam, acres in extent, were continually being churned anew by fresh cataracts. These are not seas, I thought: they are the Snowy Mountains of Australia – and they are rolling right over me. I was very much afraid.

Some time later – I had no idea how long – my terror receded into some remote corner of my mind. I must have shrunk from a reality I could no longer face into a world of happier memories,

for I began living in the past again, just as I had in my exhaustion
in the gale two days earlier. It is hard to explain the sensation.
I did not move over from a present world into an illusory one
but temporarily inhabited both at once and was fully aware of
doing so, without feeling this to be in any way strange or alarming. My handling of the tiller was quite automatic.

Mounts Kosciusko, Townsend, the broken crest of Jagungal;
sculptured summits, sweeping snow slopes streaked with naked
rock; all this mighty snow panorama rolled past like a cinema
film. It was moving because those snow mountains were simul-
taneously the too-fearful-to-contemplate watery mountains of
paralysing reality.

*I am watching, as from afar, four of us gliding down off the snow-plumed
divide, four dots in a vast whiteness. Then I am striving for balance under the
weight of my pack, skis rattling a bone-shaking tattoo over a serration of ice
ridges. We ski to a rest under a snow cornice overlooking the headwaters of the
Snowy River, where we tunnel a snow cave to shelter us for the night – a survival
exercise in preparation for my present venture.*

But why are those snow mountains rolling onward? Where
are they going? I have drifted away even further from the present
and my tired brain baulks at the effort of solving the conundrum.

*The picture blurs. I am leading a party up this same Kosciusko during the
winter lately past, something like three months ago, amid the same rounded
shoulders and rolling summits – literally rolling. My little Susie, refusing help
with her pack, plods gamely up the endless snow slope, eyes suffused with tears of
tiredness. We halt to rest. Almost at once, with the resilience of childhood,
Susie is away – laughing, her tears forgotten, the swish of her skis answering
the song of the keen mountain wind.*

The intolerable present became too intrusive to be ignored;
the past faded into the background. Veritable cascades of white
water were now thundering past on either side, more like breakers
monstrously enlarged to perhaps forty-five feet, crashing down
on a surf beach. Sooner or later one must burst fairly over us.
What then?

I wedged myself more securely on the lee bunk, clutching the
tiller lines, my stomach hollow with fear. The short sub-Antarctic
night was over; it was now about 2 a.m.

My heart stopped. My whole world reared up, plucked by an irresistible force, to spin through giddy darkness, then to smash down into daylight again. Daylight, I saw with horror, as I pushed aside the cabin table that had come down on my head (the ceiling insulation was scored deeply where it had struck the deck head) . . . daylight was streaming through the now gaping opening where the forehatch had been! Water slopped about my knees. The remains of the Tilley lamp hung askew above my head. The stove remained upside down, wedged in its twisted gymballs.

Ice Bird had been rolled completely over to starboard through a full 360° and had righted herself thanks to her heavy lead keel – all in about a second. In that one second the snug cabin had become a shambles. What of the really vital structures? Above all, what of the mast?

I splashed forward, the first thought in my mind to close that yawning fore hatchway. My second – oh, God – the mast. I stumbled over rolling cans, felt the parallel rules crunch underfoot and pushed aside the flotsam of clothes, mattresses, sleeping bag, splintered wood fragments and charts (British charts floated better than Chilean, I noted – one up to the Admiralty). Sure enough the lower seven feet of the mast, broken free of the mast step, leaned drunkenly over the starboard bow and the top twenty-nine feet tilted steeply across the ruptured guard wires and far down into the water, pounding and screeching as the hulk wallowed.

The forehatch had been wrenched open by a shroud as the mast fell. Its hinges had sprung, though they were not broken off and its wooden securing batten had snapped. I forced it as nearly closed as I could with the bent hinges and bowsed it down with the block and tackle from the bosun's chair.

Then I stumbled back aft to observe, incredulously, for the first time that eight feet of the starboard side of the raised cabin trunk had been dented in, longitudinally, as if by a steam hammer. A six-inch vertical split between the windows spurted water at every roll (it was noteworthy, and in keeping with the experience of others, that it had been the lee or down-wind side, the side underneath as the boat capsized, that had sustained damage, not the weather side where the wave had struck).

What unimaginable force could have done that to eighth-inch steel? The answer was plain. Water. The breaking crest, which had picked up the seven-ton yacht like a matchbox, would have been hurtling forward at something like fifty miles an hour. When it slammed her over, the impact would have been equivalent to dumping her on to concrete. The underside had given way.

Everything had changed in that moment of capsize on 29 November at 60° 04′S., 135° 35′W., six weeks and 3,600 miles out from Sydney, 2,500 miles from the Antarctic Peninsula. Not only were things changed; everything was probably coming to an end. The proud yacht of a moment before had become a wreck: high adventure had given place to an apparently foredoomed struggle to survive.

Part 2

Waters of Life or Death

About to re-step the mast after reinforcing rigging attachments, prior to leaving Sydney.

Welding strengthening members to Ice Bird's rudder, before the Antarctic voyage.

*Before leaving Sydney,
20 October 1972, in cockpit
of* Ice Bird *with Vicky* (left)
and Susie (right).

*The kiwi and kangaroo
painting in* Ice Bird'*s cabin.*

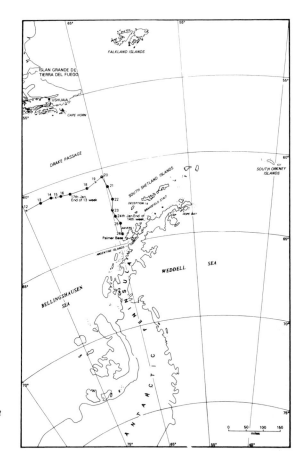

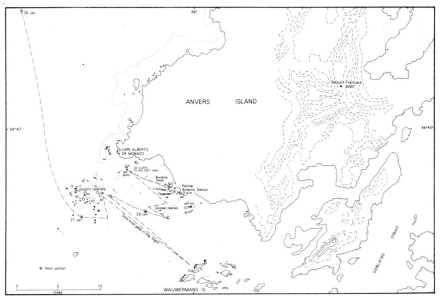

Ice Bird's *passage to Palmer.*
The boat's erratic final
approach (below) reflects the
tricky conditions, the less than
efficient rig, and David
Lewis's exhaustion.

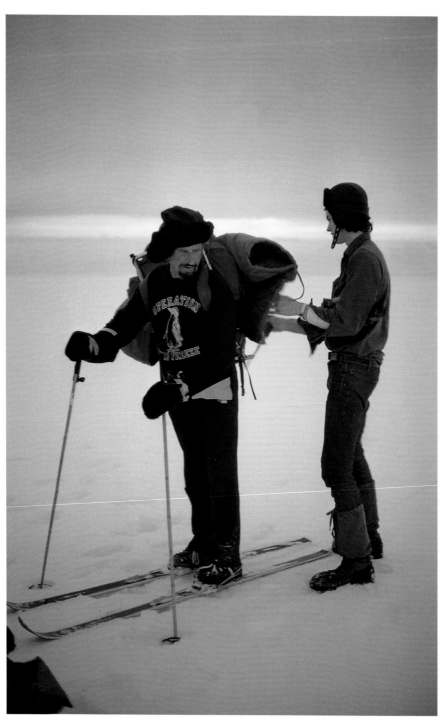

David Lewis, about to ski out to spend a night on the ice cap, along with four of the Palmer personnel.

Carrying out Ice Bird's *new wooden mast, constructed at Palmer.*

Ice Bird, *with her new mast in place, undergoing sea trials in heavy spring pack ice at Palmer.*

Soon after the launch of Ice Bird, *the Argentinians came visiting Palmer.*

Palmer Antarctic Station.

Chapter 4
Struggle without Hope

I hastily stuffed the nearest floating rag into the gap in the side of the coach roof (later I substituted sealing compound). My Omega wrist watch, kept on Greenwich time for navigation, was providentially still running. In the absence of radio time signals – I correctly assumed that the radios would all be shorted out by salt water – I must rely solely upon it for longitude, estimating its probable error as best I could.

A hurried search for gloves was fruitless. Well, gloves would be no use to me if *Ice Bird* sank. Seizing a bucket (the pump, of course, was useless) I began bailing for life.

The capsize must have occurred soon after first light, or around 2 a.m. Hour after hour I bailed until I was repeating the sequence of operations in a haze of tiredness, mechanically, like an automaton. The glass was beginning to rise, I noted dully, so the cold front must have passed, switching the storm winds to the southwest. This presumption was confirmed when ragged tears began to appear in the driving cloud wrack. Bursts of sunlight momentarily illumined a scene that, even in my then state, I appreciated was of awesome grandeur. The screaming wind had not let up in the slightest. The tormented sea was a sheet of white water that looked like snow. At least I have seen the sun again before I die, I thought.

By about 8.30 a.m. the yacht was empty down to the floorboards. Then *crash!* I picked myself up from the corner where I had been hurled when this second killer wave had knocked *Ice Bird* flat, this time over to starboard, to find her flooded again to almost exactly the same level as before. The carefully salvaged logbook, charts and sleeping bag were once more awash.

When I wearily recommenced bailing I saw that the life raft was gone from the cockpit. I was without thought; conscious only of pain and weariness; actuated only by some obscure instinct for survival. An age passed until suddenly there was no more water to scoop up. Then I was knocking out the bolts securing the floorboard battens and scooping the remaining thirty or so bucketfuls out of the bilge.

Noon. *Ice Bird* was dry again. Habit was strong. With numb hands I picked up a ballpoint pen, opened the sodden logbook and laboriously recorded the incident.

'Gale moderating to force 10–9. Heavy seas breaking against us. Everything soaked and destroyed. Must rest a little.' I finished. I had been bailing continuously for something like ten hours.

The thumping of the mast against the hull soon had me on my feet again. Thank goodness the boat was of steel. Crawling out on deck, I set about knocking out split pins to free the shrouds from the rigging screws that anchored them to the deck. The stainless steel wire rigging, like the mast itself, would have to be sacrificed: there was no way in which I could hoist aboard such a weighty tangle of wreckage nor make use of it if salvage had been possible.

So I pried and levered with a screwdriver, pinched and hammered with pliers at those stubborn split pins. The deck's motion was too violent and I was too tired to hit accurately but I carried on until the sunken mast was held by only two wires, never noticing that I had gashed my left hand deeply in two places, as the wounds neither hurt nor bled.

By 7.30 that evening I could do no more.

'Hands bleeding and very numb,' I wrote in the logbook, incredibly failing to realize what was wrong or to make the slightest attempt to warm my still uncovered fingers – and I a doctor! The numbing effects upon reasoning power of exhaustion and shock were never more apparent. 'Will have a stiff drink and try to sleep. Sleeping bag soaked,' I added in a barely decipherable scrawl. But the rum bottle was nowhere to be found. Smashed to pieces, I assumed and, after some searching, found another. It was a fortnight before I came upon the original bottle. Driven up through the plywood floor of a locker, it was still intact.

A fitful sleep of utter tiredness followed. In the morning my fingers were too numb to feel the winder on my wrist watch. My first reaction was horror. Should the watch stop I had no way of setting it to the correct time again. Result – the ending at one stroke of any possibility of navigational accuracy and the fading to absolute zero of my already dim chances. I searched feverishly for my glasses. They misted up as soon as I put them on. I squeezed out wet toilet paper and wiped them repeatedly. Now I could *see* the winder turn. This procedure was to be faithfully repeated night and morning from then on and must never, on any account, be omitted.

The wider implications of my fingers' numbness came home to me as I belatedly realized the obvious – that both my hands were frostbitten. From now on I must always keep them covered. The damp woollen gloves or mitts (I had so far salvaged one of each) I would reserve for work on deck, using slightly less damp woollen socks when below. I even learned to write up the log and open cans of corned beef with the socks on my hands.

The remaining shrouds parted of their own accord about the middle of the morning and *Ice Bird* floated free of the wreckage. I laboriously hoisted thirty-five buckets of water out of the companionway and poured them into the self draining cockpit; later in the day eighteen buckets more. I tried to force more sealing compound into the split but had little success. Every single roll of the dismasted yacht put the side decks under and sent a fresh spurt of water into the cabin.

My first pathetic attempt at rigging some sort of a sail was by cutting away the remaining fragments of the canvas dodger and wrapping them round the pulpit forward. It was ineffective. The dry fur coat and fur trousers that had been stowed carefully away in the forepeak in a waterproof plastic bag I found to be soaked, for the bag had chafed through unnoticed during the long weeks at sea. Nevertheless, I changed into them, a procedure which, because of my hands, took over an hour.

The 9 p.m. scribbled entry in the day's log sounds curiously forlorn. 'Blowing up from the west. Both hands fingers frost-bitten – attempted to warm them up this p.m. Will now try to run off before the sea.'

And a little later, 'Failed steer. Failed primus. 18 buckets.

Estimate watch 4 minutes 33 seconds fast (est. daily gain 6 seconds). Can't be sure if winder turning.'

Depressed by these successive failures, I huddled down in my sleeping bag and pressing my unfeeling hands (which seemed as little part of me as slabs of chilled meat) against my warm body, I dozed the miserable night away.

The first of December. Working in swirling snow, my hands surprisingly well protected by wet woollen gloves, I cleared away the remaining wreckage and set about rigging up a jury mast. The best spar I could find was the surviving spinnaker pole (the other had been broken when the mast had collapsed). It was an aluminium tube ten feet long, far too fragile for the job in hand, as well as being ridiculously short, but I could think of nothing else to use. Shrouds or stays were needed for support and halyards to hoist sails. An old friend, a veteran climbing rope, was sacrificed to make these, supplemented by part of a coil of rope given me by the Stewart Island Fisherman's Cooperative. A deck safety wire was pressed into service as a forestay. I was tired out by the time the task was completed, but at least I was ready to raise the makeshift mast the moment the weather allowed.

I had now time to investigate the motor. Not unexpectedly, it was useless, its electrics brine-soaked. I did succeed, with the expenditure of many waterproof Greenlight matches, in getting one stove burner going erratically and I heated some stew and made coffee over the flaring yellow flame.

'This must be Christmas,' I wrote, with my first flash of humour.

The following day, the third since the capsize, was a landmark, for we got under way. The temperature was −2°C and soft ice – frozen sea water – coated the deck. But between the heavy snow showers it was fine and the wind had at last dropped to a normal breeze. This was the opportunity I had been waiting for. I made fast the jury shrouds, one to each side and one to each quarter at the stern and led the forestay wire from the 'mast head' round the bow anchor warp roller and back aft to where I could reach it. Then, planting one end of the spinnaker pole in the mast step, I pushed the light spar upwards and hauled in on the wire forestay until the pole stood vertical, secured laterally and behind by the rope shrouds. The wire was soon made fast and the shrouds tightened down as far as they would go.

The remaining number two storm jib had next to be dragged up from below. I found by trial and error that two knots in the head of the sail reduced its length to that of the short forestay. It only remained to shackle it to the bow, clip the hanks on to the forestay and reeve a pair of sheets. Finally I crawled along to the foot of the mast, braced my back on it against the rolling, and hauled up the jib.

I dared not think how futile was the gesture. The first sights since the accident had shown the stark ice barriers of the Antarctic Peninsula to be around 2,500 miles off, farther than from New York to Seattle or from England to Siberia. It seemed flouting fate as I sheeted in the pathetic rag of sail on the ten-foot mast (the old mast had measured thirty-six feet) and, at the speed of a good one mile an hour, turned the bow towards grim and distant shelter.

Ice Bird had to be steered by hand (from inside the cabin with the tiller lines) whenever the wind was a following one but she could be left to make good her own rather erratic course in beam winds and, with head winds, she could be persuaded to point ever so slightly to windward. My compass could not function inside the steel hull because of the magnetism, so when steering by hand I had to peer up from my seat on the corner of a bunk through the Perspex dome at the strips of sailcloth I had tied to the backstays to indicate the wind direction. Steering was essentially a matter of keeping these at a constant angle.

Since the most common wind directions were approximately from north-west or south-west, the yacht's natural tendency was to sail sideways to the wind and waves (a characteristic that meant ceaseless rapid rolling – a most vile motion); her preferred direction of advance was frequently towards the south-east or north-east rather than due east and we pursued our way, often as not, in a series of zigzags. Sometimes, the wind being more northerly or southerly, *Ice Bird* could be left to her own devices and would follow roughly the desired course for as long as a day or more. At other times, when the wind was more westerly, I would have to steer by hand for twelve or fourteen hours at a stretch, only letting go of the lines to snatch up a biscuit, slice off a hunk of corned beef or answer the call of nature. Time and again, the need for sleep would overwhelm me and all hope of making progress would have to be abandoned for the time being in favour of my body's imperative demand for rest.

The numbness in my swollen hands was beginning to give way to intense and growing agony, showing that some life at least remained in them. Antibiotics offered the one hope of saving my fingers, else infection would make short work of the damaged and devitalized tissues, so I now began taking double doses of Tetracycline capsules and continued this massive therapy for several weeks. To aggravate matters, my left knee became red and swollen. The same antibiotics might be expected to control this infection too. The hope was happily realized, and the pain and swelling subsided in a few days. The Australian Antarctic medical expert and veteran of the Heard Island expeditions, Dr Graeme Budd (he himself had been badly frostbitten) had helped me to plan a joint investigation into the effects of prolonged wet cold that I was expected to encounter during the voyage. This scientific study was accumulating far more information than I had bargained for, I thought ruefully.

Whenever I was not otherwise occupied I turned to escapist novels, so that I could forget for a while the surrounding squalor and misery. But to return to the reality of chilly feet squelching in boots that I had no option but to wear day and night – since my clumsy sausage-like fingers were unequal to the task of unlacing them – to damp sleeping bag and aching hands only served to deepen my depression. The violent rolling in the virtual absence of a steadying sail was physically and mentally exhausting too. Then always at the back of my mind was the reality that I still dare not quite face: one mile an hour – and that in favourable conditions. How far to land? I pushed the thought from me.

Then even this dismally slow progress was halted. After the crippled yacht had been crawling eastward for four days, the foot of the little mast broke off in a gale; and a stormy night and day intervened before I could sort out the cat's cradle of rigging tangled around the deck and raise it again.

'Hands always pain,' I wrote.

Assessed soberly, the situation did, indeed, appear hopeless – in the middle of the stormiest ocean on earth with a makeshift mast that kept crumbling away. I silently cursed the unknown busybody who had added a particular statistic to the *National Geographic World Atlas* that I had aboard: 'World's most distant point from land,' he had written. His totally redundant cross on the map lay due north of *Ice Bird*'s position.

It was impossible for me any longer to ignore the facts. 'A shutter has closed between a week ago when I was part of the living and since. Chance [of survival] negligible but effort in spite of pain and discomfort. These last are very great. Must go on striving to survive, as befits a man. Susie and Vicky without a daddy is worst of all.'

Next day, as blinding snow showers driving up from the south ushered in a new gale, I wrote further. 'Surprising no fear at almost certainly having to die, a lot of disappointment though.'

Would all I could offer the children be memories that would soon fade and the austere comfort of the words I had written in the will made before leaving Sydney? 'In the event of my death attempting to storm new frontiers at sea . . . I want Vicky and Susie to know that I expect them always to face life unafraid, with their heads up, and always remembering to laugh. My grown-up children already know this.'

To my own surprise, I realized that the intolerable thought of the little girls left fatherless did even more to keep me striving than did the urge for self-preservation. Also, surprisingly, the expectation of dying in such utter solitude, about as far from human contact as it was possible to be anywhere on earth, did not occasion me any special despondency; since every one of us must ultimately tread this road alone.

A kind of philosophy seemed to have taken shape about this time. The chances of crossing two and a half thousand miles of Southern Ocean in my leaking, battered boat, with its ludicrous mast were too remote for serious contemplation and the far from welcoming blizzard-swept escarpments that were my destination promised no welcoming havens. I must just live for the day, therefore. The awful effort demanded by the daily struggle was worthwhile *in itself*, regardless of its hopelessness; despite its futility this striving would, in some obscure way, not be wasted.

I tried clumsily to express these thoughts in the log. 'Earning membership of humanity – must earn it every day, to be a man.' I proceeded to try for that day's quota by laboriously and painfully emptying out twenty-four bucketfuls of bilge water, clearing the jammed halyard in a snowstorm and hoisting another sail to assist the little jib. This was the storm tri-sail. The head had once again to be knotted so that it could fit the diminutive mast.

If it were not for my hands, how much more I could do, I kept thinking. But even after being outside only long enough to take a sun sight I found myself 'shouting with the pain in my fingers'. The morning of 11 December was relatively calm and I was able to get the stove going, for the first time in five days, to heat up a can of stew and make a lukewarm cup of coffee. I was depressed the greater part of the time, overtired but restless and unable to sleep soundly even when I did have the chance.

By the 12th I had become more obsessed than ever with my terrible hands. Time and again I postponed or put off altogether going on deck to carry out the most urgent and necessary tasks, all for fear of the endless minutes of torture that I knew must inevitably follow. 'Steering by yoke and line from the cabin all afternoon,' I wrote. 'Gashed and frostbitten fingers more painful now. Are they healing? Worry over water [the supply of fresh water aboard was unlikely to prove adequate for reaching land at the present rate of progress], distance, time. Sometimes just get cowardly and whimper a bit in my sleeping bag.'

Then at midnight I concluded the tale of the day's tribulations. 'SW gale, force 8, *lower four inches of jury mast crumbled*. Lowered sail and lay a-hull. Hands stand less cold than ever.'

The grim reality behind these laconic phrases had been my clawing desperately about the deck, as always on hands and knees, smothering the flapping sails with my body until I could secure them with lashings and then tightening down the shrouds to secure the mast, as I had before – only this time even less of it remained. All this was in darkness out of which streamed volleying snow pellets and stinging half-frozen droplets of spray.

I could not know then that *Ice Bird* was on the eve of another new disaster.

Did I pray? people ask. No. I longed to be able to but, not being religious at other times, I had just enough dignity left not to cry out for help when the going got a bit rough. A higher power, should one exist, might even appreciate this attitude!

I am very often asked about loneliness and I have mentioned the subject previously. Even though my prospects had now changed so radically, I was at least spared this desolate emotion. My little drama was being played out on the vast stage of the Southern Ocean with death lurking in the wings, but my solitude, while full of anguish, was never lonely.

The last day of the eighth week out of Sydney Cove, 13 December (just a fortnight after the capsize) was not a Friday. But it dawned inauspiciously enough – and continued worse. The gale that at midnight had sheered off its four-inch quota of the spinnaker pole mast, had increased until it was blowing at force eleven by 7.30 that morning – only one point in the wind scale below a hurricane. The lashings I had tied so tightly round the sails the night before were totally inadequate in a storm of this intensity. Frozen snow-filled pockets of heavy sailcloth ballooned out of the ice-sheathed ropes that confined them and proceeded to flog themselves to pieces with the abandon of demented living things. I hastily hunted out more cord and braved the icy deck to wind the cord round the tri-sail and jib, in defiance of the screaming snow-laden wind that strove to wrest the line from my numb hands.

'Dear God,' I thought, 'if only I could set even the smallest headsail to give the yacht steerage way and render her controllable in these terribly high, steep seas.' But I well knew this was a vain ambition – doubly so, because the strongest sail would have disintegrated before ever it could have been sheeted home and, in my case, the frail jury mast could never have stood the added stress. I was left with no option but to try to make the yacht steer down wind under bare poles again. And I had already experienced the futility of attempting that procedure in these Southern Ocean seas (unlike in the North Atlantic) and the near-fatal consequences of failure.

Well, no more could usefully be done on deck. Down below I made sure that nothing had been omitted from the gale routine that bitter experience had dictated. I mentally ticked off the items. Hatches fastened, washboards in place. Yes, I had secured the table by spreading across it a piece of strong nylon fishing net, anchored on one side to the port bunk board and, on the other, tied down to the floor battens. This should keep not only the table itself in place, but also the current supply of canned food stored in three boxes underneath it, even if – I hated to admit the possibility even to myself – even if the *Ice Bird* were to be capsized again. One locker only was without a catch and this I attempted less successfully to net down too. A criss-cross of cords (seamanship basically boils down to having quantities of string of all sizes – impossible to have too much) tied down my cardboard files of letters, lists and photostats, many of these papers stuck together and part-pulped from their ducking a fortnight earlier. There were few suitable points to anchor the cord to, so the documents stood to fare little better than before. The heavy bundle of damp, slimy charts – there were so many that I could scarcely lift them – had already been stuffed into the plastic bag with the fewest holes. Now I pushed the logbook in on top, and after a moment's thought, added a few rolls of toilet paper.

What else? The vital watch, of course. I wrapped it in cotton wool and placed it in a box which I wedged among the plastic bags containing spare batteries and matches in the driest locker. Next the ventilators. I stuffed each one tightly with rags. Fresh air was not at a premium that day – neither was salt water. Finally, laboriously, at the cost of many a bruise and quantities of spilled water, I bailed out twenty bucketfuls from the centre well to leave the bilge dry. This done, I tried once more to steer, but, as in the hurricane that had turned her over, the yacht generally wallowed broadside on and refused to run off before the enormous wind-torn waves, which were becoming more formidable every minute.

By early afternoon the relentless, sustained wind of sixty knots or over had built up huge hollow seas, which differed in two respects from the mighty storm waves I had encountered in other oceans – the rapidity with which they increased in height and their extraordinary steepness.

'They are *jetting* forward,' I noted at 1.30 p.m., with horror. The streaming lines of foam driving across the frothing waste were scarcely distinguishable from the opaque white of the snow blizzard that swept over them. And here and there amid the general turmoil great killer breakers collapsed like tumbling waterfalls in thunderous ruin. Sooner or later one was bound to mark us as its prey. Could we survive?

After watching in helpless misery while the remains of the self-steering gear broke up and was swept away, I made one more attempt to steer. It was hopeless. We lay, helplessly, starboard side to, rolling the decks under. I cowered down on the port bunk, back braced against the cabin bulkhead – as if to seek companionship from the kangaroo and kiwi painted there – about as far into the depths of the cabin as it was possible to get.

It must have been around three o'clock in the afternoon that it came: the dreaded shock that exploded like a bomb: that heart-stopping lift again. Then the little home enclosing me whirled round in a dizzying arc and, for a fraction of a second that seemed an age, I was standing on my head on the roof of the upside-down cabin, before *Ice Bird* crashed over right side up once more.

My preparations had paid off. True, the sleeping bag was soaked through again and my already damaged typewriter, vaulting from its restraining cords, had been smashed into a shapeless tangle of twisted keys and festooned ribbon. Sodden ships biscuits plastered the sides of the cabin and the deck head (the roof). Sultanas, peanuts, cheese and chocolate had once again been liberally dunked in brine laced with kerosene and, in the case of the first two at least, rendered practically inedible. But the precious charts and the logbook were safe and the netted table had held down most of the cans in the boxes beneath it. Blocking the ventilators had kept the water intake down to a paltry twenty-one bucketfuls. More remarkable still: the little mast, I saw with astonishment, was miraculously still standing.

So far, so good. But we had not escaped unscathed, as I realized when I tried to open the main hatch. It slid back a foot, then jammed. No amount of straining would budge it a millimetre farther. Was I trapped in a steel coffin? My heart began to race unpleasantly until common sense came to my aid. There was always the fore hatch, and the difficulty there was to keep it closed, not to open it. In a calmer frame of mind I pushed and struggled and at length succeeded in squeezing through and locating the trouble. The frame of the pram hood, made of half-inch galvanized steel piping, had been so buckled when the yacht had crashed upside down into the water as to jam the hatch by fouling the Perspex dome. In no way, without the facilities of a machine shop, could I hope to straighten it again. Fortunately, I could just wriggle my way through in my bulky clothes.

The immediate problem, of course, was how to bail. How on earth could I lift a bucket of bilge water past me when I was wedged in the hatchway, not to mention the far more delicate manœuvre of lifting the toilet bucket out into the cockpit? The answer was found by trial and error. I was able to evolve a set of co-ordinated movements that, when I removed my parka and exhaled deeply, just sufficed to allow me to squeeze the bucket up past my chest and, balancing it precariously above my head, lift it out of the hatch. Bilge water could then be unceremoniously tipped into the cockpit, though the toilet bucket required further contortions before I could gain the bridge deck and empty it safely overside.

The canvas that had covered the twisted pram hood frame had been completely torn away, but this was of little moment. Far more serious, the steel framework had been bent over until it almost touched the steering compass, which was mounted on the main hatch (incidentally, the mounting was damaged). The proximity of the steel tubing must be deflecting the compass needle out of true. This much and the fact that the deviation was easterly was apparent at a glance. But exactly how great was the deviation was a question that could only be answered much later when I had had the opportunity on rare fine days of comparing the compass with sextant readings of the bearing of the sun. It turned out to be a good 20°.

When *Ice Bird* turned over, the barometer had already started rising and, as if satisfied at having so effectively demonstrated its power, the storm now rapidly declined in intensity. The wind eased but, I noted with no enthusiasm, rogue 'killer waves' still continued occasionally to avalanche thunderously. During the night the gale finally blew itself out.

An incongruous note is struck by next day's log. '14 December. My paper is being read before the Royal Society in London today.'

This was an account of ancient Polynesian astronomy, a science that in the islanders' maritime culture was virtually part of navigation. I would much rather be there than here, I thought, wistfully – even at the cost of facing intimidating questions from ranks of eminent astronomers.

No point in wishing. Fortified by ships biscuits and muesli, I pulled a soggy wool glove up over my right hand and a freezing mitt over my left (their mates had never come to light since the first capsize) and reluctantly issued forth into chilly blustery wind under a low, leaden sky. Dubiously eyeing the split and twisted base of the mast, I hoisted a rag of sail and found my forebodings realized when more shards of the aluminium broke away. Was there anything I could do? Seated on the deck, I stared intently at the mast, willing there to be an answer, oblivious of all else except this life and death problem.

I was not wearing my safety harness, for I often omitted it these days; after all, the precaution seemed rather pointless when the ship itself was doomed. The breaking sea caught me unawares, the shock catapulting me through the air towards the vanished starboard guard wires. Here I brought up agonizingly, if providentially, against the tip of a stanchion. I felt ribs go in a blaze of breath-stopping agony and my right arm went numb as the elbow shared the impact. I can't stand any more pain, I thought, as I writhed in the scuppers, gasping for breath. But there was also relief that I had not gone over the side, where five minutes in the $-1°C$ water would have brought oblivion. Such is the mark of our humanity. There is no foreseeable way out of your predicament; you have come to the end of your tether; yet some unsuspected strength within you drives you to keep on fighting.

I dragged myself, moaning and groaning and making a great to-do, along the side deck and down below. As the wind was from the south-south-west there was no need to steer. Bilge water was overflowing the floorboards, though. Cursing mentally – drawing each breath meant stabbing pain enough without aggravating it by speech – I prized up the floor and scooped up twenty-two buckets from the well to tip them into the cockpit. The rest of that pain-fringed day and a restless, chilly night I spent on my bunk, increasingly aware of the vast difference between a merely damp sleeping bag and one still soaked from the recent capsize.

The morrow brought little relief. True this was the day I discovered the missing rum bottle projectile, which had penetrated the floor of the locker; but our poor progress, as revealed by two sun sights, gave little cause for complacency. I hoisted the tri-sail to give us a little more speed and was duly rewarded when the wire span that held the halyard blocks to the masthead parted and the sails came tumbling down. Three hours in snow showers relieved by intervals of fitful sunshine were taken up in lowering the mast and repairing the damage. I also took the opportunity of fashioning a pair of wire shrouds out of a spare inner forestay, to reinforce the rope stays.

The knife-stabs in my right side that had greeted any sudden body movement during this work on deck became less frequent once I had returned below where I could move with greater caution. But my hands! I rocked back and forth, tears squeezing out from under my eyelids. Would they never mend? Extravasated blood ballooned out each finger end grotesquely so that the finger nails were acutely angled. The bases of the fingers were, in contrast, pale but so swollen that my hands looked like flippers. On the credit side, there was as yet no sign of gangrene. The antibiotics must be taking effect, then, and the healing process beginning, though how complete it would be only time would tell – if time were allowed me. But the pain! The agony resulting from only the briefest moment of chill was worse, much worse than it had been and was lasting longer.

This was the day that my sheepskin trousers, which had shown signs of falling apart, finally disintegrated. Damp and smelly though they were, I was sorry to see the last of them; sorrier still to have to go through the awkwardness and discomfort of getting them off, then pulling over my shivering limbs the mildewed and half-frozen Dacron flying suit I had earlier discarded. How much more of this recurrent misery could I stand? Would it not be easier just to give up the hopeless struggle? And fresh trouble was in store: as I lit the hurricane lamp that evening, I saw with a sinking heart that the glass was dropping again.

I spent a sleepless night as the weather worsened. The number two storm jib, despite the knots that reduced its length to fit the short mast, was setting so badly that periodically it threshed violently. This was my best and strongest sail, a brand-new one, but because I could not immediately think up any way of saving it from the damage it was sustaining, I did not even venture outside to look. Had I done so, ways of dealing with the trouble surely would have become apparent. I would rather not record this, but the sorry fact of the matter is that I had become so demoralized and my dread of pain from fingers and ribs was so great that I did not once go on deck to experiment with the sail's sheeting for three whole days.

Meanwhile the wind rose, fell and rose again, varying between a modest force six breeze and a force eight gale. *Ice Bird* took some heavy buffets and the jib continued to vibrate. Lengths of shock-cord hooked to the tiller lines allowed me to leave them but not for long, so I sat for hours staring miserably out of the transparent dome at the happy-looking ice birds that fluttered around the cockpit. A careless one even flicked the backstay with its wing.

By 18 December a strong gale was building up steep, hollow, tottering seas. This was the third day of my shameful cowering below – I was aware of my own weak-mindedness; I even noted it in the log, but I had not will power enough to overcome it, taking refuge instead in escapist novels. At 11 a.m. one of the collapsing seas broke aboard, catapulting a volley of pots, aluminium plates and cutlery clear across the cabin.

It was five o'clock that afternoon when the much abused jib split, leaving a portion still drawing. I could have saved it had I only bestirred myself earlier. Now it was too late, so I left up the flapping remnants to give the yacht some steerage way to run before the gale, which had now increased until it was blowing at something like fifty-five to sixty knots with no sign of abatement.

Somewhat belatedly I set about the near hopeless job of trying
to stitch up the first storm jib, which had been torn almost in
two in the initial capsize. One vital item forgotten in the rush at
Sydney had been a sail-mending palm. The best that could be
done was to use a book to press the sail needle through the seams
of the tough eleven-ounce Terylene, to execute a clumsy repair
that I doubted would stand any strong wind. Meanwhile outside
my tossing steel shell the south-east gale, fresh chilled from its
passage across the polar floes, roared out ever more fiercely over
the Southern Ocean, tearing off great gouts of water bodily from
the wave crests and driving them horizontally before it.

'Trembling and fearful night,' I wrote, without exaggeration.
'Water washing over floorboards. Shriek wind in spite of blocked
ventilators and full battening down washboards.' My thoughts
can be imagined.

Blinding snow showers, sweeping across the ocean's face
before even stronger squalls, heralded dawn around 2 a.m. The
formerly hollow seas now seemed to have been flattened a little
by the very fury of the storm – but for how long, I wondered?
Then, somewhere around 6 a.m., the stainless steel luff wire of
the already split jib tore right through. Now I had to redeem as
best I could the cowardice that had kept me so long in the cabin –
now that it was much too late to save anything of the sail, unused
until three weeks ago, which was now completely split in two,
with even its bronze hanks fractured. I brought up the jib I had
mended the day before and dragged it along the deck to the forestay, where I hanked it on. But no sail could be hoisted in that
storm. Once again we were riding out a severe gale with no means
of propulsion so that the ship was out of control and the seas
tossed her from side to side at their will.

By now the cabin was well awash and fresh spurts of water
were continually being forced under pressure through the split
coach roof. It must be got rid of even at the risk of swamping
when unbattening the hatchway. Twenty-seven bucketfuls were
lifted out, every one paid for in pain: pain in my right ribs with
each gasping breath; in my hands as always; from a new bruise
whenever a wave smashed me against the side of the cabin. At
length it was done, though a worse task awaited me. For a record

three days I had held off using the toilet bucket. Now it could not be delayed a moment longer. This was a dreaded chore and a difficult feat of balance at the best of times. In a gale it was a hundred times harder. I dreaded removing my flying suit and, even more, stumbling into my filthy tattered clothes again with one wary eye on the bucket. Emptying the bucket without spilling its contents all over the cabin, myself, the cockpit or the deck was the most delicate operation but, more by luck than otherwise, it was always successfully accomplished.

Afterwards I could not rest; no relaxation being possible while the heavy seas kept crashing on to the resounding metal hull. My morale was very shaky for no respite was in sight even should we survive this particular storm without further damage. Indeed, towards midnight the storm did begin to ease but I was little comforted.

'No progress. Near despair,' I wrote. A half-forgotten fragment of poetry from my schooldays flitted through my mind and was scribbled down in the log.

> Though we are ringed with spears,
> Though the last hope is gone,
> – ? fight on, the – ? gods look on.
> Before our sparks of life blow back to Him who gave,
> Burn bright, brave hearts, a pathway to the grave.

Though I characterized this as 'corny', it did express a little of what I felt, though at times the implications of this bleak destiny would overwhelm me.

By the following morning, 20 December, except for an occasional last fling, the gale had moved away eastward. We had been nine weeks at sea. Going on deck I found that the rope forestay had parted and that several more inches of the spinnaker mast had crumbled away since the day before. When I hoisted the roughly repaired number one storm jib, the yacht had been forty hours lying a-hull without sail.

Back to bailing, only to find that the cockpit drains had become blocked, probably with pulped paper, so the cockpit needed bailing out too. Depressingly, no amount of poking about in the wet cockpit succeeded in clearing the drains. That job would have to wait for another day. I clambered down into the cabin, to discover that the socks I wore to protect my hands and keep them warm, and which were normally relatively dry, had got wet in the recent gale. All these trials and discomforts were getting me down. The perennial problem was the hopeless inadequacy of my attempts to escape from this fierce, lonely sub-Antarctic ocean.

Why was I bothering to write anything down, I wondered, as I drew the damp logbook out of its plastic bag, opened it on the bunk and scrawled painfully.

'How long will the "mast" and stays last? What sail or gear can stand such gales?' Still less could my makeshift arrangements be expected to cope with them.

All in all, the urge to make a daily record in the log was basically illogical because, now that I was facing the issues squarely, there did not really seem to be a way out. Even should *Ice Bird* continue to ride out these repeated storms without mortal damage, we were for practical purposes getting nowhere and time was slowly but surely running out before the freeze-up would render unattainable even the grim shelter we were seeking. Water, too, would be running short before long, for I had anticipated a quicker passage. The fine rain of high latitudes had been more of a dank mist and impossible to collect. Certainly some handfuls of snow had been scraped off the Perspex dome and cabin top on 3 December and made into several cups of coffee but generally the snow had been too contaminated with spray to be drinkable. The last resort – to seek out floating ice – would probably take all summer in a boat so little mobile as *Ice Bird* then was.

Yet I did have vague hopes that someone, somewhere would read what I was setting down. Even if by then I was dead of thirst and privation, *Ice Bird*, floating half waterlogged or perhaps frozen in, might be found by some whaler or expedition ship. Such thoughts were often in my mind these days, as were speculations about how revolting it would be for someone to come across my decomposing body – unless, of course, time and birds had reduced it to an aseptic skeleton or, more likely, it had been deep frozen like a Siberian mammoth's carcase.

.

If only it had been possible to erect a stout, dependable mast I could have made it. I mixed a tot of rum (a large one, I see by the log), drank it down resignedly and squirmed into my sleeping bag, for it was night now, the evening of 20 December. This was my darkest hour. But some portion of my mind was far from resigned. All at once the idea, fully formed, burst into consciousness to set me bolt upright, trembling with excitement. The key to survival had come into my hand.

Chapter 5

Future Possible: *The Fight to Make Land*

The ideal jury mast had all along been the robust eleven-foot, six-inch wooden boom. But it was far too heavy and unmanageable for me to lift upright by hand. Now I *knew* how it could be done. Would it work, though, in practice? I would soon learn the answer, for the very next morning, 21 December, the wind had miraculously dropped right away, though the sea still ran very high. There had been little sleep for me during a night spent elaborating the idea and I was early astir. By eight o'clock it was calm enough for me to begin.

The boom first of all had to be rigged with side shrouds, forestay and backstay. The wire shrouds I doubled for extra security with stout rope ones made fast to ringbolts that I bolted to the rail. The twin backstays leading to each quarter were retained and reinforced by a central wire stay improvised, like the forestay, out of a deck safety wire. This standing rigging must be doubly secure. Should this mast ever be raised, I was making sure that it would never come down again.

I would not have thought it possible to do all this, down to fitting and tightening the bulldog grips that locked the wire loops, with hands encased in a mitt and a glove. Yet that was how it was done. Halyards for hoisting the sails had next to be rove through blocks shackled to the future masthead – a double purchase for the jib, since it must be hauled up taut; a single block for the tri-sail. One end of the boom (the intended foot) was fitted into the mast step; the other, with its festoons of ropes and wires, was lifted into the boom crutch above the main hatchway.

Now for my inspiration. I detached the main sheet (the many-part tackle with sufficient mechanical advantage to haul in the mainsail against the pressure of strong winds) from the sliding horse over the rudder head and, on hands and knees, dragged it forward to the bow. Here I shackled its lower block to the fore-stay fitting and led the tail back aft to the powerful sheet winch. All these preparations, which had mostly to be carried out crouching or crawling to maintain balance on the erratically tossing deck, took from eight in the morning till half-past four in the afternoon – eight and a half hours without a single break. But too much – life itself – depended on the outcome for me to stop then.

Tense with anxiety, I began to turn the winch handle. Was the 15° angle at which the boom lay, hopefully pivoted at the mast step and supported upon the crutch at its other end, sufficient to give purchase? Yes. The boom rose a foot out of the crutch, then it slewed as the yacht lurched sharply to port and stuck fast. I could have cried. But, thank goodness, its foot had only jammed in the pin rail. On the second attempt the boom mounted steadily inch by inch to the vertical.

One hour later. An old cotton staysail folded in half along the centre seam to fit the strong, but still diminutive, new mast had been shackled on, hoisted and sheeted in. No matter that pus was now welling out of my right thumb where the bone itself had become infected. Never mind exhaustion and pain. We were under way with a reliable mast at last, one that could stand up to all the sail that I could string from it – the storm tri-sail and the lower half of a folded-over or divided staysail. That night I drank rum and condensed milk in celebration of hope reborn and, in the gentle yellow glow of the hurricane lamp, supped on corned beef that had miraculously taken on a new, delicious flavour. From time to time I peered aloft at the wind pennant streaming from the backstay and adjusted the helm with a pull on the tiller lines.

I contentedly dozed the night away, the tiller lines still in my hands. Next morning in a snow shower I hoisted the tri-sail to speed our passage. The tiller lines continued to demand my attention all that day, the following night and on into 23 December – forty hours or thereabouts – before the wind shifted into the south and *Ice Bird* could be trusted to pursue her way unaided.

How lucky I was to have reading matter, but how boring, I thought, referring to those long monotonous hours lately past. The boat had to be kept moving as fast as possible and on course.

There must be a system of priorities, which I summed up that morning. 'Not concerned with sights – only to make the best time – other problems like my last jib with windward ability can wait until, if ever, needed! . . . Finger nails beginning to loosen. Tender, tender fingers vulnerable to cold [There was some necrosis of the terminal bone in my right thumb. Care of my fingers was certainly a priority.] . . . Fluid conservation . . . Sea is not cruel, it is neutral. Depends on *me*,' I concluded.

I gazed around the cabin, remembering how once it had been so orderly and shipshape. It certainly looked a shambles now, but it was in fact an organized shambles, where everything had its accustomed place even if only on the floor. Some storage spaces were particularly unsatisfactory, like the wet locker where the tools were fast rusting – but where else could they go?

My personal papers had fared worst. The list of food stowage particulars had been pulped to shreds. Thus it was that I never did find the eggs at all. I did come across the sugar once (under a great pile of sodden cardboard, cheese and salami in the toilet compartment) and extracted one bag. I must have been dreaming at the time because I completely forgot where I had found it and, though I subsequently searched diligently, I never did rediscover the sugar's hiding place. Then there was the sheaf of addresses of people and organizations whose generosity had made possible the fitting out of *Ice Bird*. The few that had survived at all were illegible. Their loss will probably lead me to omit some very important acknowledgements and thanks – and so give the appearance of gross ingratitude.

The wind remained abeam and the yacht continued steering herself. By the evening of the 23rd I was rested and it was sufficiently calm for me to decide to cook supper. The procedure was complicated enough not to be embarked upon lightly. The spare Primus camping pressure cooker had first to be assembled (at other times I preferred to struggle with the erratic burners of the ship's stove). Everything necessary had next to be placed ready to hand for, once lit, the stove had to be held steady between my knees. Matches done up in plastic bags were kept in one locker (the driest), the methylated spirits for priming were in another. Saucepan, cutlery and the rapidly rusting can openers were heaped under the ruined chart table, the shelves where they had formerly been kept having disintegrated. Since I could not open the locker catches with my fingers, the steel sharpener carried in my knife sheath was pressed into service – as for many other operations. Nor could I, without functioning fingernails, pick up a dropped match. So it was lucky there was a good supply of Greenlights.

'A real picnic,' I described the process, in the log. No wonder I could not often face the effort of cooking, so that it was only every two or three days that I bothered to heat anything.

This time there was coffee, followed by hot canned potatoes and corned beef, the first hot things I had tasted for a week.

Next day and the one after that were both Christmas Days. My local noon on 24 December would be seven o'clock on Christmas morning back over the date line in Canberra, I calculated. What were the little girls doing and thinking, I wondered, understandably depressed. The first two fingernails to loosen were nearly off now – well, that was progress of a sort. Still I must not brood. There was the sea routine to be followed, so I set about checking the new rigging for wear and tear and tightening it where necessary. A length of wire proved to be the key to scraping out the debris that had blocked the cockpit drains. I felt better after doing something constructive. Then out of the blizzard (it was a white Christmas, right enough) floated my friends the ice birds, so I crumbled up and tossed them their share of Christmas ships biscuits. I felt less alone, seeing them circling among the silent snow flakes.

My own bonus arrived the following day, the 25th. A livid, leaden dawn, sea and sky later gave way to broken overcast, though snow showers continued all day and the snow-flitting ice birds once more shared my dinner. Rather dubious sun sights, the first for ten days, gave our position as 61° 30′S., 104° 57′W. This was real progress at last, mainly attributable to the new mast's ability consistently to support more sail.

'If only these figures are correct,' I wrote, 'this is . . . the best Christmas present.'

There was a less pleasant episode next morning, when I dis-

covered that a four-gallon plastic petrol can had burst and its
contents, emulsified with sea water, had produced a substance
that I thought resembled octopus vomit (or what I imagined this
would be like). This foul greasy liquid had blocked the drain
pipes and filled the cockpit, slopping out on to the deck as we
rolled. There was nothing for it but to scoop out all I could and
then plunge in and clear the drain. Everything became plastered
with the clinging mess, in the process. My boots were so slippery
that I could not stand without support. To make matters worse,
the petrol fumes brought on an attack of nausea and vomiting so
acute that I was forced to heave-to and rest for several hours.
Afterwards I resumed steering, still shaky and plagued by the
discomfort of my wet 'hand socks'.

The question of destination had now become a crucial one.
The bases at Deception Island in the South Shetland Islands, which
would have been the obvious choice had, I knew, been largely
abandoned following a volcanic eruption, so that ruled them out.
The longer I looked at the damp charts, taking great care not to
tear them, and read the pilot book and the latest bulletins on
occupied bases, the more convinced I became that the best course
of action was the boldest one – to continue to aim for the Antarctic Peninsula itself. The only innovation would be the choice
of the American Palmer Antarctic Station on the south coast of
Anvers Island as being much easier of access than the British
base at the Argentine Islands, which was tucked away behind a
myriad rocks and skerries, forty miles farther south-east.

Not without much doubt and heart searching as to the wisdom
of my choice, I decided on Palmer. There was a certain grim
satisfaction in continuing to make for approximately the same
spot as had been my goal from the start. After all that had happened, had I the effrontery to dare hope to save my ship and
myself and attain the Antarctic continent as well? Impertinent as
this ambition seemed, I would try to achieve it.

But sober calculation of times and distances and, above all, of
drinking water, must supplement mere determination before I
could hope to succeed.

The position regarding water was this. The seventeen-gallon
tank in the keel was empty as of 27 December, ten weeks out from

Sydney and eight since the tank had been topped up at Stewart Island. Of the water in plastic cans there remained fourteen gallons though, such was the confusion following the capsizes, that, at the time, I only discovered ten. This should be enough at my then rate of progress but to be on the safe side I decided to introduce strict accounting and rationing, at least for a time. The other alternative, sailing due south into the pack ice and there replenishing my supply, would mean a lengthy detour and the waste of weeks of precious time. Still, it was available as a last resort.

The unpleasant water rationing process opened with a twenty-four-hour period without any water at all, necessary in order to shut down kidney output to a minimum. Thereafter I adjusted my fluid intake so as to maintain a concentrated dark urine. Whenever it became pale and diluted I knew I was overconsuming and so wasting liquid. I am speaking here, of course, of total fluids, including canned fruit and vegetable juice, not water alone.

Experience showed that the quantity needed to keep me in water balance, for the three weeks it seemed prudent to maintain this regime, was just over a pint a day. I was conscious of thirst all the time but did not become dehydrated. The cabin temperature averaged round about zero centigrade so sweating was at a minimum. On the other hand, mucus streaming from my nose (every skier is familiar with this phenomenon) accounted for an appreciable drain of fluid. Long periods of heavy work on deck not unnaturally produced a raging thirst.

A period of better weather now set in, for the sub-Antarctic summer had come at last. The routines of checking over the rigging for signs of chafe, attending to the grub screws that locked the tiller to the rudder head, of adjusting the trim of the sails and, too often, steering by hand, continued monotonously. My fingers were no whit less painful after each period of exposure but profound boredom tended to replace chronic anxiety and acute terror. The books that were my only escape from sleeplessness, thirst and anxiety were becoming scarce, since I had read the best of them. The nights had become barely worthy of the name. Before the sunset finished painting the whole south-western quadrant of the sky scarlet and gold, its heraldry became joined towards the south-east with the pink and orange of the sunrise. Thus, around midnight, whenever the clouds lifted, the whole southern horizon blazed with fire.

Only too frequently, at this time, the wind fell so light that the yacht was almost or totally becalmed. This caused fresh worries about progress as *Ice Bird* crept eastward into the new year.

'Hand steering necessary every second,' I noted on 1 January, 'but moving towards life – the wind is westerly.'

Another day and – despite tears in the old cotton staysail that indicated its days were numbered and exhausting hours of hand steering – I was heartened that we had passed an important milestone: we had broken the 1,000-mile barrier; there were but 945 miles to go. The site of the first capsize had been left 1,500 miles astern.

Then came 3 January, which, besides being the end of the eleventh week out, marked the beginning of my appreciation that the voyage had entered a new phase – that of '*practical* awareness of dangers and difficulties' when there was '*some* chance'.

These problems and dangers mostly concerned landfall; knowing when land was close aboard, identifying the stretch of coast and then penetrating its icy offshore defences. Navigation would be complicated by the generally overcast skies that could be counted upon to blanket the sun at the most inconvenient moments and by the unknown error of the wrist watch. I had no option but to rely upon my assumption that the watch would continue gaining the six seconds a day that it had up to 29 November, though this was pure guesswork and might be wildly out. (The trusty Omega did, in fact, gain five seconds a day, so that it was only fifty-five seconds slower on landfall than I had calculated.) Once a successful landfall had been made the problems would multiply. The idea of having to manoeuvre the damaged and barely manoeuvrable vessel among rocks, islets and bergs, in tidal waters subject to strong erratic winds, filled me with dread. The best I could do was to take every opportunity of drying out the charts and trying to digest everything the *Antarctic Pilot* had to say about the formidable dangers attending every possible line of approach.

Doubts as to how long the sails would last (the two strongest headsails were already destroyed) also plagued me. Then my general health had deteriorated during the voyage; my bodily strength seemed to have been sapped by all I had been through – to say nothing of the condition of my hands. Could I stand up to the heavy additional demands (like steering from *outside* in the cockpit) bound to be made during the days of that final approach, I wondered? Of more immediate concern was the fact that we had strayed much too far south, almost to 63°S., into the zone of calms and unfavourable easterly winds. In fact it was on this very same morning of 3 January that we found ourselves in a new world, whose smiling face masked its real hostility; a world of sunlit, brilliant blue, calm sea, where the temperature had risen to a relative heatwave of +3°C. But the gentle breeze was easterly – dead on the nose.

For the next three days I fretted and fumed, trimmed and re-trimmed sails and repeatedly adjusted the tiller lines, while the light head winds were only interrupted by periods of calm. Then *Ice Bird* would lie dead in the water, her only motion slow rolling on the undulating glassy swells and my impatience would mount to new heights. No more than sixty miles were made good during those three days. I found the delay exasperating.

'Books (getting short unfortunately) are my only drug to hide me from reality. Sleeping badly. Thirsty all the time.'

The wind now freshened and became more often favourable but long periods of hand steering became the rule rather than the exception and these severely taxed my limited strength. On the 9th, the cotton staysail finally blew out and I hoisted another old sail, the genoa or number one staysail, having first snipped away with scissors the redundant upper half above the centre seam. The ship, which had been lying dormant while the headsails were being changed, came alive as the latest staysail was sheeted in, and steadied to the wind, her rolling controlled by its pressure.

Sights indicated a good run that day, which so heartened me that I at last took stock of my unprepossessing personal appearance. I made an unsuccessful attempt to get a comb through my hair. I even attempted to shave in cold salt water, but this too had to be abandoned.

The only thing left to me was cleanliness. 'Changed socks and pants after about a month. Feet in good condition, a bit water-logged, very smelly. Will they speak to a polecat at the base?' This occasion, and the time the sheepskin trousers had to be discarded, were the only times I took off my insulated boots. Otherwise I wore them day and night for a full two months.

The log continues, airing what had now become my habitual preoccupation. 'Landfall, and especially making harbour, won't be easy. Must try to make a good approach and then avoid impatient rush. Other thumbnail off.' The note of impatience was a salutary warning. We were now overdue and I was well aware of the anxiety this must be causing, especially to the girls and Barry. The thought of their fears – whenever I was foolish enough to allow my mind to stray into forbidden pathways – was unendurable and every instinct demanded that I hurry to reach a radio transmitter at the earliest moment, practicable or not. Such rash haste must at all costs be avoided, I realized in my more sober moments. Better to waste a week, if necessary, waiting for weather and then cautiously thread the frozen perimeter of the continent, than to rush in blindly and never arrive at all.

There followed two days of running down-wind before westerly snow squalls, two days during which I had to steer by hand for eighteen and fifteen hours respectively, but to such good effect that sights the following day, the 12th, showed that we had no more than five hundred miles left to go. I was elated and poured myself out an extra drink of canned apple juice as a bonus. Then a railway locomotive let off steam alongside the yacht and I leapt up incredulously, banging my head painfully against the hatch cover. Two sei whales, each about *Ice Bird*'s size, were swimming slowly beside her, side by side, the nearest about four yards off. Their elongated, warty heads were just awash, though sometimes they emerged far enough for the sardonically down-turned mouths to be momentarily visible. Periodically, with a hollow roar, they blew off clouds of steamy vapour in mighty exhalation. I was delighted to have their company and hoped they would remain with us, for, apart from the escorting flock (or flocks?) of ice birds and an occasional albatross or petrel, they were the only living creatures to visit us in this desolate ocean since before the first capsize.

These days, despite my poor physical condition, I was gradually becoming more my old self. It was a milestone, almost a recognition of reborn perception when I wrote on that same day, 12 January, 'Wind-blown snow. Exciting smell of the sea – only now notice it – I am coming to life again.' Rather less optimistically I added a question mark. Indeed, renewed calms, persistent fog and a return of easterly head winds soon sent my labile spirits plummeting downwards again. It was no easy task persuading *Ice Bird* to stand to windward with her minimal rig, especially in light variable winds. The whales at least were welcome company. Probably with the children in mind, I had christened them 'Sniffy' and 'Snuffy' and only wished I could tell the girls how the pair played around the yacht, weaving in and out like dolphins.

Throughout the period of water rationing chronic thirst remained a constant preoccupation. Thus the log of 16 January. 'Two fingernails came off today. Drink discipline. Sometimes I can't resist cheating. Use more water when steering at night (than when resting). One dodge is waiting till midnight (when I can begin drinking next day's quota). Try to resist temptation . . . nice tasting drinks are a snare.' But this hardship was at least ending. Three days afterwards I had in hand sufficient reserve of water (eight and a half gallons) to end rationing altogether. It turned out, as mentioned earlier, that I had resisted temptation to the extent of consuming no more than a pint and a quarter of all liquids a day.

January 17, thirteen weeks since Sydney. I was all the time conscious of the magnitude of the ordeal that must be undergone before safety could be assured. 'Day dreams: keep off these. The barrier of landfall still stands in the way of entering the ordinary world and there are enormous problems even after this (landfall) before I can see anything of the future.' Then, in recognition of how hope had been rekindled, 'But what day dreams I do have, no longer have the character of obituaries.'

Despite my best intentions, thoughts of the children tore at my equanimity. 'Keep thinking of the girls as I must be causing worry . . . But I can't hurry any more than I am doing. Can't bear to think of the girls' feelings.' (It was about this time or a little before, I learned much later, that their bright confidence seemed at last to have deserted them. They made no comment but became very quiet, moving about like little ghosts.)

A new note of pride in achievement is struck by the main entry in next day, 18 January's, log. 'Cape Horn rounded 360 miles to the north.' Fog banks and still more calms. Becalmed of all places in Drake Passage, the notorious seaway that separates Cape Horn from the Antarctic Peninsula. Not at all how one expects to round 'Cape Stiff', never mind; rounded it in 62°S., well beyond the pale of even Cape Horn latitudes. Perhaps, though, I deserved a respite, for the 'screaming sixties' had been, so far, anything but kind.

Anyway, the customary privileges of those who have rounded the dreaded cape were now mine. I wondered if I would ever be in a position to exercise some of them, like the right to drink the loyal toast with one foot on the table. But one at least was already my prerogative, and I duly entered in the log that I was: 'Now entitled to piss to windward,' then added a note of anticlimax. 'I can do it anyway in this calm.' The real problem in this latitude, I reflected, thinking of my bulky clothing, was trying to get a two-inch pipe through four inches of lagging. No wonder my flying suit was rank with the smell of stale urine.

Two days later, on 20 January, a longitude sight showed us to be in 65° 30'W. – and so to have passed further east than Palmer Station, three hundred miles away to the south. At last I could alter course directly towards our objective.

The culminating battle of the voyage – the fight to win access to the forbidden continent itself – was about to be joined.

Chapter 6
Grim Landfall

Caution – the mariner should exercise great care in navigating the area covered by this work.

Antarctic Pilot, p. 2

As if our change of course had been a signal, the wind now switched into the south-south-west, slowing our southward progress to a crawl and driving us even farther to the east. Good sights were obtained on the 22nd, which depressingly placed us a long way north. We should be well clear of the South Shetland Islands as yet, and were certainly still a long way north of the Antarctic Peninsula proper, but very soon I must begin to exercise caution lest land be nearer than anticipated – either through bad guesswork as to the error of the wrist watch or through the compass deviation (caused by the twisted pram hood frame) being different on this southerly heading.

The day's log shows a natural preoccupation with the weather conditions. 'Snow lying in cockpit. Hard put to hold to windward against lop, so grossly undercanvassed.' By 7 p.m. 'almost becalmed. Snowing heavily. Shut-in feeling from restricted visibility.' Then came the swish of speeding forms, arching half-seen through the swirling snow. They were Commerson's dolphins, small beautiful black-and-white denizens of Tierra del Fuegan waters and Drake Passage, that gave notice by their presence that my navigation was not so far out, after all.

The last remark set down that evening points to a certain depression – 'sick of waterlogged mattresses' – but earlier entries had struck an unusually positive note. 'Mended worst rents in my anorak. Mercy to be able to use fingers. Periods of acute pain less often. Hot coffee, first hot drink for a month (since water rationing) – forgot how comforting. Primus burners very dodgy.'

Most revealing, however, was this sentence. 'Plans for refit maturing.' For the very first time I was thinking beyond gaining safety and even to my long-set goal, the continuation of the voyage.

Another day of repeated snow showers followed, with the skies remaining leaden until midnight, when away to the southward there opened a window beyond the edge of the cloud roof into a sunset-sunrise that was all clear golden light. The wind was variable but mostly easterly, falling very light again during the afternoon. This was the day chosen by Sniffy and Snuffy, after a week spent in our company, to swim off westward. And with them, circling and darting in their wake, went the flock of ice birds that had been with us for so long. This was a break indeed, for, in some illogical way, I knew intuitively that they would not return. I was unable to shake off the fanciful feeling that they were ocean spirits of the drifting snow who, having escorted us safe across the waste and brought us near to land, were departing now their task was ended.

That night I slept soundly, tired out with so much hand steering, and awoke on the morning of the twenty-fourth to find that *Ice Bird* had turned around and was heading back in her tracks. Such are the trials of single-handed sailing. Because of the capricious breezes and this reversal of course I found, when I worked out our position at noon, that we had only made eighteen miles in the past twenty-four hours. On the credit side, my fingers were now capable of handling the heavy brass sextant – instead of only the light plastic one – and with this more accurate instrument available I had more confidence in my navigation.

Hoped-for stronger winds showed no signs as yet of setting in. In fact, before nine that evening, except for the occasional expiring puff, the wind had died away altogether and the silence of the sea was broken only by the swishing of the sails, as the ship rolled, and the clatter of the blocks against the coach roof. Three pintados on the water bobbed and curtsied to each other and flung up spray with their threshing wings in some private display ritual of their own. By midnight even the slatting sails and the blocks were still, but at 3 a.m. a snowstorm ushered in an easterly wind, which gradually steadied and strengthened, as I sat keeping watch as best I could (ice, as well as land, might now be near) through the brief hours of darkness.

I tried to sort out what I had read and been told about this fascinating Antarctic Peninsula, which could not be so very far beneath the horizon. It was a nine-hundred-mile-long projection of the otherwise almost circular Antarctic continent, geologically and geographically a mirror image of the Andes of South America. The ice-choked Weddell Sea forbade all seaborne access on the east, but the western coast, which we were to approach, washed by the Bellingshausen Sea, was much indented and fringed with islands and could be reached for a time in summer.

But even this accessible side, judging by the *Antarctic Pilot*, was rather like the Himalayas transported to sea level, with its peaks rising sheer to ten thousand feet. 'It is nearly all glacier covered,' the *Pilot* (p. 131) says, 'except the most precipitous peaks and cliffs, some of which form part of the coastline, the remainder of the coast consists chiefly of glacier faces.'

Mr Edward Bransfield, RN, of the sealing brig *Williams* was the first to discover the Peninsula (and very possibly the first to see any part of Antarctica) when, on 30 January 1820, in 63° 16' south latitude, 'the haze clearing', land unexpectedly appeared to the south-west. On 16 November that same year, the American sealer Nathanial Palmer in the little *Hero* 'got over under the land' at 63° 45'S. (Unaccountably, the Americans have clung stubbornly to the myth, which they well know to be nonsense, that Palmer was the original discoverer.)

These gallant captains were also ruthless exploiters. A year after Bransfield's voyage ninety-one sealing vessels were active in these waters: by 1822, fur seals had become almost extinct. The whales were more resistant, though a century and a half of continuous hunting in the Antarctic seas have so depleted stocks that only two nations, the Russians and the Japanese, little to their credit, are still carrying on mopping up operations on any significant scale.

Expeditions to the Peninsula have been legion. Of special relevance to the area we were nearing was the British captain John Biscoe's 1832 landing on Anvers Island, which he thought part of the mainland, and de Gerlache's correction of this error in the *Belgica* in 1898, by the discovery of the strait that bears his name. Much later on, between 1934 and 1937, the British three-masted schooner *Penola* under J. R. Rymill, re-charted the better part of the west coast. Of special significance to me was the fact that this extensive survey was carried out in a tiny gaff-rigged semi-open boat, that had been brought to the Antarctic aboard *Penola*. If I remember correctly what its owner, Quentin Riley, told me some years ago in Essex, its overall length was either twenty or twenty-one feet. Seeing that this cockle shell had wandered at will among the icebergs and rocks of this coast for months, why could not I do likewise? At any rate, it should have been possible, had *Ice Bird* still possessed her mast and motor.

I got up and opened the main hatch, for the transparent dome was plastered with snow. Pulling myself up by the pram hood frame, I strained my eyes ahead. It was no use. Nothing but slanting lines of fast falling snow.

Back inside the cabin, my mind returned to the desolate place where we hoped to find shelter. Even its isolation had not sufficed to keep it out of the unedifying stream of power politics. The Peninsula is claimed by Argentina, Britain and Chile. The United States and the USSR also have bases, but have sensibly held aloof from what has been, from the World War II years at least, something in the nature of an international circus act. Glancing through the record almost at random, we find:

1942 Argentine ship *Primero de Mayo* takes formal possession of Deception Island.

1943 HMS *Caernarvon Castle* obliterates Argentine marks of Sovereignty on Deception Island and hoists British flag.

1943 Argentine ship *Primero de Mayo* removes British emblems at Deception Island and repaints Argentine flag.

1943–44 British expedition removes Argentine emblems from Deception Island.

1951–52 Argentine-British armed clash at Hope Bay.

1953 British remove Argentine and Chilean huts from Whaler's Bay and HMS *Bigbury Bay* patrols Deception Island waters.

Ultimately nature itself took a hand in the Deception Island dispute and a volcanic eruption blew up the British and Chilean bases there, leaving the Argentinian one almost intact. In any case, by then the custom is said to have developed (and I will not vouch for the truth of the story) of base commanders delivering their official protests in rotation and afterwards being entertained at monumental parties. These parties so disrupted the work of the various national stations that the signing of the 1959 Antarctic Treaty, whereby all territorial claims were put in cold storage for thirty years, became inevitable.

At least the area was peaceful enough now, I thought, calculating that the treaty still had more than twenty years to run. A good thing too. The Antarctic presented obstacles enough to the lone seafarer without any additional naval complications.

By six o'clock on the morning of 25 January, I could no longer stay awake. Continuing to maintain a lookout seemed pointless, since it was still snowing so heavily that, despite the daylight, visibility was nil. The unattended yacht went bowling along southward with a fair easterly breeze abeam.

The sun was shining when I woke at nine and the white-flecked sea was a deep blue – and floating upon it, glittering with such brilliance that my eyes hurt to look upon them, were three sugar-icing bergs. They lay in a line from east-south-east to west-north-west across our course. One was tabular, another castellated and the third weather-worn and undulating.

Time to steer from the cockpit. Wearing my driest 'hand socks' under the windproof but not waterproof canvas overmitts that I had been carefully husbanding for the occasion, and with fully impervious Marlin jacket zipped up over the recently repaired anorak, I was reasonably warm. Soon a school of blackfish surfed by down the wave faces. Then bergy bits, some as big as small coasters, began to appear ahead and a good lookout became more than ever necessary. Around noon we passed through the line and, the wind continuing to freshen, quickly left astern the three bergs with their inconspicuous but potentially lethal attendants.

The elderly staysail burst around four o'clock. I reluctantly unearthed from the forepeak the last remaining big headsail that I had been saving for the final approach. It was an old-fashioned sail called a footing staysail, specially made to fit *Isbjorn*'s shortish foremast and never before used. I hoisted it with two knots in the head and set off again. It drew well. 'Going like hell,' the log records.

Still the wind kept on increasing, until a north-east force eight gale was blowing by evening, when I reefed the new staysail, 'cold, wet, anxious'. Midnight, and I lowered the mainsail altogether for, to my dismay, a strong force nine gale had by then developed. We continued south-eastward under the storm tri-sail alone.

By the time that I got below my hands were in agony. Minutes later the pain eased and I battened down fully, then listened dully as volleys of spray exploded against the steel hull and the wind's howl became a scream in the squalls. There was no way of keeping a lookout for ice in these conditions. I crept miserably and fearfully into my chilled sleeping bag, more tired than I realized because, for the first time ever, I went sound asleep in a gale.

Astonishingly I did not wake until eight the next morning, 26 January, Australia Day. The gale was still blowing but was down a little to force eight. The cabin temperature was a cheerless −2°C. Beyond the thirty-foot seas amongst which the yacht laboured, gaps in the cloud-wrack revealed icefields sweeping up to vast snow mountains and, nearer, a jagged snow-streaked rocky pinnacle and a jumble of pallid tabular bergs. Far from feeling triumphant at this first sight of land for almost three months – land which I had thought never to see again – I was appalled at the forbidding prospect. After one jaundiced look, I retired to the damp warmth of my sleeping bag and pulled it firmly over my head.

Prudence soon brought me to life again. We were closing the coast fast. By midday the truly gigantic scale of the icebergs in the foreground and of the ice plateaus and mountains behind was beginning to become apparent (though I was to continue to underestimate the vastness of the country, consistently believing we were closer inshore than we were – with dire consequences to my pilotage). The wind had continued to decline but the seas were still huge, if less dangerous, and the sun was only intermittently visible. Sun sights at this juncture were so important that I hove-to to take them. Even so, I was repeatedly jarred against the pram hood frame as I struggled for balance and the resulting observations were poor ones.

I committed myself to an option. 'Land is Brabant or Anvers Island. My bet (before working sight) is Anvers,' I wrote. Sure enough, the latitude line, 64° 21'S. did confirm it as being the west coast of the 1,000-square-mile Anvers Island, on whose southern shore Palmer Station was situated. With such rapidity did the weather moderate that we were periodically becalmed from four-thirty that afternoon onwards.

Now I really did appreciate the magnificent panorama – sixty miles of ice cap and glacier topped by serrated summits two miles high. A truly enormous berg appeared to be grounded off what I (correctly) took to be Cape Alberto de Monaco, the south-west corner of Anvers, that we were slowly nearing, and which we must round to reach Palmer. The Anvers snowfields appeared, for all the world, like level sheets of fog, filling and hiding the valleys, above which soared the lofty summits, culminating in 9,000-foot Mount Français, the highest point of the island.

I sat in the cockpit choked with emotion. Close alongside, parties of penguins called 'ark, ark' as they porpoised out of the water, landing with a succession of little plops. I was still gazing out upon the scene when the light began to fade with evening. The sky above Anvers was a pastel green and the jagged Graham Coast ranges farther southward turned pale gold. A waning moon hung over the empty land. The ice cliffs of the great bergs turned from blue to mauve to violet and then deep purple. We stood on south-eastwards towards an island that I had identified from the chart – only to find next morning that it was really just an iceberg.

The growing daylight revealed my error by 4.30 or so. I took the helm then and continued steering mostly from the cockpit all day; except in the flat calms that alternated monotonously with short-lived north-easterly and easterly wind flurries.

The rounding of Cape Alberto de Monaco would be attended with some hazard, the *Pilot* book warned. The Cape itself was 'fringed with islands and rocks, frequently with gigantic icebergs grounded between them, extending about seven and a half miles south-westward'. (p. 159) Except for a tongue of moraine forming part of the shore of Arthur Harbour, where Palmer Station was

sited, the Anvers coastline consisted entirely of 100–200-foot ice
cliffs.

I wished, for a moment, that we were still making for the
Argentine Islands described in the same work (p. 174) as possess-
ing *a peculiar luxuriance of vegetation . . . moss* covering as much as
an acre.' (My italics.) Then I recalled their formidable rocky defences and was glad enough to forgo this mossy demi-paradise.
The safest route round the cape, I decided, bearing in mind the
fickle breeze and our pathetic rig, was outside Joubin Islands at the
apex of the extensive fringe of foul ground off Monaco proper.
(I was wrong. The inshore route would have been better.)

Tension mounted very high off the first of the Joubins, which
we reached about 11.30 after some six hours at the tiller, for the
breeze died away completely, leaving the shoreward-setting
current free to bear the helpless yacht down upon the snow-
capped islet. She had drifted perilously near when a swirl of snow
flakes signalled a welcome breath of wind and we ghosted clear
of the danger. A little farther on the track lay hard by an echoing
wave-worn cavern, scooped from the base of a three hundred-foot
berg where, even on this calmest of days, surf boomed and
thundered, and the passing *Ice Bird* was rocked by the scend.

All afternoon we continued threading our way among fan-
tastically weathered, grounded bergs and rocky shoals, sometimes
passing within a biscuit toss of cold stone or colder blue ice,
from time to time, crunching through lines of brash with many
a jarring thump. 'With no engine or proper sail it was hell,' I
wrote afterwards, without any exaggeration, for at any moment
during those slow dragging hours a stray current could have
grounded and wrecked us. Those anxious hours stretched well
into the afternoon, so that it was 5.30 before the Joubins, and
their parent cape, had been rounded. Palmer base was eight miles
away across a stretch of skerry-studded water.

It might well have been on the moon, so utterly unattainable
was it. For it lay dead in the teeth of the easterly wind which,
unfortunately, was now the prevailing one, and *Ice Bird*'s ability
to tack to windward was minimal and might even prove non-
existent. The sail area was not only totally inadequate, it was also
ill-balanced. The footing staysail was so large in proportion to

the tiny tri-sail doing duty as a main, that the first gust to break each calm blew the bow round, pivoting the yacht down-wind. Not until she had slowly gathered way could I persuade her to swing reluctantly back to windward again, by which time she had lost the better part of the ground so painfully gained earlier. By the same token, the bow was readily knocked to leeward by the slap of the short inshore waves.

I was very tired, for I had been steering for thirteen and a half hours in the chill open air. An elementary mistake in applying magnetic variation, which could well have had fatal consequences, brought sharply home to me the unreliability of my weary brain. Rest and sleep were obviously essential. But where in these tidal waters, surrounded by so many dangers, could it be managed? Anchoring was out of the question; it was far too deep, each islet and shoal was the tip of an underwater pinnacle rising sheer from fifty fathoms. Safety was so very near. After all the trials we had been through, were we to be wrecked on the very threshold? Exhausted and utterly unnerved, I burst into tears.

Hot coffee – with a generous addition of rum – and a cold snack revived my spirits a little. I took a chance, having no real alternative, and dozed for two hours while *Ice Bird* drifted becalmed. When I awoke at ten, feeling rather better, there was wind again but the light had grown too dim to sail safely any longer, so I lowered the big staysail, leaving the yacht to fore-reach slowly under her tri-sail alone.

One of the unpredictable sudden changes of Antarctic weather now took a hand. Gale force gusts, easterly unfortunately, set in shortly after midnight and drove us towards a fanged huddle of skerries overlooked by a double-spired cathedral-like iceberg. I wore round (gybed) on to the port tack and, still under tri-sail, began to win clear, heading south-eastward away from Anvers Island.

As the iceberg receded, I was electrified at the sight of Palmer Station's tantalizingly inaccessible light shining brightly across the intervening miles. Perhaps they had a motor boat that could tow me in? We were moving farther away every minute. I hurriedly let off a flare, which, predictably at that range, accomplished nothing more than burning my fingers.

The violent gusts coalesced into a gale that increased until it
was howling, snow-laden, down from the mountain defiles at a
good sixty knots. The waves were steep but no more than five
feet high, for the near-by land gave shelter. In company with a
small drifting berg, *Ice Bird* fore-reached in the direction of the
snow-covered Wauwermans Islands off the entrance to Gerlache
Strait, which separates Anvers Island from the mainland. The
strait is nearly five miles across but, search as I would, once the
gaunt buttresses had emerged into the light of a sickly dawn, not
one solitary sign of a break could be detected in that sheer
mountain wall.

The desire to sleep had again become overpowering. The
dangers were obvious, for, although the gale had begun to ease
Ice Bird was still moving much too fast for safety. The visibility
(it was now 3 a.m. on the 28th) was reasonable but insufficient to
detect perils an hour or more ahead. The best I could do was to
come about, head towards reasonably open water and refrain
from emptying my bladder before slumping down on to the bunk.
Sure enough the discomfort soon woke me, and once again, but
the third time I slept more soundly and did not awaken until
half past nine. I jumped up but too late to have been of any use
because a jagged rock skerry was even then slipping by only
fifty yards abeam. A narrow escape indeed. I dare not doze again.

By eleven that morning we were once more lying becalmed off
the familiar twin-spired berg and its accompanying cold wet
rocks – two hundred yards to windward of where we had been
at eleven o'clock the evening before. Little change occurred until
two in the afternoon when a relatively steady north-east breeze
set in that bore the yacht across under Anvers – and into a tide
race among the Outcast Islands which, the *Pilot* book advised (p.
160) not very helpfully, 'should be given a wide berth'. It was a
great relief eventually to be through the islands and to be painfully, ever so slowly gaining ground tacking towards Palmer.

The breeze continued to hold. Around ten that evening a misty
drizzle set in, cloaking the dangerous rocks from my view. There
was obviously no hope of making port that night, the base being
still three miles away up-wind. There were two alternatives. Either
heave-to for the night where we were, or stand out eastwards into

the mist on a long tack, the return leg of which should bring us into Arthur Harbour. I chose the second alternative and came very close, in consequence, to losing my ship and my life.

With the steadier wind I could go below, for *Ice Bird* was now able to steer herself quite well on the wind with the tiller loosely lashed. My jerseys and flying suit beneath the impervious Marlin jacket and trousers were quite as soaked with my own sweat as were my feet, for I had been continuously 'wet suited' in full outdoor gear for some days. Of more practical moment, my over-mitts and wool gloves were also soaked – from sleet and from handling wet sheets on our frequent tacks. A month earlier and my hands could never have stood it. Now I could repeatedly spend minutes at a time in the chilled wet darkness of the cockpit before my fingers drove me inside the cabin again.

There was, fortunately, not a trace of the overwhelming sleepiness I had felt the night before. Perhaps it was the generous tots of overproof rum that I kept drinking to keep myself warm. The rum certainly did counteract wind chill and helped me to stay alert and I must have consumed all of half a bottle that night. I well know that all this is contrary to accepted ideas on physiology but these are possibly oversimplified and, moreover, take little account of the body's sometimes altered reactions in conditions of extreme stress.

Monday 29 January. Forty minutes past midnight. All at once we seemed to have become surrounded by masses of bergy bits. Peering through the murk I became aware of a loom which took form as the ghostly outline of an enormous berg, the source of the bergy bits. I came about with all speed. Several times in the next few minutes *Ice Bird* brought up hard against growlers and I blessed her steel hull. They soon fell astern, but she had repeatedly to plough through crackling brash ice that gave out a delicate musical tinkling. Hearing things again, I thought, but the explanation, I heard later, was a natural one. Air bubbles trapped ten thousand years ago in the glacier were being released as the ice melted in the sea.

With dawn close at hand and the wind at last fair for Palmer, came the moment of deadliest peril. I was in the cabin when all of a sudden I felt *Ice Bird* lift under me. We were close under the

land; this just could not be happening to us. As these incredulous
thoughts shot through my mind I was leaping for the cockpit and
the tiller. As I reached it a swelling crest broke roaring all about
us and I realized that we were in breakers over a rocky shoal.
Three times the seven-ton yacht was picked up bodily and surfed
forward through the white, frothing turmoil while I clung to the
tiller, at every second expecting the keel to strike and the adventure – and my life – to end among jagged rocks in freezing
water: within a mile of safety.

The six-foot-deep keel must have passed over the rocks with
no more than inches to spare. I was still trembling with reaction
when the increasing light at 2.30 a.m. enabled me to round Lichfield Island into Arthur Harbour and enter sheltered water for
the first time since leaving Half Moon Bay three months before.

The gallant little yacht had come 6,100 nautical miles from
Sydney in 14½ weeks. Since being dismasted 8½ weeks ago, she
had traversed 2,500 miles at a creditable average (especially
allowing for the many days without sail) of 41 miles a day.

The buildings of Palmer Antarctic Station (64° 46′S., 64° 02′W.)
were silhouetted clearly now against a tremendous looming background of ice piedmont. Torgersen Island passed to port, alive
with tiny dinner-jacketed figures, stumbling over rocks that were
ochre-red with krill-stained droppings and acrid with the smell of
a penguin rookery. There was a rock-built pier in front of the
station, made fast to which was a converted minesweeper that
later proved to be Jacques Cousteau's *Calypso*. What a little ship,
I thought, to venture into these waters. Then I laughed at my
own reaction. *Ice Bird* was no more than twice as long as her
capacious outboard dinghy.

I dropped anchor within ten yards of the sleeping motor vessel.
Then, fearing the patent anchor might drag on the glacier-
smoothed bottom of the sound, I called out.

'Is anyone awake? Do you mind if I tie up alongside?' The
saloon door crashed open and a very startled figure appeared. I
threw him a line and made fast. The first single-handed voyage
to Antarctica had been accomplished.

Calypso's sleepy and startled crew popped out of their cabins like gophers, to help moor up *Ice Bird* and to ply me with steaming black coffee and crisp rolls. My urgent preoccupation, though, was to have a radio message sent off to report my safe arrival and a tall, lean Frenchman, who seemed to be in charge, promised to see to this immediately. I had recognized the ship's name, *Calypso*. It was on the tip of my tongue to ask him if he had bought her from Cousteau when I belatedly realized that he *was* the celebrated scuba-diving pioneer and marine publicist. He would hardly, I think, have been amused at not being recognized.

True to his word he promptly dispatched the news via satellite. The *San Francisco Chronicle* reported later:

> In awed tones Cousteau told of the most amazing incident of his voyage. At 4 a.m. . . . he saw emerging from a badly broken-up boat a 'strange hirsute figure' who, he radioed, was Dr David Lewis, solitary circumpolar navigator. Both ship and man (were) in pretty bad shape but alive and in good spirits. The *Ice Bird* capsized about two months ago and broke its aluminium mast. Lewis carried on with an emergency short boom as mast and everything on board was completely soaked in sea water at freezing temperatures. He intends to repair as well as he can and sail again in the direction of the Cape of Good Hope. Incredible but true.

The thrill of being again among people temporarily overcame my exhaustion. But once the message had been sent reaction suddenly set in with overwhelming force. Palmer Base proper was still sleeping when I stumbled back aboard *Ice Bird* and fell at once into a dreamless sleep.

Around mid-morning I awoke to find a note from the base commander propped up on the cabin table saying simply, 'Your room is ready for you.' What a welcome! In one phrase it summed up the warm-hearted American hospitality that was to illumine my months at Palmer.

Indescribable was the luxury of soaking under that first hot shower; of donning clean dry clothes fresh from the Laundromat; having my hair cut (necessary before the knotted, matted tangle could be combed) – a photograph taken earlier, and later published, had an amusing sequel. A Canadian girl, who had been corresponding with me off and on about a voyage her boy friend proposed, wrote, 'I had pictured you before seeing this photo as a handsome if rugged sea dog. Now I am quite disillusioned.'

'Chow's up,' yelled the cook. We lined up for enormous steaks followed by blueberry pie and lashings of coffee. The big lounge/dining room was decorated with a notice board, emblems of Polar research ships and signed photographs of British and Argentine bases. The door to the radio room was labelled 'Radio Free Palmer'.

'You had better rack out now,' I was advised, but the excitement was too great. Afternoon found me in a Zodiac inflatable boat, crunching through the brash ice around those same Torgersen and Lichfield islands that I had passed by in the early dawn just hours before – but hours that had marked my emergence from the shadows of solitude, peril and pain. Now I was in the company of two cheerful young American scientists, my hands comfortably encased in warm mitts and enthralled at the busy world around. There were porpoising penguins, somnolent Weddell seals dozing on the stony foreshore – so unafraid that you could stroke them – and monstrous elephant seals wallowing awash. Once a leopard seal lifted its terrible head above water as it swirled away, frustrated, from the penguin colony.

We edged inshore past a berg, along whose skyline a column of penguins was solemnly marching, then poled the Zodiac through the tinkling brash to land on Torgersen Island. The inhabitants, Adélie penguins, whose eyes are encircled by round white rings, soon forgot our presence in their rookery and went on about their business. Each adult had accumulated a ring of stones around itself. While it stood gazing contemplatively into the distance, its neighbour in the rear would snatch as many stones as it could get away with. Once the victim came out of its trance and saw what was happening it would squawk and wave its flippers in protest at the raider, only to succumb to temptation, in its turn, once another's back was turned. The more acquisitive had accumulated great piles, while the least alert had been almost completely despoiled of these treasures.

Half-grown chicks, the remnants of their baby down hanging in untidy tatters over their sleek black and white coats, poked their beaks hopefully but unproductively up into those of their parents. For their long period of dependence had passed and they were now capable of fending for themselves.

We watched one group of several adults clustering about the edge of the drop-off down to the water, nudging each other with their flippers. For some minutes they continued to jostle, for all the world like commuters on a rush-hour subway platform, until inevitably one lost its balance and fell in, when the rest, craning their necks and peering down into the water, intently followed its progress to make sure that no leopard seal was lurking below. Once satisfied, all dived in without further hesitation.

'What scientific work are you all doing down here?' I asked my two companions.

'Our own field is the physiology of giant petrels and penguins. Do you know that the circulation through the feet of both makes them as insulated to cold as those rubber boots we are wearing? Then two guys are anaesthetizing leopard seals with darts, making them vomit and finding out what they have eaten.'

'What do they eat?' I asked.

'One had two Weddell seals inside it, a penguin and, surprisingly enough, krill. A bird man is expected later to sort out the Arctic from the Antarctic terns that both nest here. There is no difference between them to look at, yet, while the Antarctic ones stay put, the others fly all the way from the High Arctic, the whole length of the world down to this area every year to breed.'

Later on I saw some of the experiments set up by a group of Argentines working at Palmer who were trying to unravel the secrets of the ice fish, whose blood is mere plasma devoid of any haemoglobin, or equivalent compound. This means that its blood cannot transport much oxygen from the gills to the tissues. Is the answer an enormous heart pump driving a rapid circulation? I do not know. The study is continuing.

The marine ecology programme was an important one. This involved criss-crossing large areas of sea bed sixty to one hundred feet down with weighted cords, listing the inhabitants of each square – seaweeds, crabs, limpets, sea worms and so on – and studying their behaviour through the year. Regular scuba diving was required – in winter through holes sawn through the ice. Al Gianinni, for instance, made 181 dives, totalling seventy-four hours under water (including swimming under icebergs) in one year.

The support personnel at Palmer – diesel mechanics, carpenters, electricians and so on – who looked after the base's elaborate equipment, were highly qualified and experienced US Navy petty officers. This infrastructure was to be taken over by a civilian contractor the following season.

Walking was a pleasure that first day ashore after such prolonged, enforced confinement. It did not remain so for long. So high was the temperature maintained by Palmer's central heating plant that my feet, damaged by two months of chill dampness, day and night, inside insulated rubber boots, swelled up so much that next morning I could barely stand. And hobbling about was painful in the extreme. After a week's antibiotics to control any possible infection, Doc Spencer, the station medical officer, let me have some cortisone; this promptly shrank the bulbous feet down to normal size, though the showers of scaling dry skin that soon began to rain down from my top bunk on to my room mate caused him to mutter darkly about it being like living with a dozen rattlesnakes all shedding their skins at once.

Actually my second night ashore was a sleepless one but this had nothing to do with my swollen feet. I remained awake and restless through all the dragging hours, leaning against a window thrown open to the white night, while I worried and planned how to make *Ice Bird* seaworthy again. Scarce conscious of the sweep of berg and skerry, violet shadowed ice cliff or the spine of mountains marching away southwards into the rose-tinted sunset-dawn, I racked my brains how to make a new mast; for suitable timber was conspicuously lacking. The call to a breakfast of pancakes, maple syrup and bacon found me no nearer a solution.

The advent of the US supply ship *Marfak* a day or so later provided the answer, in the shape of two fifteen-foot lengths of eight by four inch timber – heart of spruce at that – that had been used for battening down cargo. Not only did the captain present me with the wood but also with coils of nylon rope and even a wet suit.

The first job was to join together the two lengths of timber by scarfing and glueing a joint as in the diagram.
Unfortunately the blade of the power saw was too small to make the necessary four-inch cut.

'I'll fix the mother fucker for you Dave,' offered burly, bearded Melvin Williamson – Willy – thumping me reassuringly on the back with enough force to shatter a rib.

'We'll just lubricate first with some of that Aussie rum of yours.' Willy threw his head back and gargled the fiery overproof spirit as I watched in awe. Then he made a six-foot diagonal cut into each plank, turned it over and repeated the process on the other side. The waste pieces fell cleanly away and, so keen was Willy's eye, after the surfaces had been planed, glued and clamped together, the match was perfect. A mast so joined with modern synthetic glues is actually stronger at the joint than elsewhere.

Problem number two was that the new mast was only twenty-three feet long, while *Ice Bird*'s original aluminium one had been thirty-six feet. Arthur Owens, who was the only experienced yachtsman on the base, helped me draw sketch after sketch as we tried to figure out what to do. The best solution, we eventually decided, was to use a gunter rig. Here, as shown in the diagram, the gaff (upper spar) stands nearly upright, in effect lengthening the mast. Provided that the boom (lower spar) could be pivoted to the mast by its gooseneck fitting as low down as one foot six inches off the deck, it should be possible to set the original mainsail with a single reef tied down: a more than ample spread of canvas for the boisterous Southern Ocean.

Having made our plans Art Owens and I got to work, trimming two inches off one edge of the mast to leave it with a six inch by four inch oblong section. Afterwards we rounded off the edges. The question of how to make and attach the spreaders – they would jut out sideways from a point four feet six inches below the masthead – we left in abeyance. Also postponed was the search for wire suitable for stays.

A new mast was not the only need. Rusty tools had to be taken ashore and left soaking in oil. Two young telecommunications

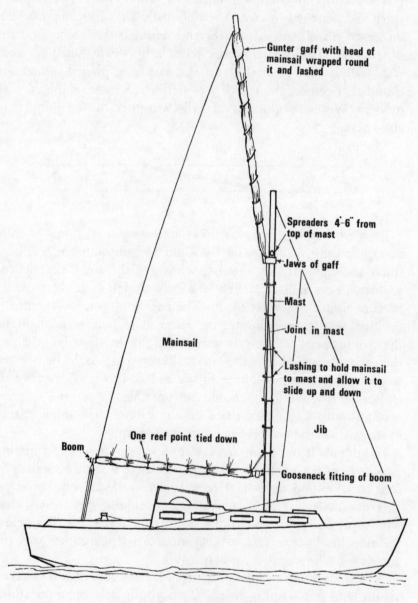

Gunter gaff with head of mainsail wrapped round it and lashed

Spreaders 4'-6" from top of mast

Jaws of gaff

Mast

Joint in mast

Mainsail

Lashing to hold mainsail to mast and allow it to slide up and down

Jib

One reef point tied down

Boom

Gooseneck fitting of boom

Ice Bird's Gunter rig.

experts, Pat Smith and Kent Yates, managed to fix the WWV time-signal radio receiver but the Racal transmitter had been too badly damaged to repair.

Once my frostbitten fingers were a little better I was able to start mending the rents in the sails. Several hours were spent each day with sail needle, wax and palm, stitching away at the heavy Terylene until the split storm jib and the frayed tri-sail had been repaired. I took advantage of fine days to paint over all the bare patches on the hull and deck to prevent rust. The bent part of the pram hood frame that had been jamming the hatchway was cut away by hacksaw and replaced by side struts. Jim Evans, the mechanic, who was to become my special friend, disappeared head first into the chaos under the cockpit; to announce in due course that no God-damned Limey motor was going to get the better of him. He would have the motor running again – but just give him time. Looking at the rusty thing, I did not believe him. But I was wrong.

One evening after supper I noticed Jim collecting meat bones – spare ribs – from our plates.

'You hungry or something?' I asked him.

'Come with me and you'll see.' Behind the buildings in a wire netting cage was a skua gull.

'Poor son-of-a-bitch has broken its wing,' explained Jim as he entered the cage and proferred an eight-inch-long piece of bone. The skua's cruel beak gaped and it gulped, leaving half the bone protruding. Since it was clearly intent on swallowing the whole thing, which threatened to emerge from its anus and impale it, we both started forward in alarm. We had underestimated the bird. Rolling a malignant eye towards us, it kept on swallowing convulsively, miraculously not choking, until the entire bone, in apparent defiance of the laws of nature, had disappeared. I still do not know where that skua put it.

These predatory birds are magnificent fliers. Sandy, the cook, was wont to toss waste pieces of meat into the air for them to catch on the wing. They would twist, turn, hover and even stern glide to snatch the morsels.

'Try holding a piece in your hand,' I suggested once, and Sandy unwisely agreed. A moment later a yell of agony and a stream of profanity announced that one skua had misjudged its bite.

'Kiwi – Limey son-of-a-bitch you get no chow after this,' howled the victim.

'What's the matter; you've got nine more fingers, Sandy,' I reassured him. But retribution was on the way. There came a soft plop on the top of my head.

'Shat you dead centre,' cried the delighted Jim.

'Get me a sling shot and I'll teach that bugger!' But the skua was already far away.

There were these light-hearted moments – many of them – but work on *Ice Bird* went on pretty consistently. Mainly thanks to Art Owens I was now equipped to work out of doors in comfort. The most sensitive part of me, my damaged fingers, were protected from wet cold and wind chill by industrial rubber gloves worn over thin, closely woven woollen ones. I was later to find these equally satisfactory at sea in Antarctic waters. In course of time I also acquired a collection of mitts to wear in the dry: American, Japanese and one pair of 'nosewipers' (so called because of the use made of the fur trimming on the backs!). A new anorak and insulated rubber boots that fitted properly were an added boon.

Inside the centrally heated base buildings, of course, the lightest clothing was more than enough; a circumstance amusingly illustrated when a party that included Sir Vivian Fuchs from the Research ship *John Biscoe* visited Palmer. All were wearing climbing boots and heavy jerseys. It was not long before they were stripping off layer after layer – and still perspiring freely.

Fire is the most dreaded of Antarctic hazards, since the pitiless environment has little mercy on men without shelter. So when the Palmer fire alarm went off with an ear-splitting clangour every man leapt to his feet on the instant and dashed off towards the site of the danger (as indicated by a winking red light on the fire alarm board). I followed more slowly, impeded by my swollen feet. A vague suspicion as to the cause of the outbreak grew towards near certainty as I descended the stairs. It *had* to be *my* stove. It was. Throwing open the machine shop door I burst in upon a striking tableau.

The centre piece was the merrily blazing stove from *Ice Bird* and standing in front of it, arms thrown wide in fierce protectiveness, was the Texan, Kent Yates. A half circle of men were aiming large red fire extinguishers directly at him.

'Stand aside, Kent,' shouted the lieutenant.

'Don't shoot! It is going out by itself,' replied the gallant and immovable Texan. And sure enough the yellow flames did rapidly die down. This incident is typical of the kind of story that more than once lies behind the acknowledgements at the end of this book. Thus my 'thanks to Kent Yates for repairing the stove' cover a good deal.

'About time I hauled ass out of here,' I muttered, ashamed at having been the cause of so much trouble. And, all unknown to me, unforeseeable events that were to involve my 'hauling ass' and postponing *Ice Bird*'s voyage back to civilization, were even then maturing.

My book, *We, the Navigators*, about the ancient techniques of the sea-roving Pacific Islanders, had attracted the attention of the *National Geographic Magazine*. Assistant Editor, Bill Garrett had telephoned from Washington to Tim Curnow in Sydney while I was still at sea.

'We want Lewis to write for us on Polynesian navigation and migrations. Will you have him ring us back?'

'He can't ring you back. He is missing in the Antarctic Ocean. He is probably dead.'

'Everyone can get to a telephone these days,' Garrett brushed aside such trivial objections.

It was now that the persistent *National Geographic* did run me to earth at Palmer and cabled their request. A radio link was established with Washington (to my regret, technical reasons precluded direct contact with Australia and the children) and Bill Garrett came on the line. Could the article wait until I had repaired *Ice Bird* and completed the voyage? No, it had to be written at once. Furthermore, they would like me to go out in the Polynesian voyaging canoes again, this time accompanied by a photographer, to obtain good colour pictures. What was I to do? I turned to Lloyd Yukkola, the base commander, for guidance.

'We can hoist *Ice Bird* out of the water with our crane and store her ashore for you during the winter,' he offered. The upshot was that the *Geographic* offered to get me to the USA, Australia and the Pacific and to return me to Palmer on the very first ship next season. They would provide a new self-steering gear (no mean consideration). The obvious advantage to me was more time to repair the yacht plus the benefit of an early start next spring. Would I be prepared to come out on *Lindblad Explorer*, an 'adventure tour' liner which made annual voyages to the Antarctic and would shortly be calling at Palmer? I agreed.

There was much to be done if *Ice Bird* was to survive the bitter winter in safety. Willy began straight away to construct a stout cradle on the jetty to receive the yacht. Once she had been hoisted into it and secured with heavy wire guys and turnbuckles, she would be out of harm's way. Meanwhile I was kept busy unloading food and gear. Barrow load after barrow load was trundled up from the wharf to the store-room and packed in crates and boxes. Perishables like eggs – several had been broken in the capsizes but none had gone bad – cheese and salami were handed over to the cook. The remaining bottles of rum were left behind to help relieve the winter solitude. The stacked boxes held more than enough corned beef, biscuits and butter to complete the voyage next season, though canned vegetables, fruit and fruit juice were low. On the other hand, there were vast stocks of soap, for I had hardly used any at all (I still cannot fathom why I took so much in the first place).

Stormy weather now set in and the Antarctic began to show its colours. Bergy bits far larger than *Ice Bird* crunched their way past her under press of wind and tide, repeatedly crashing against her hull. The ice would appear as if by magic, then would as suddenly be gone. Vicious seas threatened to chafe through or snap the yacht's mooring lines and dash her on to the rocks against which they were breaking – scant yards from the vulnerable rudder. The cradle was ready but the mobile crane would have been pulled bodily off the dockside if any attempt had been made to lift the heavy plunging boat in these conditions. Only a windless day and a flat calm would do. (Not until a week after I had sailed – feeling mightily anxious – was Willy, working in a snowstorm, able to hoist *Ice Bird* to safety).

We came nearest to losing the faithful yacht the day before *Lindblad* was due. That she survived was because of Art Owens's vigilance. A sudden gale set *Ice Bird* snubbing wildly. Art spotted that the vital stern warp had almost frayed through and struggled for more than an hour, sometimes knee deep in freezing water, to re-attach the slippery three-inch nylon. Imminent disaster had been averted but *Ice Bird* could scarce ride out the night without extra mooring lines. She was swooping and rolling too wildly for anyone to get on board and only after much effort did we succeed in hooking the railings with two grapnels and making fast their lines well above high water mark. By then evening was well advanced; my hands and feet ached and I could barely stand.

Next day, apart from a heavy residual swell, the storm might never have happened. That same afternoon, 29 February 1973, just one month after first reaching Palmer, I ascended *Lindblad Explorer*'s gangway (wearing borrowed clothes) to enter a different world. But even as I waved goodbye to my friends I realized that the months ahead would be but an interlude. True reality was at Palmer, where *Ice Bird* would await me beneath her mantle of winter snow. Only after my return in the spring to take up the voyage again would my own reality, my personal 'dreaming', come back to me.

This then is the spirit in which I propose to touch on only a few of the strange events of the ensuing eight months; for, taking place as they did in surroundings unimaginably remote from Antarctica, they were in a sense unreal. And Antarctica it was that had laid upon me the grim imperatives of a destiny that had yet to be fulfilled.

'The American we speak here isn't *exactly* the same as the way they talk Stateside,' Jim had warned me one day when we were emptying rubbish at the dump.

'You mean I shouldn't call the head of Polar Programmes a mother fucker?' I asked innocently.

Jim shuddered visibly. Having up-ended his can, he resumed, 'What are we doing?'

'Shit-canning the trash.'

'No, no, old buddy, you are wrong, we are "disposing of the garbage".'

I should have remembered Jim's warning when I crossed *Lindblad*'s crowded lounge, carrying my old anorak, now finally disintegrated, with the intention of according it fitting sea burial off Cape Horn.

'What are you doing with that thing?' asked an interested passenger. 'Shit-canning it,' I replied without thinking, then made a hurried escape in the startled silence that followed. (To cap it all, my plan was frustrated by a New Zealand ornithologist, who insisted on keeping the anorak as a souvenir!)

Part 3

The Frozen Continent

Chapter 7

Intermezzo

At first I rather dreaded the world outside. So recently had I been dwelling in the shadows at life's edge (and next season might well have to do so again), that I wondered if the sheer complexity of trivialities would swamp my newly heightened perceptions. I need not have worried. My hard-won sense of proportion, conferring a truer appreciation of fundamentals, did not alter.

We landed at Ushuaia in Argentine Tierra del Fuego and thence flew north. Anne Ryan, one of *Lindblad*'s passengers, had become my constant companion. When Cape Virgins, the eastern bastion of Magellan Strait, floated serenely by, five miles below, it was hard to realize that this was where, eight years before, we had struggled into the strait in *Rehu Moana*, in the teeth of a howling *pampero*. (See *Daughters of the Wind*, 1967, London, Gollancz.)

For some inappropriate reason my mind flits next to the airport toilet at Rio Gallegos. No common graffiti there: '*Limpiarse la Argentina, Matar uno Chileno,*' I read – 'Clean up the Argentine. Kill a Chilean.' What a neighbourly sentiment!

Then came Buenos Aires, where Anne and I parted: she to her home near San Francisco, where I was to join her later; I to wait for my visa to enter the USA. Washington next, with its two obligatory places to visit: the Lincoln Memorial by night; and Watergate flats.

The Washington-based *National Geographic Magazine* asked me for three articles: one on Polynesian voyaging (see *National Geographic Magazine*, December 1974); one on *Ice Bird*'s recent voyage (see *National Geographic Magazine*, December 1973); and another on her coming voyage. To use on this latter trip I was loaned no fewer than four cameras and given a crash course in their use.

The *Geographic*'s atmosphere of no-nonsense professionalism was stimulating, though at first the pace was a bit overwhelming. However, with Barry Bishop one of the staff, there was an immediate sense of sharing a common experience. We had dined in his home. 'Your carrying on without real hope was like us on Everest,' he remarked thoughtfully. 'We were benighted at over 28,000 feet; a 70-mile-an-hour blizzard was blowing, so we knew we must soon freeze to death.' He paused: the comfortable living room had, for the moment, lost its reality. He was back in howling darkness, gasping in the thin, barely breathable air. 'But it seemed to be more in keeping with human dignity to go out on our feet than give in.'

Then, against all probability, the storm had died suddenly away, so that they were able to survive that night of fearful cold on the frontiers of space – at the cost to Barry of several fingers and all his toes.

This will to fight on in the face of hopeless odds is, I am sure, not merely confined to dramatic situations, but is an integral part of the essence of mankind.

After Washington there was the stopover at San Francisco and, not long afterwards, the eagerly awaited family reunion in Australia. Barry was in Sydney, window cleaning to finance the yacht he was building. He was unaware that I was back in the country when I ran him to earth.

'Oh, you bloody, bloody, old fool. David, it's so good to have you back!' Father and son, two bearded men, clung together – both unashamedly in tears.

Susie and Vicky came flying down the school playground. They were so bubbling over with excitement that news of pet guinea pigs, kittens, riding lessons, tooth braces and acrobatic classes were inexorably jumbled. Only much later did they directly refer to my absence.

'People were so stupid while you were away.'

'How do you mean, Vicky?'

Susie amplified. 'They kept asking, "Don't you miss your Daddy? Aren't you worried about him?" What a silly question! I always said "No".'

The only absentee from this reunion was Barry's married sister, Anna – of necessity, her home being in England. I was amused to detect in her letters, together with relief (or was I imagining it?), a faint note of 'motherly' exasperation at the irresponsible doings of her wayward parent.

A considerable part of my time in Australia was occupied in writing the *Geographic* articles and beginning this book. Then, before I knew it, the southern mid-winter was past and I had been spirited away to the north-west Pacific on a *National Geographic* photographic expedition, back to my old friends the last of the star navigators. Hence my presence in the remote central Carolines in a specially chartered yacht with photographer Bill Curtsinger. Sub-zero temperatures of a few months back had been replaced by an equatorial steam bath.

There seemed something particularly incongruous at my being seated at a typewriter in the yacht's cabin, wearing only a breach clout, re-living the Antarctic voyage through the pages of *Ice Bird*'s logbook propped open in front of me. Time and time again the sweat dripping off my face and arms rendered the typing paper sodden and unusable.

We were anchored in the lagoon of uninhabited Pigailoe, awaiting the arrival of two big flying proa canoes from Saipan – a 420-mile sea passage without intervening land, formidable for craft being navigated without the benefit of chart or compass. (The voyage was successfully accomplished in two weeks against consistently adverse winds.)

A meal of turtle, breadfruit and coconut had left us replete. Bill Curtsinger stood up. 'Swim David?'

'No, too lazy.'

Bill slipped into the clear, tepid water. His cry came only minutes later. 'Shark!' Then, in desperate appeal, 'Help – quickly!' Otey, one of the yacht's crew, was in the dinghy almost before the shout had faded, rowing wildly towards the ominous red cloud in the water, where a black fin was circling the flailing Bill.

'*Hurry!*' The shark had struck again. A moment more and Bill, red from neck to ankles, had flopped into the dinghy. He was soon in the cockpit.

'Get under way,' I called over my shoulder, already busy with water, towels and first aid kit.

'There was only time to put my hand in front of my face, David; he came so fast.' Then, in an agonized whisper, 'Will I lose my hand?'

'It will be good as new. Good God! Have you drunk *the whole* bottle of brandy?' Eyes staring with shock, Bill concluded his story, 'I started swimming – and then it hit me again – on the neck and shoulder.'

By this time the yacht was bucking to the rollers in the reef pass and I had completed my examination and stopped the flow of blood. The shark's teeth had missed the major blood vessels in the neck by a hair's breadth and had cut only one tendon in the hand. Blood loss we could do little about in the absence of transfusion facilities but it seemed to have been controlled in time. The other great complication of shark bite – infection – we did have the means to handle: massive doses of antibiotics. I recalled that the last time I had used these drugs had been to treat myself for frostbite.

The Tetracycline capsules worked as well as they had on that grim earlier occasion. By the time Bill reached Yap (and an airport) four days later, his wounds were clean. We emplaned rather shakily having, in our relief, over-indulged in chilled beer and betel nut. Flying hour after hour towards Hawaii (and first class surgical facilities) sobered us.

It was well after midnight when we got to Hawaii, much too late to trouble any of our friends.

'Kahala Hilton for us,' Bill decided. 'The magazine picks up the tab.' The desk clerk at the $50 a night hotel gulped as he eyed my sole piece of luggage: a big, battered cardboard box patched with adhesive tape.

'Are you,' he queried diffidently, 'aware of our charges, Sir?'

'Yes, they are exorbitant, but I'm not paying.'

Next morning Bill began his hospital treatment. His ordeal was a long one but his injuries healed completely, leaving no permanent disability. Perhaps the punchline to his story was his editor's greeting, 'What pictures of the attack did you get?'

These events took place in July. August was spent at the farm of my Sydney benefactor, Jack Muir. The children rode while I typed some chapters of this manuscript, at a folding table set up in the barn. By September the scene had shifted two thousand miles in space, through an aeon in time.

Central Australia: the nearest sea coast 1,000 miles away; red sandhills, armoured with needle-pointed spinifex grass, stretch to a horizon that unrolls endlessly before the lurching Land-Rover. A far off escarpment lifts above the level skyline and climbs steadily up from the rim of the world like an island rising from the sea.

'Putardi hill.' The Aborigine beside me gestures ahead. 'I spear kangaroo there one time. My hunting dingo catch him. 'Nother time,' Melali continues, 'I spear emu from rock hide at Putardi spring.' Two hours later we pull up under a gnarled mulga. Putardi spring's green reeds contrast vividly with the baking rock walls behind. The emu hide is still there.

'This a honey ant dreaming,' Melali explains. 'The honey ants camped here in the Dreamtime and made the spring. You wait. I sing them to let us drink.'

'We really *are* Honey Ant People now, aren't we?' Eyes shine with excitement in Susie's and Vicky's dust smeared faces as the chant ends.

'Yes, you proper Honey Ants now,' and off they scuttle like their namesakes.

We are privileged at being taught the Aborigines' skills in their proper context – the profound spiritual world of the Dreamings, conceived and refined over fifty thousand years. It is hard to realize that this man of my own age has spent the greater part of his life as a naked stone age – mesolithic – hunter.

This brief glimpse into the wellsprings of mankind was the last diversion. The southern spring was come and with it the time for the second round.

A television interviewer asked why I was determined to resume the Antarctic voyage after so narrowly surviving. The reason was not easy to define. 'I hate to leave a job half finished.'

'But what right have you to throw your life away and leave those girls fatherless?'

This was a harder question. 'I intend to come back,' was the best I could manage; in truth, I was haunted by doubts and fears. In an attempt at clarification I jotted down my feelings.

'If the worst has to come there will at least be a record left behind – a simple human one of fighting despite weakness and fear. Then, too, this grant of perhaps borrowed time has seen Barry, Susie and Vicky through important stages. If I learned anything last year it has been passed on to them.'

I had to be satisfied with this because practical issues soon overrode these self-searchings. My one really nightmare dread, of encountering another hurricane-force storm, could best be countered by careful preparation. RRS *John Biscoe* was the first ship due to arrive at the Antarctic Peninsula. In her hold, thanks to the ever helpful Merton Naydler, would be the following replacements: a tiny thirty-square-foot storm jib made of twelve-ounce Terylene and roped all round; a masthead wind speed indicator; an Aries wind-vane self-steering gear; a Honda generator; a Japanese wick stove (purchased in the Carolines); a new carburettor and coil for the motor; courtesy flags; the 1974 Nautical Almanac; a life raft (so heavy and cumbersome that I had it shipped straight back from Palmer).

A cable from London brought appalling news: there would be no room for me on *John Biscoe*, so I must wait six weeks for the next ship. All along I had been dreading the sheer physical effort involved in refitting *Ice Bird*. This six weeks' delay, amounting to a full half of the three months summer season, would mean a disastrously late start. I had been assessing possible dangers in the knowledge that the main strings of planning were in my own hands. Now too much was outside my control, escalating the risks. I felt trapped on a course towards disaster unless early season transport could be arranged.

I bombarded Sir Vivian Fuchs and Mr Gipps of the British Antarctic Survey, the US Polar Programmes and the *National Geographic* with cabled and written appeals. For instance:

To W. Garrett,   17 August
Assistant Editor, *National Geographic*.
Dear Bill,

Further to my letter about the perfidious Limeys (8th August),
Fuchs has confirmed his inability to fit me on the first ship, the
Biscoe. Now everything depends on Phil Smith (Assistant head of
Polar Programmes). I haven't heard yet if he can get me on *Hero* . . .
I do hope you can help persuade them to take me. The photographic
part of the trip will inevitably suffer most if I am forced to rush my
preparation and cut short the time spent in the Antarctic Peninsula
region. I want to get good pics. I also want to get back in one piece
– I am pissed off with survival situations.

Yours etc.
David

This was thoroughly unfair to Fuchs and Gipps who, by dint of
much rearranging *did* eventually find room for me on *Biscoe*, which
I was to join at Montevideo, at the expense of one of their own
scientists. My unavoidably tardy letter of thanks read in part:

Dear Fuchs,   5th October

Your letter of 28th August, together with Gipps' later cable only
reached me yesterday, having been following me about central
Australia – presumably by camel mail. You must have thought me
very rude indeed not to have acknowledged either. I had not realized
what transportation difficulties you face . . . I know I seem to be
bringing down enough gear to rebuild *Ice Bird* but I am suffering
from an overdose of caution after last season's frolics.

Thanks again, etc.

The phone rang in my University room in Canberra. 'Customs
speaking. What about this $2,000 worth of Japanese equipment
that has arrived consigned to you?'

'I'm afraid you must have the wrong person.' But he hadn't.
Then I remembered. I had met Dr Tetsuya Torii, head of the Japan
Polar Research Organization on *Lindblad*, when he had offered to
send me a suit of quilted synthetic Teijin fibre clothing, a Polar
sleeping bag and an underwater watch. People are lavish with
offers they forget to follow up. Not so Dr Torii.

At the air terminal I unpacked a fur-lined parka, overtrousers, underwear – all of quilted Teijin fibre – snow boots, fur cap, mitts and the Seiko diver's watch.

'Well, we can't have you landed with full import duty on this lot, that's certain.' The customs officer was being more than helpful. 'Tell you what. Perhaps my boss can authorize this as a re-export to Antarctica.' He was as good as his word. By dint of, I suspect, straining regulations, the Australian customs waived import duty altogether.

All too soon it was time to leave. The farewell party staged for me by Barry and Tim was traumatic, so that it was a forlorn adventurer who boarded the Quantas 747 next morning en route for Montevideo and rendezvous with *John Biscoe*. With me went the Japanese gear, a down sleeping bag and a rucksack given me by the Australian sports firm of Paddy Pallin, a pair of made-to-measure American 'Oneida' insulated boots, four *National Geographic* cameras (2 Nikonis underwater and 2 Nikkormats), assorted clamps to attach them to rails or stanchions and a generous supply of film.

Drab, rain-swept Montevideo on the muddy Plate – why did postcards depict these yellow waters such an unlikely blue? – matched my mood. It lightened appreciably, however, when three British Antarctic Survey men joined me. Or, rather, two joined me at the hotel while the third, in a gallant attempt to make up in advance for the womanless months ahead, repaired to an establishment known as the Red Lion and was seen no more until the ship was about to sail.

'If those birds at the cat house aren't enough for him,' commented the Stonnington base commander, 'he can always have a last fling with "Sea Lion Annie" in Stanley.'

The British survey personnel are professional explorers. More than any others in West Antarctica they come nearest to being inhabitants. The same adventurous men return south time and again; eighteen months in Antarctica, then six months outside. The secret of their confidence and identification with this stark land seems to be their mastery of snow and ice climbing, crevasse rescue techniques and long distance sledging. As an example of their toughness, one of my Montevideo companions, the massively built Ian Smith, once broke through spring ice to survive an

David Lewis, shortly before leaving Palmer on the second leg of his journey.

Waving goodbye to Palmer as the voyage continues in the spring of 1973.

David Lewis, shortly after leaving Palmer.

The dangers of Antarctic photography. As David Lewis took this picture, the ice floe on which he was standing drifted away from his boat.

Near unnavigable pack ice meant David Lewis had to resort to pushing and pulling Ice Bird *through part of Penola Strait.*

Beset in Penola Strait.

Leaving Penola Strait and just about to enter Le Maire Strait.

Above and below. *Poling through the ice floes in Penola Strait. This method of propulsion worked well, until a moment's inattention while taking photographs saw the boothook disappear into the icy water.*

incredible one and three-quarter hours of sub-zero immersion. He was eventually able to drag himself, still unaided, out on to firm shore ice. That fearful ordeal had done nothing to dampen his enthusiasm.

The little red research ship *John Biscoe* (a taxi driver once drove her captain right past her, thinking her a tug) reached Montevideo on 28 October and sailed again two days later. A brief stop at Stanley in the Falkland Islands was long enough for me to acquire a coil of rigging wire, a spar for a gaff and blisters from tramping the peaty moorlands with the radio operator. Then the ship ploughed on into the south.

Peter, the Welsh bo'sun, set to work splicing my rigging, twice carrying on into the early morning hours, while his compatriot, the carpenter, ignored a snow storm sweeping the for'ard well deck to fit jaws on the gaff. The mate, himself a noted single-handed yachtsman, helped me assemble and test the self-steering gear and the captain took me mile by mile through the charts, pointing out anchorages and special hazards. No wonder I have fond memories of *John Biscoe*.

A few days more and ice blink, reflected up on to the under surface of the overcast between snow showers, revealed the position of two of the South Shetland islands. On 9 November, Anvers Island, its every peak and icefield imprinted indelibly on my memory, was abeam to port when the ship crunched into the pack. The BAS men rushed from one side to the other, as excited as children home for the holidays.

'There's a leopard seal on that floe.' All stampeded with their cameras. 'Look, Gentoo penguins!' They scurried off to find the best vantage point. The myth of the imperturbable Englishman was effectively demolished.

Three hours later at eight in the evening we nosed out of a fog bank and dropped anchor in the ice-covered bay off a Palmer base almost unrecognizable under four feet of snow. This snow and the amount of winter pack still firmly entrenched so far north, was unprecedented for the time of year. It was only too apparent that 1973-4 was going to be an exceptionally severe ice season.

My old friends, who had wintered over at Palmer, accorded me a really heart-warming welcome. Art, Willie and Pat had left, or were going out on *Biscoe* while Erb and Dallas were newcomers. The others were the same. Apprehension about the monumental task of making *Ice Bird* ready for sea was banished for a time. But not for long. The practical problems were daunting. A major refit, which would have taken a first class yacht yard two or three months, had to be attempted in little more than one – and in, of all unsuitable places, Antarctica. This would clearly be far beyond my capacity to carry out alone. It could only be done if the Palmer station crew were prepared to sacrifice the very limited spare time left them by their own programme.

They were.

In the morning I made out a list of things that had to be done. The details themselves may be of interest only to sailors, but I think the sheer volume of what was ultimately accomplished in about the bleakest environment on earth must forcibly strike any reader who even skims through the items. In any case, the best tribute I can pay to my friends' efforts is to give at least part of the list here. What follows is by no means exhaustive.

LAST SEASON

Mast and supporting cradle made by Willie, helped by Arthur and David.
Primus repaired (Kent).
Pram hood repaired (Paul).

THIS SEASON

Outside

Make spreaders and fit them to the mast with steel strops and wooden pegs (Pete and David).
Sand and Varnish mast and spars (David).
Make and fit steel gooseneck attachment for boom (Jim).
Make and weld into position on deck a new mast step (Jim).
Straighten and free damaged rigging screws ['Turnbuckles' in American] (Dallas and David).
Rig mast with stays, blocks, strops and halyards (David).
Fix masthead wind speed indicator or anemometer (Kent).
Make spinnaker pole (David).
Repair fore hatch hinges and make new securing bar (David).
Waterproof hatches with foam rubber strips (Al and Kent).

Repair bracket of outside steering compass (Kent).

Shackle emergency steering wires to hole bored in rudder for the purpose and bring them up to rail – in case rudder shaft should break (Jim and David).

Mount self-steering gear – a long job (Jim and David).

Weld crack in side of cabin coach roof (Jim).

Straighten bent stanchions (Jim).

Repair wire rails and rig safety wires to clip safety belt to (David).

Chip off paint and rust from the hull [a perennial job this, mostly done by Erb and Sandy].

Erb and Sandy did most of the painting that followed the laborious preparation of the steel hull – red lead and anti-fouling paint underwater, non-skid paint for deck, cabin steps and floorboards and the topsides a vivid yellow in place of the original blue (I had come upon two drums of zinc bichromate yellow buried in the snow).

'*Yellow Submarine* should be her name now,' suggested Erb. I shuddered. 'Please, no more submarines for me.' The paintwork was topped off by the ship's name in bold letters along the side and on deck (Lloyd) and a penguin on either bow (Jim). *Ice Bird* looked very smart.

Inside

Repair motor [This was a long complicated job.] (Jim).

Electric wiring; repair and replace (Gary).

Fit new inlet to bilge pump (David).

Repair five locker hinges (Dallas).

Weld cabin steps (Jim).

Replace sink waste pipe (Jim).

Repair broken chart table (Erb).

Mount boat compass on cabin table (David).

Make new galley shelves and a food box to fit under the table (Jim and David).

Make a catch to hold the cabin table in position should we capsize again (Jim).

Fit catch to lid of No. 1 port locker (David). [This was the only unsecured locker and it had disgorged an unbelievable number of articles during the capsizes.]

Radio repairs (Pat and Kent). [This proved a thankless task in the case of the transmitter, which never worked again. Only the WWV

time-signal receiving set and my elderly transistor could be mended.]
Clear cockpit drains and check inside piping (Jack).
Repair heads (Jack).

The detailed instructions for using the complicated yacht lavatory
that Jack inscribed on the inside of the door of the heads ended
with the bottom line. 'If you can read this you are shitting at
45°.'

Once *Ice Bird* had been launched and the mast stepped and
secured, the setting up of the rigging and the adjusting of the
sails to fit the new short mast would fall mainly to me.

The last item on the list, and one all too easy to forget, was
'take photos'. What a bugbear those pictures were until I hit on
a happy solution. This was to hand out rolls of film, mostly to
Kent, and ask him to photograph everything conceivably connected with *Ice Bird*, making sure to mark each cassette with his
name and address for *Geographic* credits and payment. In this way
I could feel the request to take photographs was less of an im-
position. The same procedure was adopted later at the Argentine
and British bases. So it came about that Kent kept popping up
in the most unlikely places, like perching at the edge of the snow-
covered roof in a gale, busily snapping away.

All this activity was soon in full swing. 'Practical things occupy
every minute,' I wrote in my daily log, then added a sombre note,
'but my background fears have a near-nightmare quality.' And
indeed they often did wake me out of an exhausted sleep. These
fears were less of ice hazard (though I was later to learn to dread
bergs) than of the lonely storm-lashed seas I must traverse between the last continent and inhabited land.

However, there was but little spare time to ponder. No laconic
job list could do justice to the actual work involved. The mast,
for instance, had assumed a spiral twist during the winter. Since
the spreaders, if they were to do their job of angling out the
shrouds, must lie fair athwartships, the mast's warping added an
unwelcome complication to their fitting.

One thing that pleased me was how well my frost damaged
fingers stood up to the hard usage, only the ends of the nails
crumbling away a little. However, my feet tended to swell, so I
decided to try walking barefoot in the snow for a short distance

each day, to improve their circulation. Feeling rather a fool, I tried to do this unobserved. All went well until a morning when the ramp between the buildings was coated with fresh snow.

Gary burst in to breakfast. 'Have I been seeing things? There's *footprints* out in the snow – proper footprints, I mean, with *toes*.' He looked round at us belligerently as if challenging disbelief. Then his finger pointed accusingly at me.

'It has to be David. The son-of-a-bitch is the only one of you mothers to be that crazy.'

It seemed prudent to test out *Ice Bird*'s small two-man inflatable tender, that was bundled up in the forepeak, since it would provide my only means of getting ashore from the yacht. Huge snow flakes were settling gently out of a leaden sky when I began blowing it up with a foot pump. A lovely snow petrel came ghosting silently out of the murk, as unsubstantial as the flakes themselves. It landed and moved easily over the snow on its large feet. Then it scrambled up on to a pipe line and began to pick its way along it with a preoccupied air. I stopped pumping to watch what was coming. Snow petrels always took this same route. Sure enough, at each join in the pipe it caught its floppy feet and stumbled only to make a flailing last-minute recovery. It never learned.

'What's that thing's name?' Kent was looking down at the rubber boat.

'*Condom*.'

'You can't call it that.'

'Why not? – it is short for "Condominium".' So *Condom* the little craft has remained though, truth to tell, the name had only occurred to me on the spur of the moment.

We launched her when she was fully inflated; or rather tossed her off the jetty on to a floe. I clambered down more cautiously with the oars and proceeded to drag the feather-weight boat across the ice, jumping the narrow gaps between the floes, looking for a patch of relatively open water.

The 'Little People' were out in force that day. A group of round-eyed Adélie penguins were gazing pensively along their tilted beaks up into the overcast. A few were frankly asleep: upright little statues, each head tucked under a flipper. Gentoo penguins, resplendent with their orange beaks and feet, were on the move, waddling erect or toboganning along rapidly on their tummies. At an upended floe each in turn would gather itself together for the six-foot upward hop, afterwards resuming its dignified progress.

I launched *Condom* in a broad lead full of tinkling brash and gingerly climbed in. The frail-looking boat functioned much better than I had expected and seemed to be in no danger of being punctured by the sharp spicules of ice. This was most encouraging for, should *Ice Bird* be crushed by pressure of rafting floes, *Condom* would be my only insurance of safety.

There were several occasions when, too tired to work any longer, by ten o'clock or so, I donned skis and plodded up the ice piedmont until its folds hid all signs of man. In summer so near the Polar circle there is no real darkness, right through the white night. I would stand for a while, leaning on my ski poles feeling weariness and strain drain out of me as I absorbed strength from this harshly beautiful land.

To the left the Grahamland mountains marched away southwards, their west wall breached by the cataclysmic cleft of Le Maire Channel. This gateway to the south was my goal. In front, the sea was ice covered, the level expanse disrupted by up-jutting bergs and skerries. A sharp crack as a serac split away from the ice cliffs below; a seal's bark; all else was silence. At length, spiritually refreshed, I would push off into the gathering chill wind of speed and hissing snow – and all too often fail to spot a hummock in the flat light and end up struggling, cursing, out of the hole I had made.

On yet other evenings I would join the rest at the movies. There was a year's supply of no less than four hundred films at Palmer. Their bulky cartons filled the indoor vehicle garage completely and left no room for the bulldozer and fork lift both of which had to winter outside. Not altogether surprisingly, when the expected spring thaw failed to materialize and the machines were hopefully dug out, they refused to start. Snow clearing and stores moving had to be done by hand.

The more than adequate supply of films and the very high

standard of comfort in general – maintained by a plethora of elaborate and expensive equipment – rendered the base virtually a detached portion of the USA set down in an alien environment and as far as possible insulated from it. No one had mountaineering experience, so overland travel was ruled out; Zodiac boat trips were strictly confined to islands within a two-mile radius. The scientific scuba diving programme was, however, an exception in being extremely physically rigorous (Al's dives have been mentioned earlier). The fact remains that this 'enclave' philosophy did contrast markedly with the approach of the easy-going and highly mobile British (and to some extent the Argentines) who operate efficiently on a shoestring budget, at a fraction of American costs.

Jim Evans, who was an Antarctic volunteer and my closest friend, felt not a little restricted by this confinement to the close environs of the base. One way he found of relieving his claustrophobia was to sleep on board *Ice Bird*, even before she was launched. I could usually be persuaded to join him, for it was cosy enough lying in our sleeping bags in the cabin. We would talk half the night away or else listen to taped music in companionable silence. There is a letter from Jim in front of me now. 'Those evenings, Ole Buddy,' he writes, 'will always rank +1.' But *Ice Bird*'s cabin was still too enclosed for Jim.

'Why don't we sleep out on the glacier one night?' he suggested. Thus it was that Jim, Kent, Al, Dave and I set off up the icefield on skis around ten-thirty one evening. We counted six seals sleeping on the floes, I see by my diary. Close 10/10 pack ice extended everywhere to the horizon. The ice blink was only broken in the distant west, where water sky (the dark reflection of open water) indicated the pack's edge. We halted some one thousand feet up on the ice piedmont, made rather token windbreaks out of our packs and spread our sleeping bags out on the snow. Cheese, rolls and a flagon of wine were produced, while from inside our bags we watched the southern sky flame red and gold – sunset merging with sunrise. The shadowed ice cliffs had turned to deep purple.

What with my Japanese quilted clothing and my very efficient sleeping bag, I was warm as toast – almost too hot for comfort –

and slept soundly all night. I was shaken awake about nine in the
morning by my shivering companions who were struggling into
their packs.

'Stay here all day if you like, you hibernating kangaroo. We're
going down now for hot showers and chow.'

This break from routine took place at the beginning of
December, when the painting had been finished. *Ice Bird* was
ready for launching as soon as there was any open water, but
it was not until 4 December that a sleet-laden easterly wind blew
the pack clear of the jetty and a little way out into the bay.

The whole base was mobilized. The mast was carried out to the
pier and laid down in the snow, its festoons of rope and wire
rigging all labelled and temporarily tied in place with thin cord
to prevent an unholy tangle developing. Wire lifting strops were
put round the hull and I donned the wet suit *Marfak*'s skipper
had given me, in readiness to dive down and unshackle the strop,
that passed between the keel and the rudder, once *Ice Bird* was
afloat.

Jim hauled on a lever in the crane's cabin and the seven-ton
yacht lifted easily and swung out over the edge of the dock. He
extended the jib of the crane until the yellow boat hung clear and
had begun to lower away, when it happened. The crane tilted
forward. There was a horror struck gasp before Jim let go with a
rush and *Ice Bird* took the water with a splash. For one agonizing
moment the crane still teetered before it settled back on to its legs.
A white-faced Jim emerged from the machine's cabin.

'How about taking off those lifting strops or are you Limey
mothers scared of water?'

'At least I don't go swimming in a crane, you Yank nut.' We
were all badly shaken by the narrow escape from tragedy.

I pulled on my mask and snorkel and climbed down into the
sea. To my surprise there was no shock of cold and, by the time
the wire strops were off, I was enjoying myself. Al joined me and
we began playing water polo with a lump of ice.

'When you mermaids decide to come out we can get on with
stepping the mast. We haven't got all day,' called Jim.

Al and I hurriedly showered and changed, then joined Paul,
Pete and Gary on deck, to guide the mast foot into its step and

attach the wire stays that would hold it firmly in place. Each stay's lower end had to be looped around a deadeye in a rigging screw; secured with bulldog grips, served with marline and parcelled with adhesive tape. The forestay and three stays a side had to be made fast in this way. The pair of runner backstays being rope, simply had to be knotted to eyebolts.

By supper time it was done. We straggled back to the base and the champagne I had been saving for the occasion – all rather subdued at the memory of Jim's narrow escape. *Ice Bird* was left rocking gently in her proper element, already lightly powdered by the snow that had begun to fall, the stars and stripes fluttering from her starboard spreader and the red ensign astern.

Two days were needed to fit boom and gaff and bend on sails. The biggest problem was how to accommodate the triangular Bermudan mainsail to the roughly quadrilateral gunter rig (see diagram p. 112) without cutting up the sail. It was partially solved by rolling the head of the mainsail round the gaff and lashing it into place. This only just allowed the mainsail to be set with one reef permanently tied down, though hoisting the heavy gaff was not easy and at best the boom tended to droop against the pram hood frame and foul it. Would this rather makeshift arrangement stand up to a good blow and how efficient would it be to windward? There was no way of knowing, for the pack ice had returned and *Ice Bird* was immovably beset.

The foresail situation was hardly more satisfactory. My biggest headsail, the Genoa (technically a footing staysail made originally for the lost *Isbjorn*), set perfectly. Unfortunately there was no intermediate-sized sail, the next smaller being the little storm jib I had earlier mended at Palmer. This lack would leave the yacht seriously undercanvassed in winds too strong for the Genoa. To make matters worse I had doubts as to how well the stitched-up jib would set, and the only alternative was the even smaller storm jib I had brought with me on *John Biscoe*.

Sooner or later an opportunity must arise to try out the sails. Meanwhile pressure of heavy ice floes against the rudder was giving increasing cause for alarm. There was absolutely nothing to be done about it but to hope for the best and get on with loading stores and equipment. This time, having learned my lesson, I was careful to stow clothes, important books, cereals and so on in small plastic bags. The kangaroo skin fur coat that had been presented to me performed its last role: it was cut into strips for tying along the rails to prevent chafe.

'Looks pretty smart,' said Jim approvingly, 'but you really should have used mink.'

We improved the cabin decor by adding an Adélie penguin to the kangaroo and the kiwi in ambiguous juxtaposition, then wrote along the bulkhead, 'Repaired in Antarctica by Trained Penguins.'

The impending arrival of the US research ship *Hero* necessitated the yacht's moving to a new mooring to make room. This she accomplished under her own power despite the 10/10 pack, alternately backing up and then going full ahead to ram apart the close set ice floes. Though *Ice Bird* proved an excellent mini-icebreaker on this 45 minute, 500 yard maiden voyage, it was obvious that penetrating the 15 miles of heavy pack between us and open water in Gerlache Strait would be far beyond her capacity.

Hero herself only got through with difficulty. She was due to sail on 12 December, carrying most of my friends with her to South America en route to the USA. By then I too would be ready to sail, but how to get out? I was most reluctant to accept the captain of the *Hero*'s offer of a tow, for fear of damaging *Ice Bird*. The only alternative to waiting for conditions to alter would be to try to follow in the big ship's wake, taking advantage of the passage she broke.

I had to be satisfied with this plan, but nervous tension kept mounting and I was physically very tired. My damaged left hip took this opportunity to play up. The X-ray taken by the Station Medical Officer was hardly encouraging, revealing as it did several nasty looking pieces of detached bone.

Some opening up of the inshore pack to 6/10 occurred on 10 December and provided the first opportunity to try out *Ice Bird* in relatively open leads, along which she zigzagged merrily under power. The breeze was too light to tell much about the set of the sails and the ice was still too dense to allow of the self-steering gear being tried out or the compass swung. This latter

omission was to come near to having the most serious consequences. All in all the hour's excursion was enjoyable and
encouraging.

Everything changed radically next afternoon on the eve of
departure. The fresh north-easter we had been hoping for
materialized and like magic the ice was gone. Now was the chance
to carry out the plan I had been secretly nursing. This was to sail,
not at first for home, but as far into the south as the ice conditions
would allow. Instead of heading northwards around the Antarctic
Peninsula on the first leg of the long haul towards Australia, I
would initially go in exactly the opposite direction. For how could
I dream of wasting the opportunity of seeing as much as possible
of this fascinating continent? I had suffered too much in getting
there to be satisfied with a fleeting visit.

My immediate objective would be 'Argy', the British base at
Argentine Islands, forty miles to the south beyond the spectacular
Le Maire Channel. An added attraction was that *John Biscoe*, after
landing me at Palmer, had damaged her propeller in an unsuccessful attempt to reach 'Argy' and no other ship had as yet succeeded
in getting there. It would be ironical if *Ice Bird* were to succeed
where *John Biscoe* had failed. A radio message from the British
base, reporting that navigable channels had opened between the
floes, showed that the idea was not altogether impracticable.
(Next evening they were to come on the air with a very different
picture – but by then their news was too late.)

The open water and the 15–20-knot breeze gave the opportunity for a real trial sail under canvas, and a great success it was.
The mainsail functioned better than I had expected. To quote
from the first page of the log: 'Mast etc. seem to stand well. Rig
goes well to windward.'

Last-minute preparations took up a good part of the night,
leaving scant leisure for philosophizing. There was not much
time to spare, since both vessels were to set off on their separate
ways at five a.m. Anne was coming south again on *Lindblad
Explorer*'s next voyage, so all exposed film was parcelled up and
left for her to collect and forward to the *National Geographic*.

There was one thing more to do before I could seek my bunk:
write a letter to the Secretary of the US Navy. It need not be

quoted in full; my debt to the men of Palmer must be sufficiently obvious by now. But here is the last paragraph.

I am now about to resume my voyage . . . should this trip ever come to be considered praiseworthy, I would like to suggest that the reconstruction of the yacht in the Antarctic has been an epic achievement. Any successes *Ice Bird* and I may subsequently achieve are due to the efforts of the men of Palmer Station and, in small token of appreciation of the debt I owe, the yacht now bears a plaque inscribed,

> 'Ice Bird
> Palmer Station
> Antarctica.'

(The plaque was in fact a washboard at the cabin entrance and the yacht's name and 'home' port were also stencilled on the transom.)

Then I stretched out in my sleeping bag for a few hours' rest, very conscious that *Ice Bird* and I were on the point of setting out towards an unknown future.

Chapter 8

Beset

Morning. 12 December.

'Wake up you degenerate old man, it's a quarter of five already.'

An obscene grumble from me.

'Now, that's physically impossible for me to do. Here, drink this.' Jim guided a mug of scalding coffee into my hand as I groaned and sat up, noting with a jaundiced eye that the sun was shining as it had been for most of the night. Since I was already wearing nylon briefs and jeans, socks, vest, shirt and heavy wool jersey, dressing consisted merely in pulling on a pair of waterproof trousers, insulated boots, parka, fur hat and gloves (thick industrial rubber ones worn over a thin woollen pair). Miserably tired, I stumbled up the three steps of the companionway ladder.

A light northerly breeze was ruffling the surface of the bay; and Bismarck Strait outside, except for scattered bergy debris, was ice free. There came the faintest stirring of excitement. So far my luck was holding; the first part at least of the road south was open and the wind was fair.

Still alongside *Hero* I hoisted the mainsail with its unwieldy gaff, then the genoa. Willing hands helped me cast off. Cameras clicked. My stomach gave a sudden lurch of emptiness at parting from such loyal friends, who expressed their own feelings after the manner of men everywhere.

'Piss off Limey and don't come back.'

'Just call me up Yank when your horrible floating coffin breaks down and I'll take you in tow.'

Ice Bird drew away. The other side of the channel loomed; it was time to come about. Tiller hard over, weather headsail sheet cast off, a hasty grab for the winch handle to trim the flapping genoa and the wavelets were rippling along the yacht's side as she gathered way on the new tack. Brash ice crunched and tinkled under the forefoot. A glance astern showed that *Hero* and Palmer Base had already dwindled. No time for nostalgia; the skerries, ice-capped islands and grounded bergs strewing the next part of the route demanded every bit of my attention. The moment was hardly opportune to connect up the as yet untried self-steering gear, since the many obstructions necessitated constant changes of course and the wind was fickle. In fact common prudence would suggest I unship the vane's lever arm, which projects down into the water, lest it be damaged by ice – but I did not think of this at the time.

Preoccupied as I was with trying to get the best out of the yacht's makeshift gunter rig and of navigating unknown and difficult waters, all at a time when I had been abruptly thrown back on my own resources, I felt exhilarated to have at last the chance of learning at first hand what I had studied in theory for so long – the arts of an ice skipper. *Ice Bird* had been re-born. In only one month last season and a month and three days this spring, she had been transformed from a near-wreck into a ship fit for that exploration of the Antarctic coasts that had all along been my aim. We, *Ice Bird* and I, were once again an efficient team.

The start was auspicious. The 'Banana Belt', so named by the cynical British, was so far living up to its reputation for good weather. Easily identifiable landmarks made position fixing easy. I was steering towards Cape Renard twenty miles away, a sheer red rock tower capped rakishly by a tip-tilted glacier. It signposted Le Maire Channel. Looking back I could see how the almost equally spectacular Gerlache Strait was beginning to open out between the glaciated peaks of Anvers Island and the stupendous continental escarpment. Danco Coast is the name given to the more northerly portion of the mainland peninsula; the southern part, towards which we were now heading, is Grahamland.

Before long the motor had to be pressed into service, for the wind fell lighter and the way grew ever more tortuous. Icebergs are easily avoided, always provided you can see them, I mused, circling one stranded monster. Pack ice was another thing altogether, since it could obliterate every bit of navigable water. Moreover wind and current pressure could buckle twenty-foot thick floes like cardboard or cause them to override and raft over each other.

This seems as suitable a place as any to enlarge further on the varieties of ice found at sea. Icebergs and their smaller cousins, growlers and bergy bits originate, of course, on land. With something like three-quarters of its bulk submerged, a berg drifts slowly northwards whenever the summer thaw releases it from imprisonment in the pack, gradually weathering into fairy-castle shapes or turning turtle as its stability is undermined by the waves and ultimately melting in warmer seas. Or else it may ground, commonly on the hundred fathom line, which is six hundred feet down. Here its voyage ends unless it breaks up. Immovably stranded, its two-hundred-foot cliffs erode through the years into pinnacles and purple caverns of ever more fantastic beauty, until in the end the pale sun wins its predestined victory.

Pack ice, as mentioned earlier, is formed by the surface of the sea freezing. Fortunately for me, the floes that I encountered were generally old and near to melting and were generally only four to six feet thick.

Pack appeared likely to be the immediate problem. By 11.30 a.m. we were approaching Le Maire Channel. Under motor alone, for the rock and ice cliffs that towered close aboard had cut off every breath of wind, we weaved in and out between the lines of floes that almost but never quite choked the approach to the defile. The tidal current was perceptible. Were we going to encounter pressure where there was no room for manœuvre? I stood tense at the tiller, envying the relaxed Weddell seals dozing on the floes and the Gentoo penguins preoccupied at their fishing. Every now and then the motor would miss a beat and my heart seemed to stop with it. This maritime canyon was no place for a breakdown.

I jerked my head up, startled at a sudden rumbling roar from above. Staring up the mounting succession of ice fall, cirque and snowfield, my eyes at length found the snow cloud that marked where a hundred ton serac had just tumbled into ruin. The strait, narrow enough at the best of times, became effectively constricted to a mere ribbon as the only lead narrowed. Worse still, the open water channel began to trend right under the left-hand ice

cliffs, which were now fully exposed to the disintegrating effects
of the midday sun. I had no idea of the extent of the avalanche
danger, but the question was academic since there was no other
route. I had to try this way. It seemed an age that we nosed along,
the rattle of the exhaust booming back from the ice cliffs, the
while I apprehensively divided my attention between the half-
tide rocks and looming seracs to port and the sinuous ice edge
opposite.

At last *Ice Bird* chugged round a corner (the engine's beat had
now steadied, thank goodness) and crunched through a line of
brash out into the sunlight. This was a place where the passage
widened out to receive a heavily crevassed mainland glacier. The
time was 1.30 p.m., two hours since passing Cape Renard. We
had come almost to the start of the real narrows, the four-mile-
long Le Maire Channel proper.

At this point I noticed that the plywood wind-vane was gone.
Clearly I had failed properly to screw home the securing bolt.
Ignoring the unworthy thought that there were still three spare
vanes aboard, I turned back along our wake and was lucky enough
soon to retrieve the inconspicuous varnished board.

Back on course, we soon reached the bend that had so far
hidden from us the throat of the pass. A berg which, judging from
its water-smoothed surface and vertical tide marks, had but
recently turned over on to its side, had cleared an open space in
its fall. We crept past it, rounded the corner and there ahead
stretched the narrows – no more than half a mile across, flanked
by three-thousand-foot walls. That first glance conveyed the
absurd impression of there not being room enough for *Ice Bird*
to pass. Yet, as I well knew, even large icebreakers used the
channel.

The deeper we penetrated the more I marvelled at the wild
beauty of this place. Sun-warmed rock buttresses ribbed the
dazzling snowfields of the eastern wall but, on Wandle Peak
opposite, the westering sun had already cast the hanging glaciers
into purple shadow. Ice floes slowly gyrated with the current.
The 'ark ark' of porpoising penguins and the engine's staccato
echo were the only sounds to break the silence. Then came the
thunder of a nearby ice avalanche. I watched the water boil as

the great blocks rained down, and saw the pack heave up alarmingly. No need to worry: the spreading undulations were so quickly damped down by the ice cover that no more than a few gentle ripples reached as far as *Ice Bird*.

I will not attempt to enlarge further upon this unforgettable scene or the effect it had upon me. In any case Le Maire Channel crops up again later in this story, even if in rather different circumstances, so I will content myself with recording that the pack was kind, no denser than 6/10. In two and a half hours of rather circuitous motoring we traversed Le Maire Channel and emerged into the open around four in the afternoon. I heaved a sigh of relief. Surely the way would be easier now that there was more room to manœuvre! The rest of the route to Argy lay along Penola Strait between the sheer Grahamland coast to the east (on the left hand) and a screen of islands and rocks some four miles out to seaward. The largest of these, Hovgaard and Petermann, with their attendant skerries, stretched south for about ten miles. The small low Argentine Islands, where the British base was situated, began five miles south of Petermann.

I was soon disillusioned. The pack became progressively more dense and it even appeared to be moving in behind to block off the way we had come. In preparation for the backing and butting aside of the ice that seemed to be in prospect I shut off the motor so that I could, rather belatedly, disconnect the vulnerable self-steering lever arm and refuel. After the abrupt cessation of engine noise the stillness seemed unnatural. *Ice Bird* floated motionless in the centre of a mirror-smooth polynia – a patch of clear water in the pack.

There had been 26 US gallons of petrol aboard that morning, 20 of them in four 5-gallon jerrycans lashed to the rails forward. Eight hours under power had used up 6 gallons. Lugging one of the jerrycans aft and emptying it into the fuel tank through the filler pipe on deck, I could not help comparing the ease of this operation, now that the waves had been damped down by the ice, with its awkwardness in a seaway. Twenty gallons of fuel remained in hand, more than enough to take me to Argy, I thought, as I pressed the starter button and the motor stuttered into life.

The only possible way past Hovgaard Island was along the

I.B.—K

shore lead, the tenuous tidal gap separating the fast ice frozen to
the shore from the free drifting pack farther out. The prospect of
traversing it was far from inviting. Ugly looking boulders everywhere projected through the fast ice and it was a reasonable de-
duction that other rocks lurked close beneath the surface outside
the ice margin. Nevertheless, all went well until *Ice Bird* ran out
from the shelter of the southern tip of the big island and, without
warning, we found ourselves in real peril.

Jagged skerries were suddenly all around us and the pack was
innocuous and quiet no longer. A heavy swell from the open sea
was causing the ice floes to collide and buckle, battering them
against the rocks and swirling them in the savage backwash. The
little yacht lacked the power to make any impression on pack such
as this. She was surged helplessly back and forth, bringing up
repeatedly against the bigger floes with stunning force. For the
moment she was completely out of control. I could only pray
she would not be dashed against one of those grim islets, to be
pinned down and, in all probability, pounded to pieces.

But the same swell that threatened *Ice Bird*'s imminent destruction was to prove her salvation. As the floes cannoned together
in one place leads opened up temporarily in another. Two floes
ahead parted. I slammed open the throttle; a floe dealt the hull a
tremendous buffet; then we were moving – out from that fearful
place. More by luck than good judgement I managed to zigzag
along one lead after another until we reached deep water and
quiet pack in the lee of Petermann Island.

Once again there was no alternative but to follow a shore lead.
Three miles down the coast the island's precipitous cliffs gave
way to gentler slopes and there, unexpectedly, stood a solid
looking little building. I studied the chart more closely. Yes, there
it was, marked 'Refuge Hut'. I hoped devoutly not to need it but
its presence was comforting nonetheless.

I was determined to avoid at all costs the potentially dangerous
southern tip of Petermann Island and so started to work across
in the general direction of the mainland Coast through a
series of narrow leads. We were well out into Penola Strait by
the time Petermann Island had fallen astern. This would have
been all very well because, save for some scattered bergs and a

few skerries several miles away, the strait was free from obstruction. Unhappily the pack was now so close – eight- or nine-tenths ice cover, I judged – as to be all but unnavigable. The very few leads that remained all tended eastward towards the tumbling mainland glaciers that spilled down from the continental ice cap and led away from the hummocked Argentine Islands, now in tantalizingly plain view. And even these last leads were closing fast.

I was unaware until many weeks later that the Argy base personnel had spotted *Ice Bird* through their binoculars. Nor could I know that they had just radioed to Palmer that the previous day's wide leads had closed up again. Not even a strengthened expeditions ship, they warned, could hope to reach Argy. I had reached much the same conclusion.

By 6 p.m. we were virtually beset but I wasted another two hours and much fuel in fruitlessly charging floes that the weight of the yacht's overriding bow could never hope to force aside – because they were packed so tightly that there was no place for them to go. There being no point in trying any longer, I shut the engine off at 8 p.m.

The petrol tank was nearly empty again, the last few hours at full throttle in close pack having been prodigal of fuel. Eleven gallons all told had been consumed in that day's eleven hours' motoring. There were fifteen gallons left. I refilled the tank, attended to such routine maintenance as tightening the stern gland and took bearings to fix our position. Time for a last look round. There was still no wind and it was very warm, a remarkable +7°C., that I was not to experience again for more than two months. The sky remained cloudless, though a faint haze shimmered over the ice. Westward and southward, glistening under the low sun, gently heaving hummocked pack and its captive bergs stretched away into infinity.

A few slices of bread and cheese were all I could stomach that evening. One duty remained before I could seek my bunk, to complete the logbook record of this eventful day. I wrote:

Beset in Penola Strait. 65° 12′ S., 64° 07′ W.
Very tired. At the helm, mainly in ice, 15 hours.
Distance 33 miles.

Next day I woke periodically only to go back to sleep again, for there was not only that first day's weariness to make good but, more important, all the tiredness that had accumulated during the exhausting refit at Palmer. Between 8.30, when I woke up first and noted that the yacht was still close beset with some pressure and was nearer the glaciated mainland coast, and 2 p.m., the log contains only one word (entered later): 'slept'. The ice pressure had eased by two o'clock. Narrow lanes of water were visible between the floes. The decision, whether to tackle the 9/10 pack or remain where we were and save fuel, was solved by the view from aloft. There were no patches of clear water. Within the hour the pack had closed in again.

Nevertheless there had been one important observation. The floes had loosened at high tide. From now on I must adjust my strategy accordingly. As a first step I must be ready to get under way by three o'clock next morning, which I judged would be just about the time of high water.

This having been decided, there was nothing more constructive to be done than to go to sleep again. Hunger awakened me at seven-thirty, when I ate a similar supper to the night before. Then, feeling a little demoralized by my helplessness and the enforced inactivity, I retired to my bunk once more.

I was up and about according to plan by three next morning, 14 December. I had slept, with only short breaks, for the major part of thirty hours. It was calm and sunny, with a temperature of $-2°C$. To my delight I saw that the floes were spaced much wider apart than the previous afternoon. The intervening water was itself lightly frozen over but the new ice, being barely half an inch thick, presented no problems. I got the motor going at once and, with high hopes, began picking a way towards Argentine Islands. Fifteen minutes later the engine stopped abruptly.

I am no favourite with motors since I lack the natural mechanical aptitude necessary for getting on really good terms with them. Nor had I had much occasion to delve into *Ice Bird*'s engine, Jim having been the one who got it going at Palmer. Now I was really on my own. With the help of the instruction manual I soon traced the fault to a block in the fuel line, but taking down and re-assembling the carburettor in that cramped space without dropping some vital part into the bilge, was not so easy. The job, therefore, took me some time and, before the engine could be got running, the pack had closed in once more. There was yet more trouble. The end of the throttle cable had broken off. It slipped out repeatedly when I tried to replace it so in the end I had to be content with an engine that ran at a third throttle and whose speed could not be varied. Still, at least it *was* going.

Paradoxically, I began to feel much more confident now than at any time since leaving Palmer. Here was something that I found particularly difficult and had tackled on my own more or less successfully. I had 'earned my keep'.

Heightened morale encouraged me to get on with things I had been neglecting. After a general tidying up of the cabin I decided that this was an excellent opportunity to ease my conscience with the *National Geographic* by taking 'indoor' photographs. The absence of movement, so unprecedented at sea, and the strong light provided conditions too good to miss. All along I had been taking pictures in the cockpit with a Nikonis waterproof camera, loaded with Kodachrome II, clamped to the stern rail. A string which I constantly kept tripping over worked the shutter. The result was a high proportion of pictures of my own rear.

Hopefully the cabin shots would be a little more varied. The Nikkormas had a delayed action shutter release, which would be an improvement on the string. I clamped one to the forward cabin bulkhead. It had been loaded with High Speed Ektachrome pushed to 400 A.S.A. to obviate the need for flash, a practice I adhered to subsequently with apparently good results. I proceeded to immortalize myself shaving, writing up the log, plotting bearings on the chart and making my first hot meal and drink on the Japanese wick stove – even though this involved no more than heating water and a can of stew. The kettle proved to be leaking, so I cursed and tossed it overboard, forgetting for the moment that the sea outside was solid. It bounced along in the direction of two very startled Adélie penguins who squawked in alarm and fled.

This incident gave me the idea of taking pictures of the trapped *Ice Bird* from alongside. An ice-axe driven into the snow provided a useful camera stand for the other Nikkormat. There followed an enjoyable twenty minutes of actuating the delayed release and then plunging across to the yacht so as to be posing nonchalantly alongside when the shutter finally clicked.

High tide that afternoon saw some loosening of the pack but so little that, after an hour's effort, we were no more than a quarter of a mile in a straight line from our starting point. Our situation had actually worsened for we were right in the track of a line of bergs that appeared to be ploughing southward through the pack. Bearings on the land showed later that it was the bergs that were stationary and probably grounded while the pack was moving northward. But which was in motion was irrelevant to our predicament. We had to get out of the way. Twenty minutes' pushing and squirming through gaps carried the yacht the necessary five hundred yards to safety.

Only just in time. Without warning the pack snapped shut like a vice round *Ice Bird*. From time to time the whole mass would begin to surge violently to and fro. Perhaps a distant berg had overturned. But after a minute all would become still again. It began to snow. It was then that I blessed the designer for the yacht's wedge shaped underwater cross-section because, as the pressure increased, she was squeezed bodily upwards. Her steel frame merely groaned and creaked a little but the stout craft was clearly in no danger at all.

The lack of a functioning radio transmitter was annoying: this was because I feared that my failure to reach Argy might be causing needless anxiety, rather than because of *Ice Bird*'s being beset. Certainly she was amply enough supplied, carrying as she

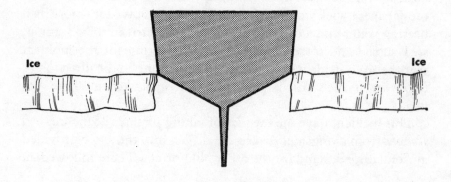

did a good six months' food, even if variety were limited, and thirty-nine gallons of water (and this old pack had long since become fresh water ice). There was meths enough – four gallons – to heat up a hundred Primus stoves. I had exchanged what survived of my original paperbacks at Palmer. So light reading matter was no problem. The only item that was short was kerosene, a mere quart. Palmer had inadvertently used up the rest. Still, cold food would be no novelty. In fact, of course, the unusually persistent summer pack had to disperse soon – in a matter of weeks at most.

There was no immediate risk of the yacht's being damaged in the ice, much less wrecked or crushed. Nevertheless, such unpleasant possibilities did exist and it would have been irresponsible not to have thought out in advance ways of surviving the loss of my ship in the continental pack ice.

These emergency plans hinged on the fact that Antarctic Peninsula bases are not very far apart. The ultra light *Condom* could easily be carried, either inflated or folded up in a rucksack, over ice floes or across land and could be used to cross considerable stretches of coastal water in fine weather. Thanks to that not altogether purposeless overnight glacier trip from Palmer, I knew that my sleeping bag was more than adequate in the open. Add an ice axe, a knife, emergency food and, above all, the patience to wait for really calm conditions, and only incompetence or very bad luck could prevent my reaching safety under my own steam. At the present moment, of course, there was that most convenient refuge hut on Petermann Island.

The other dire contingency, foundering in mid-ocean through storm or collision with an iceberg, was less well covered. In fact I had no plan at all. The circular rubber raft, which I had sent back to England from Palmer as too cumbersome, would in any case have been useless. It was only capable of blowing along helplessly until its fabric perished – long after my own demise. In the Appendix, I have enlarged on the need for a steerable raft for ocean yachtsmen but, so far as I was concerned, *Ice Bird* must continue as her own lifeboat in the open ocean – and we must studiously avoid bergs.

These days beset in the pack seemed to flow into one another, the blurring of time in the absence of normal seagoing routine being accentuated by the continuous daylight. Despite the steel plates protecting the cabin windows and cutting off two-thirds of the light I could still read down below at any time of the night. The hours of high water, with the consequent loosening of the ice, became the significant twelve-and-a-half-hour markers. Thus, only my wrist watch and the log entries indicated that another day had come when I started the motor at 1 a.m. on 15 December.

It was colder now, —4°C. and snowing heavily. New ice had formed between the floes. High time to replace my thin jeans with warm Japanese quilted undertrousers. Once more the patient zigzag south-westward towards Argentine Islands was resumed. The penguins were still asleep at this hour, either erect with head beneath flipper or prone. At the yacht's noisy approach they would wake in a panic and dash off, leaning forward with flippers held stiffly out behind, to plop head foremost into the nearest lead. Once a seal poked its head up close alongside, choked in surprise and coughed up a stream of water, then hastily dived.

When the eventual closing in of the pack put an end to the morning's endeavours, another half jerrycan of fuel had been used up. Apart from what was left in the tank, only ten gallons remained in reserve. To set against this we were now, I estimated, in 65° 22'S., so there *had* been fair progress. Argentine Islands were only four or five miles off. (This modest success had been duly noted by the British watchers on their hilltop, with the unfortunate sequel that, when RRS *Bransfield* relieved them a fortnight later, she generously steamed another ten miles down Penola Strait to see if the yacht had been carried farther in the direction she had last been seen heading.)

The pack failed to loosen at all that afternoon. The temperature remained below freezing. Snow began to fall again and continued heavily all night. Nevertheless, I was pleased at our progress and looked forward with anticipation to the morrow. I could not know that 65° 22'S. was to be *Ice Bird*'s southern limit.

Shortly after eight next morning, 16 December, the snow clouds rolled away and the sun broke through, rapidly melting the accumulated snow on deck. The ship was still heavily beset.

But it was not this that caused my consternation. The familiar Penola Strait landmarks had vanished. It took a moment to recognize the island to seaward as Hovgaard and to realize that the whole pack must have drifted quite a few miles north-eastward during the night. Not only had the last three days' painful efforts been wiped out, but we had lost as much ground again as had so laboriously been won. The steadily changing bearings of the land confirmed that the drift was still continuing.

There was only one possible decision. As the log stated:

In view of the drift of pack, am abandoning Argentine Islands objective.

Will try to return north along Le Maire and on to Almirante Brown. [The Argentinian station at Paradise Bay on the mainland side of Gerlache Strait.] Worries pack, motor, petrol.

With such an inauspicious start opened a most memorable day.

For the moment initiative lay with the pack. *Ice Bird* was fast beset and nothing I could do would move her an inch in any direction. The small leads, in defiance of the bright sunshine, were still frozen over. Everything glittered and sparkled. What a picture the bright yellow yacht must make, I thought, against the shadowed blue ice of the Grahamland escarpment! Dropping down on to the ice with a camera, I began casting about, hopping from one floe to the next, in an effort to obtain the best vantage point. Yes, there was an ideal floe – even if the lead was a trifle wide. I crouched down and jumped.

Good, I had made it easily! I got to my feet jauntily and looked back. The lead was already a good ten feet across and was widening rapidly. The momentum of my leap had been trans-mitted to the floe with a vengeance. Now I watched in dismay as *Ice Bird* receded beyond a growing expanse of water. Recollection of the effects of immersion in sub-zero sea water were not re-assuring. How to get back? With an effort I held down incipient panic and studied the situation more carefully.

My floe had by now come to rest against the opposite side of the newly formed polynia. Would any of the adjacent pans bear my weight? Not worth the risk, they all looked rotten. Therefore my floe must somehow be induced to go back. There being nothing to paddle with, I lay down gingerly on my back near the edge of the floe, put both feet against its dubious neighbour, glanced round to confirm that the angles were right and shoved off hard. The floe slid forward sluggishly, gyrated and came to rest at the edge of the polynia again but, this time, a little nearer *Ice Bird*. Heartened, I got up and took the photograph that had led to all the trouble, lay down again and repeated the manœuvre. After the third push the floe floated up to the yellow hull. I grasped the stern rail as if it had been my salvation (as indeed it was) and clambered thankfully aboard.

Almost imperceptibly the pack kept on drifting northward. For half an hour it was racked with violent sheering and rotatory movements, but when these ceased, as suddenly and mysteriously as they had begun, it had opened out a little. A faint southerly breeze began to stir, so hoisting the genoa seemed worthwhile. Then it was the motor's turn but this ran so erratically as to have to be shut off almost at once. With a sigh of resignation I got down to the job of stripping and cleaning the fuel line, fluently cursing the dollops of melting snow that periodically plopped down from the boom to splatter over the disassembled engine.

Meanwhile *Ice Bird*, with the genoa still set, was drifting through the interstices in the 9/10 pack. Every now and then I would scramble up from below decks, push away the currently obstructing floe with a boathook and direct the yacht's bow into a crack between pans that she could gradually force open by the gentle tug of her headsail. The engine adjustments took all of one and a half hours, so it was noon before all was done. The effort had been more than worthwhile, because I had at last succeeded in re-introducing the throttle cable into the carburettor. An immediate ten-minute trial confirmed that the power was indeed much increased. Mightily relieved, I switched off and sat down to a lunch of corned beef, ships biscuits and coffee.

By one o'clock I was back on deck surveying the situation. It had not altered materially. We were still in Girard Bay between Hovgaard Island and the continental shore, though now the entrance to Le Maire Channel was open ahead. The glittering floes revolved slowly in the sunshine, gradually opening up short and narrow leads. Surely these could be utilized, given sufficient patience. But how? Certainly not by wasting precious fuel and taking the risk of straining the temperamental motor for the meagre results possible in such near-unnavigable pack.

The obvious answer was to get out and push. I stripped off my quilted anorak and clambered down on to the snow-covered ice.

Two o'clock came and passed and I was still pushing. Sometimes I had to put my shoulder to the transom, or else I would grip one of the stanchions and haul from alongside. Yet again, the bow would have to be guided into an opening. Often it was easier to pole from on deck with the boathook. Transient puffs of wind bellied out the genoa to add their quota. We seemed not to be getting anywhere until I noticed that a group of frozen-in berglets, which had been some distance ahead, had fallen a long way astern.

This original form of yacht propulsion deserved to be immortalized, I decided rather smugly, and began to record samples of my efforts with a camera propped up on an upturned bucket out on the floes. I was re-setting the shutter after having taken a shot when an ominous plop sounded back at the yacht. The boathook, which had been leaning up against the bow, had disappeared and a new lead of uninviting dark water had opened between me and the vessel. Here was the morning's predicament all over again. The experience gained earlier enabled me to regain *Ice Bird* by the same method as before, but now I was thoroughly cured of any penchant for further overside photography. I resolved to cling closer than a leech to the yacht in future.

For all these good intentions, it was not long before I had an even worse fright. While pushing hunched over from astern, the floe on which I was standing split and slid away, so suddenly that I was barely able to retain my balance on its rocking remnant. Working my precarious way from floe to floe towards safety was anything but easy and the experience forcibly brought home to me how rotten much of the ice had become. I must be far more careful and must strictly confine myself from now on to poling (with a dinghy oar in lieu of the lost boathook) from the security of the foredeck.

A fresh series of rotatory movements without any discernible set pattern now began to take place, first in one section of the pack then in another. Ice avalanches were coming off the cliffs ahead and I devoutly hoped that no unpredictable vortex would set us over beneath them. Fortunately none did so. *Ice Bird* re-entered Le Maire, from which she had emerged with such high hopes exactly four days and a half-hour earlier, in mid-channel at 4.30 p.m. The pack's density was much more variable and, once inside the pass, its drift speeded up. I was still fending off and pushing with *Condom*'s little oar, assisted by occasional zephyrs.

Worries – about being trapped against some obstruction and ground down by the irresistible pack or bombarded by ice avalanches – now faded. The pack swept steadily on, while tiny waves began to ripple along the hull as the wind wafted us across the increasingly frequent polynias. Once again I fell under the spell of Le Maire's grandeur. The camera began clicking again, only this time from the cockpit. But I soon despaired of capturing anything like a true image of those soaring precipices. As to the busily waddling and diving penguins and the somnolent seals, the former moved too fast to catch at the right moment, while the latter seemed always to be in the wrong place or too far away. Moreover, camera work was continually interrupted by the need to steer or pole off. Still the time passed enjoyably enough and it seemed but a moment before it was half-past six and we were rounding the final bend in Le Maire Channel proper, in much looser pack.

The motor could with advantage be started and, half an hour later, I hoisted the mainsail to make full use of the stiffening breeze. The ice became progressively more scattered as the mountain walls fell back on either hand, until at 8 p.m., Cape Renard came abeam to starboard and we sailed out into the open waters of Bismarck Strait and finally left behind the main body of the pack.

Since the wind, if still light, was fair the motor could now be shut off. With the sun shining as brightly as ever I hove-to to replenish the petrol tank and lay out ten fathoms of anchor cable, in somewhat premature preparation for arriving at Almirante Brown, still twenty-five miles to the north. When we got under way again I continued steering from the cockpit at first but later, as the temperature dropped, retired to the shelter of the companionway, where I propped myself up against the hatch coaming, holding the tiller lines with mittened hands. What water had splashed into the cockpit or on to the side decks froze solid. There was still too much ice about to risk trying out the as yet unfamiliar self-steering gear. I grew increasingly weary.

Alertness was essential, however. The hollow boom of swells rolling into caverns worn in the icebergs along our track spelled out a clear warning, if any were needed. More menacing even than the bergs were the growlers, whose bottle-green wave-worn silhouettes were only barely distinguishable as they wallowed awash like submerging whales. Fortunately the grumbling, gurgling noise that they made as they rolled to and fro was audible a good way off from a sailing boat. Was this the origin of their name, I wondered? Bergy bits, being much higher out of the water than growlers, were easier to see. All those with level standing room were peopled with sleeping penguins, stacked side by side like ninepins, who woke and craned their necks to watch us pass.

Soon after midnight the fifteen-mile wide Bismarck Strait was behind us and we entered the northward-trending Gerlache Strait, keeping well over towards the eastern or Danco Coast side. I hove-to again then, for coffee and biscuits and in order to study the chart in the shelter of the cabin. Landmarks had become hard to distinguish despite the continuing full daylight, because the cold white light cast no shadows once the sun had set. It might be difficult to locate Canal Lautaro, the channel into Paradise Bay, and I needed to memorize all the prominent features.

In the event, Bank Island separated itself from its background three hours later and revealed the sought-for sound. I hauled in the main sheet, put the helm over and gybed the mainsail; then, steering rather erratically by pressing my bottom against the tiller, I brought the genoa across and ran in through the entrance. No sooner were we inside than the wind died and the motor had to be started.

I had expected to be able to spot the base at once, but a full hour passed before I managed to pick out its radio masts, so dwarfed were they by the vastness of the continental massif behind. A good many Antarctic bases, among them Palmer, are located for convenience on off-lying islands. The Argentinian scientific station Almirante Brown, on the contrary, stands on the Antarctic mainland itself. This was an added point of interest for me because, although I had sailed literally within feet of the continental coast in Le Maire Channel, I had not yet actually landed upon it.

It was five in the morning before I reached the station, having come thirty-six miles since beginning to break out of the pack the previous day. I thankfully throttled back the engine and let *Ice Bird* coast past the sleeping base, while I wondered if there were anywhere to tie up or whether to anchor instead. A bearded figure appeared and waved. I swung the tiller hard over and headed in towards the tiny jetty where he was standing. He called out, but I could not distinguish the words above the noise of the engine. His meaning was soon enough to be made clear.

Unforgivably, I neglected to look over the side to check that it was deep enough for the yacht's six-foot draft. Had I done so it would have been immediately obvious (the water being clear) that the bottom was shoaling fast. There came a grinding crunch under the keel, a series of bumps, and *Ice Bird* stopped abruptly. After surviving all the dangers of the pack, she had been run hard aground.

Chapter 9

Ice Blink

The bearded one, who turned out to be the mechanic and whose name was Armando, had by now been joined by two companions. All three jumped down into a perilously rocking dory and rowed gaily out to my rescue. We tried rolling *Ice Bird* from side to side and pushing off with a twelve foot sweep that I had acquired from *Hero* on the principle that it might come in handy. On the present occasion it proved ineffective, though it was to stand me in good stead later on. It was at this point that Armando showed his acumen.

'*No problema – el mare subiendo,*' he remarked. Did *subiendo* mean that the tide was rising or falling? I could not remember, but the word sounded suspiciously like 'subsiding'. Armando's gestures soon resolved the issue. The word for falling was *bajando*, not *subiendo*. We could safely drop the anchor and go ashore to breakfast in the certainty that *Ice Bird* would float off in her own good time.

The atmosphere of the base was relaxed and pleasant and I spent two very happy days there. The temptation to accept a pressing invitation to stop over Christmas was strong but I was all too aware of the shortness of the summer and the thousands of miles of Southern Ocean that stretched ahead. Having taken the resolve, I wasted little time in contemplating the superb view. After a few hours' sleep in the bunk allotted to me I was taken on a tour of the base. Hugo, a marine biologist who was also a keen photographer, agreed to take pictures with *National Geographic* film, just as Kent Yates had done at Palmer. He subsequently passed the rolls on to Anne when the ubiquitous *Lindblad Explorer* called – and was able to dine with her on board. The rest of that first afternoon was spent in sailing *Ice Bird* to and fro before an icy amphitheatre, past the cameraman in his dory, and in testing and making adjustments to the self-steering gear.

The wind-vane steered the yacht perfectly, but only so long as the wind remained strong. Once let it drop even to force three, the level of a good sailing breeze, and the gear failed to operate. I was never to succeed in diagnosing the cause and so had no choice but to accept the exasperating limitation. The designer has since suggested that some vital component must have been damaged in transit. Exactly similar gear installed on other yachts has always been trouble free. He was right: Barry later found that the balance weight was missing.

One of my first preoccupations on landing had been to ask that Argy be informed by radio of my change of plan and present whereabouts. Here I came up against the almost total lack of communication between the different national facilities for, while the British and American bases were in daily touch on 4067 KHz in a session appropriately dubbed the 'Goon Show', the Argentines could not transmit on this frequency. An attempt to relay a message via *Hero* failed also, with the result that *Bransfield* had to make that unnecessary search in Penola Strait.

Miscellaneous tasks took up the morning of the 18th. The depleted fuel tank and jerrycans were refilled. A bulky ten gallon drum of rather dubious petrol, which would have to be filtered before use, was lashed to the rail as a reserve. Most welcome was an ample supply of kerosene. The only snag was that most of it was in two fragile fifteen-litre glass wine jars. I could only string these up in the forepeak from a complicated cat's cradle of cords and hope for the best. The plastic fresh water bottles were replenished but the built-in main water tank could be left undisturbed, since its contents were frozen.

Fuel and water apart, *Ice Bird* was so amply stocked with Australian provisions (augmented with canned bacon from Palmer) that there was simply no room to stow the great box of foodstuffs prepared for me by the hospitable Argentines. Barring two bottles of *vino tinto*, it had regretfully to be left behind.

Five miles across Paradise Bay from Almirante Brown stands the Chilean base, Gonzalez Videla. Unlike its neighbour this was not permanently manned and housed only a small summer advance party. Again in contrast to Brown, Videla is a military establishment. Some of the Argentines wanted to pay their opposite numbers a visit, so a lively party set out after lunch in *Ice Bird*. The flags of Argentina and Chile flew together from the starboard spreader. Hugo took the helm and, skilfully avoiding the numerous bergy bits, excitedly called my attention to the abundant bird life. Much in evidence were the familiar Antarctic species: penguins, skuas, terns, snow petrels and *gaviota* gulls. But here they had been joined by more oceanic types: pintados and Wilson's storm petrels. Almost unique to the area, and most striking of all, were the flightless blue-eyed cormorants, whose brilliantly coloured eyes fully justified their name.

I hoped to take this opportunity to swing the compasses – the original steering compass mounted in the hatchway and the new US boat compass set up in the cabin. Unfortunately my Chilean chart of Paradise Bay lacked the detail necessary for lining up on well defined landmarks. A rough check, which was all that was possible, satisfied me that the outside steering compass was relatively accurate, while the one in the cabin was being deviated by the attraction of the yacht's steel sides to the tune of some 12°. How wrong I was would only become apparent a fortnight later.

The buildings of Gonzalez Videla were nearly hidden by falling snow when we dropped anchor and pushed off in the deplorably unstable Argentine dory we had been towing. We were duly shown round the base and afterwards regaled with a drink that was new to me – canned strawberries in red wine. More memorable was the scene at our departure.

The base is built on a penguin rookery. As we pulled away from the shore, our hosts came to the salute and launched with gusto into the Chilean Air Force song – and the serried ranks of Gentoo penguins behind stood at attention as though in parody. We became so helpless with mirth as to almost upset our dory.

I had been planning on an early departure on the 19th but had belatedly found unacceptable slop in the tiller's attachment to the rudder shaft. Repairs, which involved boring holes in the hardened steel shaft, occupied the kindly mechanic, Armando Guzman, for most of the day. I divided my time between assisting him and sorting out charts for the next stage of the journey. There were

I.B.—L

still a hundred miles of Gerlache Strait to go, a stretch totally devoid of anchorages, according to the knowledgeable captain of *Biscoe*. We would then turn into the much broader two hundred mile long Bransfield Strait between the Antarctic Peninsula and the South Shetland Islands, where there was a Soviet base named Bellingshausen that I hoped to visit. The next four hundred miles to Signy Base (British) in the South Orkney group would be due east across the mouth of the notoriously ice-choked Weddell Sea.

Sextant navigation would soon be needed. With this in mind, I had been checking my watches against radio time signals for more than two months. Despite the Seiko's very modest gain of two seconds a day against the Omega's eight, the former was subject to erratic fluctuations while the latter's rate kept regular. Thus the Omega was designated 'ship's chronometer' for another season, with the Seiko a most comforting stand-by.

Armando finished at six-thirty that evening but despite the hour I determined to leave at once. After all, one time of day was as suitable for departure as another, for continuous daylight still prevailed – though the nights would soon begin to draw in as our northing increased and as the season advanced.

'*Buen suerte. Vaya con Dios,*' called my friends, as I motored regretfully away. Two hours later, well out in Gerlache Strait, I shut off the engine and hoisted sail to a fickle wind, too light to allow of self-steering. A breathtaking panorama unfolded. The strait varied in width from five to fifteen miles and, apart from stray remnants, it held little pack. But ice there was in plenty; bergs sculptured into fantasy, countless bergy bits and lines of brash, tracing current junctions like the driftwood of kindlier climes. Mount Français, on Anvers Island in the west, brooded nine thousand feet above the Bellingshausen Sea, separated from us by the jagged crest of Wieneke, while from the precipitous Antarctic Peninsula opposite, great glaciers and ice fronts everywhere swept down to the sea.

The hours slipped by while I steered from the cockpit, amazingly warm in my quilted jacket and insulated boots, for with the gentle wind coming from astern the air was almost still. A science fiction novel intermittently held my attention. Then the genoa would need booming out or the time would come to gybe. Close attention was needed to identify landmarks shown on the chart, both to keep constant track of our own position and to check the compass (though at this I was no more successful than before).

Midnight came and went. Nothing moved, except the yacht ghosting along and some fluttering storm petrels. The peaks that overlapped and hid the channels, encircling the horizon, now began to glow in pale pastel shades. It was while I was committing this rather poetic description to the log that we hit a small berg head on.

'Lucky the wind *was* only force one,' I added to the note I had just made, after fending off.

By 2.30 a.m. I could no longer keep awake. Selecting a reasonably ice-free patch I lowered sail, glad of the knowledge that, in the virtual absence of wind, yacht and bergs would drift equally with the tide.

I awoke at seven, feeling jaded, and made a leisurely breakfast of muesli and coffee before getting under way an hour later. All went well at first, though heavy clouds rolling towards us down the strait from the north-east, boded ill. Their gloomy advance guard arrived at ten; the wind swung round abruptly to dead ahead and sharply strengthened. The sailing honeymoon was over. From now on, beating hard into the teeth of the wind would be the order of the day and *Ice Bird*'s new rig would need to prove its mettle.

In no time at all a short steep sea had built up, into which the yacht laboured, and whose breaking crests masked the now viciously plunging ice masses. The stronger squalls blotted out land and berg alike with a curtain of snow and spray. The actual air temperature was not really low – zero centigrade – but, what with the all pervading wetness, the wind cut through me like a knife. How well would the mast stand up to this first real test? My heart was in my mouth. There was one bad moment when I noticed that it was bending at the gooseneck. I hove-to, replaced the after rigging screws (they had been bent in the first capsize) with lanyards and, first on one tack then on the other, tightened the weather shrouds. This seemed to cure the trouble.

The time was obviously come to introduce a proper seagoing routine. I donned waterproof overtrousers and safety belt, battened down the fore hatch and re-lashed the heavy ten gallon petrol drum, before letting draw the sheets and resuming our wet and uncomfortable progress. I was not altogether dissatisfied at the thirty-five miles that had been hardly won since morning, when I finally lowered the headsail at midnight.

That anxious night – it snowed continuously and I had to get up every hour or so to put about lest we fore-reach into one or other side of the strait or into a berg – made me regret not having brought along an alarm clock. How simple it would have been to set it and be able to sleep soundly for no matter how short a period. Having lacked such elementary foresight I was too tired to get going properly until nearly noon next day.

Attempts to readjust the gooseneck fitting and to peak up the clumsy gaff were not entirely successful. The mainsail persisted in sagging, so that the boom came into violent contact with the steel frame over the hatchway (and all too often with my head) each time we tacked. The improvised gunter rig was proving adequate but far from perfect. The veteran storm jib, that I had so patiently stitched together at Palmer last autumn, confirmed my worst fears as to its efficiency by vibrating madly whenever it was sheeted in hard. Before long I would reluctantly have to replace it by the even smaller new storm jib. By evening I was feeling more optimistic about the mast itself, putting down to seasickness brought on by the unaccustomed motion, my earlier exaggerated fears of its breaking. So far it was standing up to the not inconsiderable stresses of windward work against short, steep, breaking seas. Conditions might well be kinder among the longer swells of the ocean.

The strong winds began to ease and I took advantage of the gentler conditions to take photographs. Soon periods of calm, during which we had to motor, began to alternate with erratic breezes. The sky overhead remained gloomy and overcast, but far back to the southward the sun was still shining over Paradise Bay. Goodbye, 'Banana Belt', I thought.

It was while we were motoring peacefully over a gentle swell and I was musing on the idiosyncrasies of the rig that, happening to glance down into the cabin, I was appalled to see that its floor was awash. Where could be the site of this disastrous leak? The hull itself or the sealing of some opening – stern tube, sink outlet, heads? The last proved to be the culprit. A valve had given way and sea water was siphoning in through the flushing inlet, over-flowing the pan and streaming out over the floor and down into the bilge. I hastily closed the main seacock and set about the formidable chore of pumping out. No fewer than eight hundred strokes were needed.

Midnight passed. It was now 22 December. I felt very weary but comfortable enough in the cockpit in my heavy spray-proof quilted parka, fur hat and mitts, the tiller tucked under my arm, while I clumsily spooned sweet corn out of a can and tried to spread iron-hard butter on to biscuits. We chugged past an ice-capped promontory, to come upon a sight that sent me hurrying below for a camera. A symmetrical snow cone, Hoseason Island, was being perfectly mirrored by ice blink on to the level under-surface of the cloud banks. I only hoped there would be light enough under the 1 a.m. overcast to make the picture worthwhile.

Another hour at the helm was all I could manage that night. Although the persistently contrary winds had prevented us from clearing Gerlache Strait as I had hoped, we were come to within twenty miles of the outlet. There was more sea room and there seemed to be less ice about than before. I shut off the motor, lowered the genoa and sheeted in the mainsail. One last look round, then down below to wind the watch and write up the log. The entry ends, 'Three shopping days till Christmas.'

After a few hours of broken sleep a routine glance outside brought me fully awake to the unwelcome realization that the time for dozing had passed. Heavy fog compounded with falling snow had cut visibility to nearly zero. The wind was fluctuating in strength, though in direction it remained obdurately contrary. Despite the unpromising conditions I hoisted the headsail and set off blindly on the port tack, altogether ignorant of what lay more than a hundred yards ahead. A submerged, wickedly breaking rock was the first object to materialize out of the murk. I came about in some haste, my uneasiness in no way allayed, for I could not identify the rock on the chart and our exact position was obscure. A further preoccupation was with the wire mast stays. Not being of proper yacht quality, they were stretching so badly that the rigging screws might soon be unable to take up the slack. Naturally, every creak and groan from the straining mast set me worrying afresh. Probably the real trouble with me was lack of sleep, because none of these problems were really serious and our progress in the circumstances was not bad at all.

From ten o'clock onwards matters started improving. The fog lifted briefly at times and the snow showers became intermittent, so that some landmarks could be made out – the Alpine silhouette of Trinity Island to starboard and Hoseason's snow pyramid to port – as we beat patiently out from Gerlache Strait. Once a school of killer whales cruised by, the fog magnifying the height of their already lofty dorsal fins into the semblance of submarines' conning towers.

As one steep-sided iceberg came abeam, I was surprised to see that a group of Adélie penguins had somehow managed to establish themselves half-way up. How they had got there was a mystery that clearly intrigued their colleagues, a constant succession of whom kept shooting out of the waves, only to fall short, so that they slid helplessly back down the precipitous slope, squawking indignantly. These hopefuls were still at it when they dwindled from sight astern, but none I saw had made the ledge.

The log that day is full of references to the prevention of chafe, improving the set of sails and tightening lanyards. It records the wind's inconsistencies and many dubious identifications of islands and capes. Well out into Bransfield Strait, a late afternoon calm provided the welcome opportunity for four hours of the soundest sleep since Almirante Brown. Much refreshed, I set off again, heading north-east now, diagonally across Bransfield towards the Russian Bellingshausen base, which lay at the head of a twenty-mile deep fjord on King George Island in the South Shetlands.

Though the South Shetlands and the South Orkneys farther east lie north of that West Antarctic mainland which *Ice Bird* was now leaving, they are fully as 'polar'. They are included in the *Antarctic Pilot*, 1961, 3rd edn., Hydrographic Department, Admiralty, London. This work covers, by its own definition, 'The coasts of Antarctica and all islands southward of the usual route of vessels'. What business had I, I wondered suddenly as I studied the volume, to be sailing a little thing like *Ice Bird* 'south-ward of the usual route of vessels'? More relevant, however, than any such idle speculation was the rather chilling information on page 213 that instruments in a sheltered location on King George Island had recorded a gale a week, and snow or sleet on two days out of three through the year. To prove that even the Admiralty may have its lighter moments, the same passage concluded, '... the climate may be regarded as healthy'.

The area soon began to live up to its reputation. The wind strengthened, drew ahead and plastered the yacht thickly with unpleasantly wet snow. What a boon were my present warm clothes. What a contrast to last season it was, to be comfortable and dry even in such miserable weather. I felt profoundly thankful. The afternoon's sleep enabled me to keep going through the night. It was not until noon next day, 23 December, that uncertainty as to our position in the continuing fog, rather than tiredness, made it prudent to heave-to to await clearer conditions. These did not eventuate until four o'clock next morning, Christmas Eve.

Then the sky suddenly began to clear from the west, uncovering in quick succession the unclimbed peaks of Smith Island, the ice-sheathed mainland and the snow-streaked volcanic ash slopes of Deception Island to the north-east. The weather change brought with it a fair westerly wind, before which we ran rapidly down on Deception. This flooded crater, whose sole entrance between beetling red cliffs is called Neptune's Bellows, had recently become the site of renewed activity. I passed as close under the cliffs as I dared, hoping to observe something of the eruption, but I was disappointed. Nothing but wreaths of mist, which could equally well have been steam, were visible from seaward.

Once past Deception Island we closed the ice cliffs of Living-stone island, beyond which lay King George. The sun was still shining but the favourable wind was steadily dropping and ominous fog banks hovered in the offing. Sure enough, by evening we were fog-bound and becalmed within sound of surf breaking against the foot of the ice cliffs and the periodic thunder of avalanches.

I looked enviously at the group of penguins who were mocking our helplessness by porpoising gaily past the motionless yacht, and was uncharitably elated when one tripped and somersaulted, to land on its back with a splash and a startled 'ark'. My feelings were very mixed as I heated up one of the few cans of sausages in honour of the festive season. There was natural disappointment at being alone instead of at a base as I had hoped, nor could I help missing Susie and Vicky, who would be just about waking up on Christmas morning in Australia (allowing for the time difference). But things could so easily have been '*much much* worse', I confided to the log. After all, exactly a year ago my chances of regaining land had seemed negligible.

After supper I started the motor, only to hear it splutter into silence. There was water in the fuel, I found. Barely had I finished draining the carburettor, when a brisk tail wind sprang up and sent us racing towards the east. Unfortunately, since the fog remained as thick as ever, we were little better off. For the sake of prudence I had to draw away from the coast, with which I quickly lost all contact. By early Christmas morning I calculated we had made sufficient easting, so I cautiously closed the land, nosing through the fog until the shore of an ice-sheathed promontory became visible. Its upper slopes and the peaks and *nunataks* (rock extrusions through the ice) that would have aided identification remained impenetrably shrouded. Even though I suspected that this could very well be the right place – the cape on King George at the mouth of my fjord – there was no means of confirmation.

I had no alternative but to heave-to and wait with what patience I could muster in the chill fog, now joined by soggily falling snow. 'Merry Christmas,' I wrote sourly in the log. Nothing much changed for the rest of the day. I dared not, for fear of impairing my vigilance, take more than a glass of Argentine wine with my modest corned beef Christmas dinner. The final log entry at midnight is a laconic, 'Goodbye, Christmas'.

A brisk westerly, bringing a prompt clearing away of the fog, ushered in Boxing Day and confirmed that we had in fact been lying off the correct fjord the previous morning, but had been set well down to leeward since. My attempts to tack back to the entrance in the teeth of violent squalls and a powerful current made but little headway, so that by noon my patience was at an end. The two hundred-odd miles from Almirante Brown had already taken a week. Was it worth spending several more days beating towards Bellingshausen when the whole Southern Ocean remained to be traversed and the brief summer was passing? I reluctantly decided to give up the idea of visiting the Soviet base and squared away for the South Orkneys, four hundred miles to the east.

The strong wind suited the self-steering gear very well. So efficiently did it handle the steep following seas, that I could fry bacon and heat up beans at my leisure, without having to do more than scan the white-caps ahead for signs of ice. Skirting King George Island at a brisk five knots, we came to the open Scotia Sea as the afternoon began to wane. My heart warmed to the little flock of ice birds that promptly took up station astern; perhaps this augured well.

I was disillusioned soon enough on that score. The wind headed us, then fell away altogether, leaving a violent lop that set the sails slatting and slamming. One unexpected lurch hurled me against the camera clamped to the stern rail; fortunately a replacement was available. Long before dusk, snow showers had blotted out King George and the bergs that punctuated the horizon. As a reminder of changing latitude, there were several hours of real darkness that night. Much the same conditions persisted until past noon the next day, so that little progress was possible. Then things altered with a vengeance.

A sudden 45-knot (force eight and nine) westerly gale plastered *Ice Bird* with snow and sent her careering along, crashing through crests and lurching down into troughs. The food cans in the lockers were rattling, I wrote in the log, 'like a grocer's shop in an earthquake'. I was very nearly flung overboard when I was changing sail. Rather late in the day, I resolved always to wear a safety belt in future. The gale was hardly playing fair, in that it did nothing to disperse the fog. To add to my deep sea teething troubles, the weighty ten-gallon petrol drum burst its lashings and catapulted clear across the deck to end up in the lee scuppers. Its potential value seemed rather less than its capacity for mischief. With some effort, I heaved it overboard. The next casualty was

the rail around the top of the Primus stove, against which I
bounced, breaking it and very nearly my ribs as well!

This opening gale of the resumed voyage was of brief duration.
By evening it had moderated, leaving the yacht buffeted this way
and that by the toppling residual swells. Before I had time to
secure it, the gaff swung so violently to one side as to split the
jaws right away.

The accident was not altogether disastrous, for I had already
begun to contemplate dispensing with the gaff. It was very hard to
hoist in a seaway (it once took me more than an hour to get it up
properly) and did nothing to improve the windward set of the
sail. I would substitute the double-reefed mainsail set directly on
the stumpy mast. The resulting sail would be tiny but easy to
hoist and efficient in shape. I set to work at once, but it was a
long time before the final product emerged from a welter of
experiments. Eventually the rejected gaff had been secured in the
scuppers, in case there should be some further need for it, and *Ice
Bird* had become once again a Bermudan sloop – albeit a ludicrously
undercanvassed one.

Inadequate sail area apart, the only other snag with the new rig
was that the boom drooped so badly that I had to lift it bodily
over the pram hood frame every time we gybed or tacked. Once
sheeted home, however, the little mainsail set very sweetly.

In the midst of these proceedings the radio antenna fell victim
to my clumsiness. I tumbled against it with force enough to
tear it down from its attachment aloft. There would be no more
time signals until we reached sheltered waters and someone (it
turned out to be the agile cook at Signy) could climb the mast to
replace it.

The fog grew even thicker as 27 December passed over into
its successor. For the moment, no land was near by; bergs were
the potential enemy. Eyes being of little use, I concentrated on
listening for breakers. A sudden crash from the forepeak made
me start nervously, then I relaxed at the realization that it came
from inside, not out. One of the fifteen-litre glass jars of kerosene
had broken. Why now and not in the gale? I was no nearer an

explanation when the broken glass had been patiently located and cleared away and the surviving jar re-suspended. Despite re-peated swabbings with detergent, the cabin floor remained as slippery as an ice rink. Meanwhile the fog persisted. It was early afternoon before it grudgingly parted.

Five miles to starboard were the icefields and *nunataks* of Elephant Island, about the bleakest and least inviting place that could be imagined. Yet it was here that the gallant crew of *Endurance* found refuge of a sort after their ship had been beset and crushed in the Weddell pack. From one of those coves Shackelton had set out for help across the Southern Ocean to

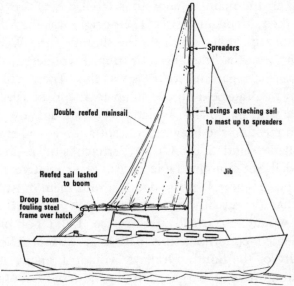

South Georgia in the hastily-prepared ship's boat, *James Caird*, so much smaller and less seaworthy than *Ice Bird*. Surely, this was the greatest of all small boat voyages. The last act of the drama, the rescue of every single man of the crew, had been played out in the lee of that southern cape. As if to emphasize the finality of this sixty-year-old drama, the curtains of fog closed in again and did not reopen.

Experimentation with the new mainsail kept me busy next day. Well used as I now was to performing complex tasks on a pitching deck in bulky clothing, I was still very clumsy. I underestimated the width of my bulbous insulated boots, for instance, and so kept on getting them stuck. When trimming headsails the fingers of my gloves would become cleated in with the sheets. My fur hat had developed a genius for slipping down over my eyes whenever both hands were occupied. Nevertheless, given patience, the jobs eventually got done – and, thanks to the gloves and protective clothes, in reasonable comfort.

The next two days were much more pleasant, for they brought a temporary return to 'Banana Belt' conditions at their best – clear skies, blue seas, sparkling bergs. Fair winds put the daily runs up into the seventies and the self-steering gear operated most of the time. Such ice as we encountered was widely scattered, consisting in the main of enormous tabular bergs several miles long and their attendant debris. Their origin was the Filchner Ice Shelf a thousand miles south on the shores of the Weddell Sea. How many years had they been drifting, I wondered?

The position regarding icebergs was this. There had not been very many in Bransfield Strait and up to Elephant Island, which was in line with the *Pilot's* predictions. We should now, however, have been meeting the heaviest concentration anywhere, because this Elephant Island–South Orkneys stretch is the main outlet for the Weddell Sea's innumerable bergs. Their relative scarcity in the very place where I had reason to dread them most led me to assume that the usually much more open waters beyond the Orkneys would be virtually free of ice. I did not bargain on unprecedented conditions this particular season. The immediate vicinity of the South Orkneys would, I knew, be packed tight with grounded bergs from the hundred-fathom line inwards, but this was a different question from ice drifting in deep water.

The fine weather interlude was too good to last. It gave way all too soon to head winds, calms and consistently overcast skies that precluded the taking of sun sights. New Year's Eve followed the pattern; a cold grey day of freezing snow showers and fluctuating winds that demanded constant sail changes. Not even the champagne I opened lightened my rather gloomy mood, well expressed in the year's last log entry, 'Berg to starboard. Happy New Year – ugh!'

As day followed day, not only did the sun remain obstinately in hiding, but the mist grew progressively denser: 1974 was not opening auspiciously. I became increasingly anxious lest we miss the South Orkneys altogether. I could hardly hope to beat back against the prevailing westerlies; and failure to call at Signy would give rise to considerable anxiety. Besides, our water must be replenished. In default of sights, dead reckoning was my only means of navigation and this in turn depended above all on the accuracy of the steering compass.

My 3 January reckoning placed the largest of the South Orkneys, Coronation Island, some fifty miles *eastward* of us. I could scarcely believe my eyes when the fog banks to the *north* parting briefly that afternoon, revealed vivid and unmistakable ice blink. On such a scale and in that latitude this had to be a reflection of ice-covered land, and the sole candidate was Coronation. The matter was soon put beyond doubt by the appearance of a misty mountain crest.

Had it not been for the one-in-a-hundred chance of that providential clearing of the fog in that particular quarter we should have sailed right past the islands, fifty miles too far to the south. I came about with all speed, but not before a jarring impact against a sizeable bergy bit had unsettled me still further. Whatever had gone wrong? Such a monumental error was unprecedented.

To anticipate a little, the careful compass swinging that was carried out at Signy, brought out a startling fact. The deck-mounted steering compass, on which I relied, had a 21° error on easterly headings. The supposed easterly course that we had been following for days was, in fact, 21° south of east. In contrast, the despised cabin compass was accurate. I had been more than lucky to have glimpsed that ice blink.

All night and on into the next day we worked our way northward through the mist. Ice became increasingly abundant and some lightening of the mist in the early afternoon showed that we were crossing an east–west line of very large bergs. Beyond them I counted more than fifty others. This could be nothing else but the hundred-fathom line.

An hour later ice blink could be made out on the port bow, shortly followed by the emergence of the western tip of Coronation itself. Easier in mind, I continued to close the land, winding

in and out between the slightly smaller bergs that now lay everywhere. Some trick of light gave to their granular-textured ice
cliffs an extraordinarily artificial appearance, exactly like icing
sugar. I was less concerned with appearances, however striking,
than with keeping clear. In general I was successful, except for
hitting one emerald-green growler that the self-steering gear,
which seemed to possess an uncanny collision avoidance capacity,
must not have noticed. With the onset of evening all the bergs
abruptly turned a deep Prussian blue. The unearthly beauty of the
scene was unforgettable.

I took in the staysail at midnight, for rest rather than for sleep,
because we had to come about every half-hour to avoid fore-
reaching into a berg (I was told later that over a thousand could
be counted, at any one time, from the hill above Signy). The wind
died and snow began silently drifting down.

Growing daylight on 5 January provided enough visibility for
us to get under way with the engine at 3.30 a.m. It was still
snowing and the mist was as thick as ever. A cloud-wrapped wall
of ice and rock did appear dimly about five, but this did not help
me to locate Normanna Strait, a narrow gap between Signy and
Coronation, through which we must pass to reach the base. The
land's appearance was no help at all, it being quite as ice-sheathed
as the Antarctic mainland. (Signy in 60°S. has, in fact, a 65°
climate, by virtue of the proximity of the perennially ice-covered
Weddell Sea.) It was then that I thought of calling the bergs to
my aid.

I recalled that the chart showed a pronounced indentation of
the hundred-fathom line close west of Signy, deep water extending
as far inshore as the mouth of Normanna Strait. The shallower
margin ought to be outlined by big grounded bergs and the
indentation be relatively clear of ice. I scrambled up on to the
boom to seek confirmation. Sure enough, there was a mile-wide
ice-free corridor to starboard leading in towards the land. *Ice Bird*,
aided by the brisk following wind that had sprung up, was soon
speeding along it. 'Going like hell,' I wrote exultantly.

A picturesque group of chinstrap penguins on a square little
berg touched my photographic conscience. I stepped over to the
helm, brushed clumsily against the camera cord and added yet

another to the mounting collection of snaps of my behind. By the time the shutter was reset the penguins were very near, and the reason for their evident determination to remain exactly where they were – in the precise centre of the berg twelve feet above the sea – became apparent. A leopard seal was swimming round and round their refuge, raising its powerful head out of the water and emitting low roars of hungry frustration. Quite what the seal hoped to achieve was obscure, since the chinstraps were obviously in no hurry to oblige.

At 9 a.m. I gybed to enter Normanna Strait, thankful to find it free from pack (but alive with countless cape pigeons and cormorants). Two hours more and Signy base came into view at the head of a cove. Then all at once, in a flurry of activity, I was lowering the main, restraining the yacht from charging the rocky shore and dropping the genoa. For a few more yards she carried her way, then the anchor splashed down.

One of the men ashore was immediately recognizable as my Montevideo companion, Ian Smith, the hero of the one-and-three-quarter-hour immersion episode. He was, characteristically, waist-deep in water, supervising the construction of a slipway. As the base commander scrambled aboard in a wet suit, it really seemed as if I had come to some amphibious institution. But my welcome from these Antarctic professionals, who obviously loved their bleak land, was so warm that my habitual shyness thawed at once. Within minutes I was feeling thoroughly at home.

I was fortunate in finding a keen photographer, Ian Collinge, who straight away began conscientiously to record everything I did – though some of his action shots I could have done without. For instance, there was my hasty retreat from a newly awakened elephant seal and, even more ignominious, my rout by a cape pigeon guarding her burrow (she vomited half digested fish with uncanny accuracy). These misadventures apart, I found Signy's wildlife fascinating. The holes of nesting petrels and cape pigeons honeycombed a stony hillside, green with mosses and coarse grass, that overlooked the main buildings. Ponderous elephant seals slumped snoring against the walls of the outboard engine shed and emitted every conceivable variety of bark, growl and roar as they disputed choice boulders on the foreshore or drifted, awash, in the shallows.

The living quarters were well designed and comfortable. I was given a top bunk in one of the little four-man rooms, which somehow seemed more appropriate to Antarctica than the far more spacious accommodation at Palmer. Racks of skis, crampons, ice axes, aqualungs and wet suits testified to the active life of the base. Two clinker wooden dinghies lay at moorings but the Nansen sledges and 'skidoos' had been placed in store for the summer. The whole atmosphere was relaxed and informal but the responsibility and keenness of everyone was obvious.

After lunch, without fuss or bother, the entire base turned-to to help me. While my dirty clothes were whisked away to be laundered, willing hands ferried the plastic water-cans ashore, refilled them and stowed them in the forepeak. There were fifty-six gallons in hand when every receptacle had been filled. At half a gallon a day, this was sufficient but left no great margin for disaster. I decided to keep a careful check on the rate of consumption and to be sparing from the first. Lastly, my well-thumbed paperbacks were replaced by new ones.

Aboard the yacht itself, the stretched shrouds were set up afresh and the radio antenna replaced. Then we motored out into the bay to swing the compass. On our way back to the anchorage we witnessed a small tragedy. The massive jaws of a leopard seal snapped shut on a careless penguin and dashed it from side to side with tremendous violence, until its neck was broken and the skin ripped from its body in a maelstrom of bloody foam. The seal paid us not the slightest attention as we drifted close by, photographing the grisly scene.

Very grateful for so much help and more than satisfied with the day's work, I sat down, that evening, to write farewell letters. I would have been equally complacent about the future had it not been for a most disturbing radio conversation with *John Biscoe*. She had encountered an enormous concentration of bergs in usually ice-free waters off South Georgia. The season, I was warned, was abnormal. It might be necessary for me to re-route north of the South Sandwich Islands, a detour that would take *Ice Bird* right out of sub-Antarctic waters and lengthen the voyage by literally thousands of miles. I resolved to give the much more direct southerly route a try and only go north if I must.

Whatever the exact route, there was need for all reasonable haste. We had come no more than a pathetic 730 miles from Palmer and I now knew just how greatly ice could slow down a single-hander. Signy would be the last port in West Antarctica (the part of the continent in West longitude or roughly below South America) and it would be the final stepping off place; for East Antarctica, below the Indian Ocean and Australia, was perennially ice-bound and offered no haven.

Anxious as I was to be off, conditions next day were impossible. The mossy hillsides were knee-deep in new snow, which was still swirling down on the wings of a vicious north-easter. A party of us did go out for a sail in the white-mantled yacht, but seasickness soon cut short the outing and the photography that had been its main object. I spent the afternoon sleeping and, after supper and a slide show, slept on through the night as well.

By morning on 8 January, the wind was back in the west and the air was only normally misty. Against my half-hearted protests the cook insisted on putting aboard more canned meat and vegetables, a bottle of whisky and, even more welcome, a sack of fresh onions.

At midday I said my farewells. All was well prepared – except for the human element. I felt forlorn and insignificant, in dread of loneliness, fearful of ice and storms; above all, tormented by uncertainty as to the morality of deliberately tempting providence by again putting my life in pawn. The base's full complement gathered on a high bluff to wave goodbye. That little group, standing in the snow and growing smaller and smaller as *Ice Bird* ran before the wind, would be my last contact with humankind. Then the bergs hid them from view and I was utterly alone.

Chapter 10

Berg and Storm

A *foehn* cloud tablecloth covered the peaks of Coronation and spilled down into the defiles. The waters inshore were studded with countless medium-sized bergs and brash debris from the Weddell Sea pack. Further to seaward, icebergs up to five miles long marked the hundred-fathom line, outside of which I still hoped to find clearer waters. As fast as yesterday's snow melted from the decks, it was replaced by drifts piled up in the scuppers by northerly squalls. Once the sun had set around ten o'clock and had been replaced by the full moon, the moonlight played the heart-in-mouth trick of turning wave crests into menacing small ice. The continuing snow showers did not help, either.

I kept going right through the night and on until full daylight, hoping vainly for some thinning out of the bergs that would allow of *Ice Bird's* being left unattended while I rested. Though our latitude at noon was nearly a degree south of Signy's, so that we must be well beyond the edge of the continental shelf, the bergs remained as concentrated as ever. There was no way to obtain sleep except to bring the yacht to a standstill, at the cost of precious mileage; so I reluctantly lowered the headsail and hove-to under the hard-sheeted main. The wind now headed us from an unseasonable east. Since I neither desired to recross the hundred-fathom line to the north, nor to run foul of the Weddell Sea pack in the opposite direction, I remained hove-to for the rest of the day.

It was one o'clock in the morning when the noise of surf brought me abruptly awake. Within seconds I was in the cockpit, barely conscious of the wet snow under my stockinged feet, struggling to cast off maliciously tight tiller lashings. *Ice Bird* had drifted down towards the weather side of a berg, which was now barely a dozen yards distant. Only the backwash from the swells reflected off the perpendicular façade had kept us off the berg. Feverishly, I paid out the main sheet, put the helm hard over and gybed clear with scant feet to spare. I was shivering when I went below again, and not with cold.

After changing my socks and switching on the WWV radio for a time signal, I took a stiff drink and felt better. Then I returned to my bunk – this time, however, to doze more lightly and maintain a more frequent lookout. Sound sleep and safety, it seemed, would be incompatible as long as bergs remained numerous.

I very soon found out that even wakefulness was no sure safeguard. That very afternoon, while I was preoccupied with working out a sight and *Ice Bird* was moving slowly to windward in no apparent proximity to any of the scattered bergs, one of them crept up on us unawares. Some change in the yacht's motion must have warned me to rush on deck, because the berg was towering right above us and, again, only the waves reflected back on themselves from its weather aspect were holding us off. This time I needed to back the staysail to bring the yacht's head round. For one agonizing moment the bow hung poised above an icy underwater ram, then the backwash, rather than my own manœuvre, swung her. First bow, then stern, cleared that green wall with no more than six inches to spare.

An onion-and-corned beef stew steadied my shaken nerves. Seeing that it would be some little time before they were needed, I spent the next hour in unshackling the bow anchor and chain and stowing them securely below. The wind remained in the east and each iceberg we skirted was replaced by another. Fog shut in towards midnight and did not once lift for sixteen hours, and then only to be replaced by snow storms and whiteout and afterwards by fog again.

Ice Bird became like a ghost ship. The freezing fog sheathed her rigging with ice; her decks grew ice-glazed – and murderously slippery. Though the conditions had assumed a kind of fantasy nightmare quality, the peril was all too real. Fog, alternating with equally impenetrable whiteout concealed the ever present bergs, while the hours of darkness grew in length and variable head winds and calms prevented us from getting anywhere very much at all.

Extracts from the 11 January log, chosen almost at random, bring back vividly this anxious time – including the dread sensation of being trapped in a chain of circumstances that could so easily lead to irretrievable disaster.

7.15 a.m. First break in fog. Had passed close to large berg in night. Wind heading us almost back along our track.
8 a.m. fog again.
11.30 – passed big tabular [berg] in fog without seeing it, fog thinner at the moment.

Afternoon brought mention of ice forming in the fresh-water cans; the sheer impossibility of looking into the stinging wind-driven snow; and every entry included reference to bergs, always bergs, whether 'dead ahead' or 'three to port' or elsewhere.

Even more indicative of the real dangers are notes such as this one for 1.30 a.m. 'Passed very near a big berg while I slept. Close shave.' And the next morning's comment, 'Snowing hard, −2°C., big ghostly tabular berg to port. Sleep has been interrupted by token lookouts. Has been a *desperately dangerous gamble* but it paid off this time.' [log's italics] 'Desperately dangerous gamble' sums it up pretty well.

All day we continued to plough eastwards, while I maintained a strict lookout. By evening, when the fog thinned a little and uncovered twelve bergs in the immediate vicinity, I was in sore need of rest again. Since no really ice-free open space offered itself, I had no alternative but to heave-to in the best one I could find, all too conscious that we might, as easily as not, drift into an iceberg while I slept. But since I could no longer keep awake there was nothing else for it. Before dropping on to my bunk I penned in capitals and underlined a last fatalistic comment: 'RUSSIAN ROULETTE – Here's hoping!'

It was midnight when I awoke. Ranks of misty bergs ringed us around in a deceptively innocent-seeming amphitheatre. Gentle snow flakes flickered down. Somewhat rested, I got under way. *Ice Bird* stole silently across the floor of that mighty amphitheatre into a dawn that for once was clear save for snow showers, skirting ever and anon glistening white symbols of beauty – and fear. The very biggest, I noticed with awe, were reflecting their own individual ice blink on to the patch of sky directly above them. But before the day was ended we would be sailing through a different world.

That evening saw *Ice Bird* dashing along through the misty darkness amid cascades of spray before a rising westerly gale. My warm quilted clothing was soaked through before ever I thought to exchange the heavy parka and fur-lined mitts for waterproof Marlin jacket and rubber gloves.

The steadily increasing strength of the wind and the need for a vigilant ice watch kept me fully awake right through that night and the following day, 14 January. I could not have kept going so long, of course, had not the wind-vane been handling the steering. By 4.30 p.m. the gale had increased to force nine and *Ice Bird*, even under her little storm jib, was beginning to yaw and steer wildly as she ran down the face of the towering seas. I deemed it prudent, while retaining the jib, to stream a sea anchor astern to steady her.

This was in line with the 'gale technique' I had worked out in the light of last season's experiences. *Ice Bird* would be steered before gales under storm jib as previously, and again at an angle for ease of control, rather than dead down-wind. But this time I would trail a sea anchor behind to hold the stern up to the seas and to help prevent the yacht from slewing round broadside on. Steering would be the job of the Aries vane gear, whose power in strong winds far outstripped my own strength. It possessed the added advantage of being impervious to fatigue. (Experience has generally confirmed my reasoning. The sea anchor's warp would have to be prevented from fouling anything. It is true the device failed to prevent, though I believe it mitigated, the final disaster, but then I was steering with the less efficient tiller lines.)

My own sea anchor, prepared in advance at Palmer, was made up of two tyres weighted with a small anchor, streamed at the end of thirty fathoms of two-inch nylon. The warp was coiled ready on the afterdeck and parcelled against chafe with the last of the kangaroo skin coat. The tyres and anchor were lashed to the stern rail.

All that was necessary on the afternoon of the 14th was to cut the securing cord, lower the contraption over the side and pay

out the warp. The drag was appreciable and *Ice Bird* ran far more
steadily with the vane in complete control. Evening drew on,
bringing with it no abatement of the gale. Worse, now we had to
run the gauntlet of the bergs through squalls of blinding snow.
Any contact with substantial ice would be instantly fatal in the
seas that were running. The spray was being dashed a hundred
feet into the air each time a wave smashed against one of the rock-
like monsters. 'Keeping desperate lookout for ice – the lethal
factor in this near whiteout,' I wrote fearfully.

To my unutterable relief, the snow showers ceased before
midnight, but the temperature was well below zero and, in the
early morning hours of 15 January, a freezing mist began to
reduce visibility again to danger level. Then at long last the gale
began to moderate. The risk of being rolled over by the still
dangerous seas if I took in sail and let the yacht lie a-hull, seemed
preferable to further risking collision with ice. After all, a capsize
could be survived, being smashed to pieces against a berg could
not.

Lowering the jib and leaving the sea anchor still trailing and
the yacht to its own devices, I crawled, wet and shivering, into
my sleeping bag. Periodically I looked out to make sure that no
large ice was near, but I altered nothing for the rest of the night
and on through the following day, while the gale slowly eased.

The cause of the disastrous misadventure that now occurred is
uncertain. It probably was impact with ice, gone unnoticed in
the slamming swell, or perhaps the sea anchor warp snagged the
casing and somehow caused it to shear. At any rate, when I looked
out at 4 p.m. the precious self-steering gear was in ruins, broken
beyond any possibility of repair.

A sizeable segment of the main supporting frame was gone,
and of the system of levers and gears there remained not a trace.
The sea had swallowed them all. Only a well equipped engineer-
ing factory could replace the lost parts and repair the shattered
frame.

Profoundly depressed by this heavy blow, I remained miserably
hove-to until the next day, 16 January, when I hauled the sea
anchor back aboard, hoisted sail and took my place at the tiller
lines, which were henceforth to occupy the major portion of my

waking hours. We were exactly a week out from Signy and the moment was opportune for a review of strategy.

A disappointing 325 miles had been made good to the eastward. The options as to course remained open, since the South Sandwich Islands were still 200 miles ahead. A route going north in 'Australian' latitudes would, because of the earth's curvature, be twice as long as one through the southern sixties. But the ice conditions made survival, rather than distance, the prime consideration; and there was a limit to the number of narrow escapes I could hope to get away with. The immediate problem was how best to escape from the icebergs into waters where I could keep sailing in safety day and night. I decided to start tentatively working northwards and see what happened.

The probable lengthening of the voyage emphasized the importance of conserving drinking water. So far, the log showed I had been using less than two pints a day: an acceptable figure.

The prospect of hand steering to Australia was daunting. But I had done it last year for two months, so could do it again. There was the comforting knowledge that, with head or beam winds, the helm could be adjusted so that *Ice Bird* would look after herself. Down-wind she demanded continuous attention and the nearer a dead run the course, the more the care needed to prevent her from broaching-to. Thus the favourable west winds I had so longed for, and which would generally prevail, would exact their toll in soul-destroying hours of monotonous concentration.

The first twenty-four hours without the vane were encouraging, the run from noon on the 16th to noon on the 17th being seventy-six miles. But this ground was won at the expense of a whole night's exhausting vigil and was only made possible by clear weather. I counted bergs to pass the time and before I tired of the game we had passed fifty in seven hours, the concentration showing no signs of diminishing. Hot drinks were at a premium, being prepared by a process of hurried dashes to stove and lockers. A major preoccupation was how to keep my fur-lined and quilted mitts from becoming soaked, through contact with the wet steering lines, for the only drying agent was my own body heat. I found no real solution and the mitts remained damp.

Whenever the outlook ahead was reasonably clear I would thankfully get out of the bitter wind and steer from the edge of a bunk by the compass mounted on the cabin table – now a boon beyond price. Frequent trips to the hatchway to scan the sea were, of course, necessary. The chill of early morning found me shivering in the companionway, easing myself into the least uncomfortable position. The concentration of decaying bergs through which we were sailing was for the moment so dense as to preclude even a visit to the heads. My notes in the log grew understandably scrappy.

I had to give in eventually and lower sail to sleep. When I awoke it was evening and a heavy fog effectively ruled out another night under way. Instead I spent it dozing fitfully, lying fully clothed on top of my sleeping bag, and was not sorry when morning came. A 'friendly neighbourhood berg', in the log's words, and a party of chinstrap penguins welcomed me back on deck when, still in heavy fog, I sleepily hoisted sail.

Thirty-nine hours later the fog had not lifted. *Ice Bird* floated becalmed on a polished ebony sea. It was eleven o'clock at night and very dark. All at once I became aware of the rumble of breakers somewhere off in the mist. I listened tensely, trying to decide the direction. Then it came again, but this time much louder, through some acoustic rift in the fog – the crash of surf. The illusion that the current was sweeping us down upon it was very strong. I well knew this could not be so, since, in the absence of wind, yacht and unseen berg would drift at exactly the same rate; but I was frightened. I had been tinkering with the motor earlier and it started at once.

Ice Bird began to glide rapidly through the darkness. But which way had she turned while I was busy with the engine? The exhaust effectively covered the noise of the breakers. Could we be circling back into danger? I lost all sense of direction and, for a moment, became prey to absurd panic. Then, pulling myself together, I switched off the motor until I had located the sound again (we *had* curved back towards it) and, holding a torch to light the compass, set off again in the opposite direction until I judged we had gone a safe distance.

Nor did I ever catch a glimpse of the berg that had caused so much worry, for the fog was still as thick as ever when I hoisted sail to a light south-easter in the morning.

Such a very dense fog I classified as 'one page fog'. The system was this: I would sit reading in the cabin, if necessary steering by the inside compass; after finishing each page (or two, in 'two page fog') I would put the book down, step up into the hatchway and peer intently ahead. I grew to detest this monotonous routine, but could think of no better way of keeping a regular lookout and remaining warm in the interim. I found that a continuous watch of more than half an hour in the companionway left me chilled to the bone. Assessing the fog's density was difficult and only reliable when confirmed by an actual ice sighting. I was to have a sighting that particular morning with a vengeance.

First I stared out and saw nothing. Then something unreal in the texture of the fog made me look again, and there it was, a pale, ghostly monster dead ahead, no more than two hundred yards off. I reached down and slammed the tiller hard over. *Ice Bird* pivoted on her heel and ran down-wind past the face of the berg and rounded a corner into its lee, to be promptly becalmed in the wind shadow. There she rocked helplessly to and fro among the small ice debris for ten minutes, before a series of savage little squalls, plummeting down from the hidden crest, laid the yacht over and drove her clear.

A welcome change from fog to light mist in the afternoon brought relief from the constant watchfulness. I was happy for the moment to have left behind the grey confines of fog. But the absurd delusion persisted, that the place where we had fled the unseen berg in the darkness would remain forever intact and unchanged, like some gloomy forest, from which we had escaped.

Largely to bolster my own morale I shaved (my beard is normally confined to my chin), a painful process, as I did not feel justified in using more than half a mug of hot water. My first intention, to re-use the shaving water for coffee, was abandoned after one glance at the mixture of stubble and lather. I could not stomach it. Not long after this praiseworthy effort the wind changed, so that I had to take over the tiller lines until 10 p.m., when the presence of some very large bergs and the increasing darkness caused me to lower sail for the night.

This practice of taking down the sails at nightfall was now becoming routine, though visibility was not often good enough to permit me to keep on so late. A few anxious nights spent staring blindly into the blackness soon convinced me of the wisdom of choosing an open space in which to spend the night in good time, while the bergs were still visible and their distance away could be judged. The plan paid off in security. True, a nocturnal wind change did once set the yacht uncomfortably close to a pair of bergs that had earlier been to windward but this was an exception. Unfortunately eight hours, the average time spent motionless, was a sizeable chunk to lose out of the twenty-four.

At first light on 21 January, I managed to overcome my extreme reluctance to leave the warm sleeping bag and drag myself awake and on deck into the bitter 5 a.m. cold. Once the sails were up and sheeted and before taking the helm to head down-wind, I confided my plaint to the log. 'Jesus! What an effort,' I wrote. The next entry was at half-past four in the afternoon and I underlined it; 'Hand steering all day.'

Those eleven hours of steering (by no means an exceptional stretch) left little time for anything else apart from reading, snatching hurried snacks and taking and working out the only sun sight the roof of stratus allowed. The food was limited to what I could reach from the box under the table without letting go of the tyrannical tiller line: corned beef, from which I cut slabs with my knife; biscuits eaten butterless; chocolate – all garnished with little balls of fluff from my woollen gloves (my fingers and fragile nails, still tender from last year's frostbite, had to be protected even when I was below).

This sun sight was typical enough to serve as an example of the two I usually shot (each sight gave one position line, their intersection was needed for a fix). The appearance of shadows in the cabin first alerted me. Sure enough, a pale disc was discernible behind thin overcast.

I hastily collected together the sight form, a biro, my glasses and some toilet paper and heaped them on the lee bunk where they could not roll off. Lifting the sextant out of its box, I scrambled up into the cockpit, clipping on the safety line as I went. Wedging myself as securely as possible and steering with one foot on the tiller, I snatched the sight as the yacht rose to the crest of a wave and immediately checked the time. Or tried to – the sleeve of my parka had, as usual, slipped over the wrist watch and I had to count the seconds while I prized back the sleeve.

Repeating the time of the sight to myself, I slid back into the cabin and scribbled down the figures before I forgot them. But I had to wipe my glasses with toilet paper, remove them and wipe them again, before I could read the sextant scale. The next operation, after replacing the instrument in its locker and putting the yacht back on course, was to work out the sight. Holding the tiller line in my left hand, I turned over the pages of the nautical almanac with the gloved fingers of my right and, equally clumsily, entered the figures on the sight form. Only at the final stage of plotting on the chart, did I abandon all attempts at steering and concentrate on angles and intercepts. This afternoon sight put us in 34° 10′ West longitude and, coupled with dead reckoning, made our run for the past twenty-four hours (including the seven spent hove-to) a better than average seventy-seven miles.

To my relief, the wind soon backed after this. The helm could be left to itself, until dusk and bergs suggested the advisability of taking in sail.

How dramatically the face of the sea could change! In the evening a score of rather featureless hummocked bergs had littered the horizon. I awoke next day surrounded by shapes of unreality – turreted gothic castles, a 'bugs bunny' (christened for the ears) and one soaring ice tower, breathtaking in its purity. Making sure a camera was loaded, I sailed up to them – narrowly avoiding a collision, in my photographic over-enthusiasm! Somewhat deflated, I squared away towards the north-east.

The Southern Ocean showed yet another of its aspects next day, a south-east gale, as wet and cold and ice-anxious as its predecessors. It was noteworthy, in that *Ice Bird* struck a glancing blow against a bergy bit without damage and for the first view for a fortnight, of the unshrouded sun. This marked the end of the second week out from Signy, with no more than three hundred miles added to the tally.

Two rather featureless days followed. On the third, the fog came back and did not lift for the next thirty-six hours. 'I hate fog,' I confided to the log, adding for good measure, 'I have been personifying bergs for a long time now, they are totally malignant.' I had proof of their spite that afternoon, when the 'one page fog' into which I was staring, took on in my tired eyes the semblance of a wall of pale ice across our path. It needed a moment for me to realize that that was exactly what it was, and then there was barely room enough to turn away. 'The next to last tot of whisky,' I noted regretfully, as I drank with a none too steady hand.

The fog seemed more terrifying than ever after this incident, but there was to be no immediate relief. It persisted through the afternoon, the night and on into the following day, when even near gale-force winds failed to disperse it. This last was hardly fair. The deceptively unsubstantial-looking sentinels in the mist were menacing enough without the vilely rough sea that tossed *Ice Bird* mercilessly. One tortoise-shaped mass that loomed up to windward was half dark green and half milky-white, the parts being separated by a diagonal, brown cleavage plane. The swell boomed like a foghorn from some hidden cavern in its interior.

Just as I finished adjusting a fairlead on the lee rail, a wave broke clear over the yacht, drenching me in an icy cascade. As I retreated, cursing, scarce able to see through the water running off my wet fur hat, the elastic in the waist of my overtrousers took the opportunity to break. This final indignity, when I was already thoroughly worn down by the fog and the bergs, was the last straw. I began to cry. There was too much at stake – and too many things to do – to indulge in self pity for long. But it was not until evening, when the mist had thinned enough for me to pick out an ice-free patch in which to heave-to, and a hot meal was inside me, that my depression lifted a little.

Nevertheless, irrational terrors of bergs plagued my rest and ensured that I slept very little that night. I awoke, jaded and tired to be greeted by the unwelcome sight of renewed fog. Hoisting sail in the murk, I took my place at the absurd tiller lines, hauling on first one, then the other. What a primitive arrangement it was! Tiring to handle and incapable of keeping direction with any degree of precision. Not for the first time, I bemoaned the lack of an inside steering wheel, a device far beyond my reach.

Then came the inspiration.

Columbus never saw a steering wheel in his life. His flagship *Santa Maria* had been steered with a whipstaff. This *was* a device that I might possibly improvise. All morning I turned the problem over in my mind and by afternoon I believed I had worked out a practical system of lines and blocks, also what to use for the whipstaff itself. It only needed a reasonably fine day and a beam wind, in which the yacht could manage herself, for the work to commence.

For the present, though patchy mist replaced the fog, the wind stayed obstinately astern and kept me glued to the helm. There was ice in plenty about, though most of it was small and tabular bergs were wholly lacking – indicative, I hoped, of impending decay. Confirmatory evidence was soon forthcoming.

Cleaving a bank of mist, *Ice Bird* emerged into the open. As far as the eye could see were strewn the ruins of the mighty disintegration that the earlier signs had foreshadowed. Some of the ice was in the ultimate stages of staghorn or cauliflower-shaped weathering, or else polished smooth into rounded growlers. But by far the greater part of what littered the ocean was splintered fragments – from the size of an office block down to slivers – that looked like the products of some cataclysmic explosion.

The parent berg must, indeed, have been enormous, for we were more than an hour passing through its debris. Even if this marked the end of a deadly enemy, I was sad at the collapse of such grandeur.

That night I slept soundly, for once, to be astir again at daybreak, all eagerness to get on with my brainchild. A whipstaff is, in effect, a vertical tiller, which is moved from side to side and actuates the rudder through a line linkage. The installation did not take very long, as the run of the lines and where the blocks should be attached had already been thought out. A hole bored in one of the cabin floorboards served to pivot the whipstaff, which was nothing else but Colin Putt's ice axe. The result was the contraption shown in the diagram – and lines everywhere, like a spider's web. I scribbled down one comment only: 'Oh Columbus!'

Odd as it undoubtedly looked, the arrangement worked well. Its added leverage more than halved the physical effort of using

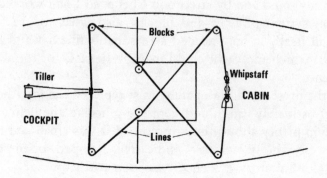

Whipstaff

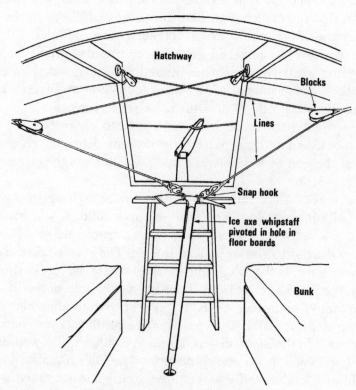

View in cabin looking aft

the tiller lines; it was simple to use one-handed and the course steered was far more accurate. The whipstaff was a real boon.

In the last few days, another problem, indirectly connected with steering, had become increasingly troublesome. None of the five gallons of water I had consumed in the last three weeks had been used for washing myself or my underwear. The natural result, aggravated by having to sit so long at the helm, was an extremely sore inflamed bottom. How was I to soothe it without wasting precious fresh water? Once again, inspiration came to my aid. Remembering Marlon Brando, not in the film *Mutiny on the Bounty*, but in *Last Tango in Paris*, I anointed myself liberally with the best Australian butter – and found immediate relief.

On 1 February, two days after sailing through the wreckage of the disintegrated berg, I really did see the last of the icebergs; a forlorn little trio in the morning, then no more. Extricating ourselves from the ice and passing the South Sandwich islands had taken us much farther north than I had ever anticipated, to 52° 21'S., equivalent to the latitude of the English Midlands in the other hemisphere. The time at hazard since Signy had been twenty-three days and the distance 1,030 miles. Although the bergs themselves were behind us, the nightmare remained; a week later I was still dreaming about them.

Saved from the need always to lower sail at nightfall, I began to make better progress: 445 miles in the fourth (part iceberg) week from West Antarctica, though only 390 (due to gales) in the fifth. I kept on heading at first in the same direction as before, having abandoned my original intention of turning south again, once the berg-spawning Weddell Sea was left behind. We had been forced too far north for that. The ice had played havoc with my timetable so far and progress would continue to be slow, restricted by the hours each day that I could steer before the increasingly prevalent westerlies. These delays ruled out the great circle route to Australia – the shortest – because the stormiest area round Heard Island could not now be traversed before the onset of winter. I decided, therefore, to continue north-east into the forties and take the longer, but hopefully kindlier, route through these latitudes. In the fifth week, knowing we must be well clear of the ice, I turned due east.

The days began to merge. There was the time when I spent every waking hour of four days at the helm, only to find that the yacht's nocturnal antics had reduced the returns from so much effort to a miserable fifty-five mile average. Memorable was the freak wave that roared down from nowhere. It knocked *Ice Bird* flat and myself clear across the cabin. Yet the weather had not been particularly rough at the time. It became a little warmer, so that some of my heavy clothing could be discarded, but the seas beneath the leaden overcast remained grey and wind-whipped after we turned east.

The sixth week opened with a north-west gale of such abrupt onset and extreme violence that the yacht, under no more canvas than jib and storm tri-sail, was laid right over. The tri-sail had to come in. Horizontal rain and spray hid all but the nearest rollers as I crawled along the deck and cast off the halyard. The sail did not budge. Neither was it going to, I saw, for the upper lacing had got foul of the top of the shrouds and no amount of tugging was ever going to bring the sail down.

I doubted my ability to climb the mast at the best of times; now *Ice Bird* was plunging like a bucking horse. There being no alternative, I clipped the safety belt to a shroud, took my knife between my teeth and began to climb. The clumsy insulated boots were a great hindrance and the mast's wild gyrations threatened, every second, to fling me off into the sea. At last I was at the crosstrees, unable for the moment to do more than rest my aching arms. Then, clinging on one-handed, I used the last of my strength to saw through the tough nylon, then slid to the deck exhausted. I marvelled how necessity had given me energy and guts enough to do something far beyond my normal capacity.

Relentless sameness characterized the days that came after this gale. I was more than glad of the ample supply of light reading, augmented at Signy, which helped shorten the long hours at the helm (the winds were nearly all from astern now) and provided some escape from reality. The depth of this need for escape came as something of a surprise. Unexpected too, was the loneliness: a feeling I had never known before at sea. The previous season must have drained me more than I knew.

Realizing that I was beginning to brood over-pessimistically –

Above and below: *A Nikkormas camera with a delayed action shutter release enabled David Lewis to take photos of himself in the cabin of* Ice Bird *while at sea.*

Paradise Bay, Antarctic Peninsula.

With the frustration of inching through pack ice gone, Ice Bird *and David Lewis set sail off the Antarctic Peninsula.*

Arriving at the British base of Signy in the South Orkneys.
This was the last Antarctic stop on Ice Bird's *voyage.*

Icebergs were a constant threat once Ice Bird *escaped the pack ice and reached open sea.*

Sailing under jury rig off Cape Town.

Arriving at the Cape Town yacht club.

about the little girls, our lack of a permanent home and the mess
I had made of life generally – to a degree that showed I was losing
my sense of proportion, I made a conscious effort to ban all
disturbing thoughts. I kept my mind in blinkers, either 'switched
off' in the worlds of light books, or concentrated on the techni-
calities of the job in hand. I tried not to count the miles that lay
ahead.

One other important factor contributed to my nervous state.
The capsizes that had so nearly killed me the summer before had
left me in terror of gales: I lived through each one in an agony of
fear.

In practical terms, I actually felt more confident in my handling
of *Ice Bird* in gales than I had before. The sea anchor-storm jib-
whipstaff system seemed to work. There was also a routine for the
onset of a gale. The table was lowered and secured to cover over
the ready-to-use food box. Charts, sleeping bag, logbook and
spare clothes were put inside plastic bags. The two stoves were
tied down; socks and rags were stuffed into the ventilators and
everything movable stowed away. No precautions, however,
could safeguard the mast.

The northerly ice-free route seemed to be paying off. Steadily,
if with maddening slowness, the noon positions crawled eastwards across the chart. Still, monotony was preferable to hurri-
canes. By half-way through the seventh week, our easterly course
between the 45th and 44th parallels had brought us to a point
eight hundred miles below, and a little to the west of, the tip of
Africa. I could comfort myself with the knowledge that the tracks
of the worst storms normally passed a good way farther south –
but then, this was no normal year.

The first intimation that something right out of the ordinary
was on its way was the plummeting of the barometer on the
evening of 23 February. Before the 24th was an hour old, the
severe northerly gale, which accompanied the warm front of a
deep cyclonic depression, was upon us, bringing fog and stinging
rain. By 3 a.m. it was at its full force nine fury. By 6.30 a.m. there
was not a breath of wind at all. I was terror-struck.

This was the dread eye of the storm; the deceptively quiet
hurricane vortex, whence few small boats had emerged. The

night's strong northerly gale would be as nothing compared with what must abruptly terminate the temporary lull – the 'dangerous semicircle' cold front coming in on the wings of a gale of unimaginable ferocity from the opposite quarter.

The huge waves, released from the weight of the wind, reared skyward in toppling pyramids that almost stood *Ice Bird* on end. The stillness was uncanny. I made sure that the sea anchor warp was free and that the storm jib was hard-sheeted. Then I waited.

At half-past eight the expected line squall screamed out of the south-west at an initial velocity of 50 knots, or force 10. An hour and a half later it was blowing a consistent 70 knots (force 12) and gusting to 80 knots – nearly 100 miles an hour (force 13), the top of the anemometer scale. Force 12 is a hurricane.

'Fear and dread. God help us,' I wrote, and put the log away.

The glass began to rise and the sky to clear, but this was simply a cold-front feature. The hurricane continued unabated. The anemometer needle came hard up against the 80-knot stop more frequently than ever until the wind broke the instrument around noon. The seas grew steadily higher and broke ever more furiously. I crouched over the whipstaff, my eyes glued to the strip of vibrating sailcloth outside the dome that was my wind direction indicator. We were running down-wind at an angle to the enormous, heavily breaking seas. Twice during the afternoon the yacht was knocked down flat. Both times she recovered, but this was the writing on the wall. Even should the hurricane wind moderate soon, the waves would not, and forty-foot monsters all around were now tumbling into surf. Ironically, around 4 p.m. the wind did start slackening.

Crash! My world was submerged in roaring chaos as a mighty hand rolled *Ice Bird* over, not ungently, upside down. I slithered round the side of the cabin as she went, and ended up in a heap on the ceiling. Then, just as smoothly, the yacht righted herself by rolling back upright the same way and I slid back with her. It was 4.15 p.m.

I could see from below that the backstays had gone; there was little doubt as to what I should find on deck. The mast had broken midway between the foot and the spreaders, and the pieces were floating alongside. The joint that Willy had scarfed was intact, the break being higher up, I noted with glum satisfaction. Never in my life feeling less like doing so, I took a number of photographs while I salvaged what I could and made sure that the remaining wreckage was well clear of the rudder and the propeller. Down below, the time-signal radio was broken. Otherwise, there was not much damage. Very little water had got in. But dejection and disappointment threatened to overwhelm me. It needed all my will-power to put them aside and to set about making positive plans. Australia could be ruled out as it would be touch and go over fresh water. Cape Town was the obvious port to aim at.

Lying in my sleeping bag, I worked out the main points. Once the yacht was jury rigged, her initial course should be due north, lest the westerlies sweep her right past Africa. The rig itself would need to have sufficient windward ability to cope with the Cape of Good Hope's unpredictable weather. Somewhat cheered at having made a small beginning, I was able to relax and sleep reasonably soundly.

The dismasted yacht was tossing wildly enough to make one's footing precarious when I dragged myself from my bunk in the morning and, dubiously fortified with cold coffee, resolutely put behind me lost hopes and set to work. The broken mast was stripped and the rigging disentangled and coiled, a physically exhausting task which extended well into the afternoon. Next came the jury mast. The boom was again the basis, but this time (to enable more sail to be carried), it was extended three feet by the gaff. The overlapping spars were clamped firmly together with oversized jubilee clips (hose clamps) supplied by the *Geographic* for camera clamps, reinforced by rope seizing and a fixed halyard to prevent slipping. At this stage the wind increased and it became too rough to continue working. I went below, uncertain if worse was to come and expressed my dread, 'God grant this isn't another gale.'

To my relief, 26 February brought much calmer weather. Even so, it took from 7 a.m. to half-past four in the afternoon to equip mast and 'topmast' with ten stays and three halyards between them. Then came the moment of truth. Could I raise the boom with the gaff's added weight? The method (main sheet forward with tail to sheet winch) would be the same as last year. After the second attempt had ended in the spars nearly braining me, it seemed probable that I could not. I massaged my aching head and tried once more. *Ice Bird* tried too. For the crucial first lift she poised momentarily on an even keel. The rest was easy. By six o'clock, the mast was erect and stayed. 'Never remember such exhaustion – but happy,' ends the day's log.

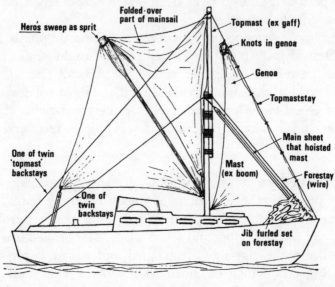

Jury Mast

The 27th was the end of the seventh week out. It was also 'sail day'. The mainsail was the original folded over and held out from the mast by *Hero*'s sweep, which at last came into its own as a sprit. The genoa, with two knots in its head, set on the 'topmast' stay and the jib on the forestay. We got under way that afternoon.

A gale, fortunately short lived, had my heart in my mouth the next day. Progress thereafter was reasonable if not brilliant, being slowed by light airs and calms. The rig functioned well, the continual flapping of the folded-over part of the mainsail being more annoying than harmful. An unexpected success was to get the engine going again – rather irregularly, but no matter – after drying out and a good deal of general attention.

One calm tempted me into pumping up and launching *Condom* in the cause of photography. Attached to the yacht by a long line, I rowed away gingerly, disturbed by the inflatable's evident desire to fold over in the middle. Just as my target filled the view-finder, the first gust for hours bellied *Ice Bird*'s slack sails and she began to move, dragging me bounding along in her wake. I soon had my fill of taking pictures. 'Very dodgy,' I summed up the incident.

There was now time soberly to consider longer term plans, and the inescapable conclusion was depressing. The voyage would have to end in Cape Town. The major part of my dream – to make the first solo voyage to Antarctica and to return thence to an inhabited country – would have been brought to reality. But the last stretch across the Indian Ocean to Australia, must needs be abandoned. There was more than one compelling reason. Even a minimum refit in Cape Town would take months. It was well into March and my next research appointment, which had already once been postponed, was due to begin in April. Currently I had no income and money was short. Lastly, Susan and Vicky had been without me quite long enough.

Though the unpalatable decision was unavoidable, it did nothing to restore my precarious emotional stability. My self-control threshold in the face of day-to-day difficulties became so low about this time that minor irritations twice set me shouting and crying with frustration. Despite the desolation of my loneliness, I had paradoxically come to dread renewed contact with human beings and the complexities this entailed. In fact, the things that so worried me were not real problems at all but merely such trivia as the dispatching of telegrams. My sheet anchor was the hope that a firm friend from my previous visit to Cape Town (see *Children of Three Oceans*, 1969, London, Collins), the down-to-earth veteran mountaineer, Bob Hinings, would be at home to look after me.

Not that the whole story has as yet been told by any means. Long spells of hand steering were often called for in those last weeks, thirteen hours on one occasion, a marathon sixteen hours on another. The nearer to Africa, the more carefully had wind and current probabilities to be weighed. I was fortunate in obtaining a time signal from a South African station on the little Sony transistor, for accurate navigation was now at a premium.

My intended landfall was a section of coast between Quoin Point and Danger Point, sixty to ninety miles south-east of Cape Town. By mid March, the risk was no longer so much of being carried east into the Indian Ocean past Cape Agulhas (the southernmost tip of Africa, a degree south of the Cape of Good Hope), as of being swept by the powerful Benguela Current too far northward up the west coast, and right past Cape Town.

Twenty-one days after the dismasting, during the night of 18–19 March, I began hopefully peering ahead much too early (as I always do). It was not until 2 a.m. that the darkness was broken. The loom of first one then another flashing light appeared on the horizon, to signal the imminent end of ten weeks' solitude. I carefully counted the faint rhythmic pulses, re-checked with the chart, and wrote, 'Loom of Quoin Point Light bearing 30° before the beam to port. Another loom more distant? Danger Point, bears 20°.'

With daylight, the blue pyramids of mountains, appearing to rise out of the sea like islands, could be seen, and a massive cloud tablecloth, which could only be covering Table Mountain. Cape Town was still a long way off: sixty miles, according to the noon sight; though this was confirmatory only, as Cape Point was by then in plain view. The yacht ran swiftly down-wind while I divided my attention between steering, consulting the chart and preparing for port. The anchor had to be got ready as an insurance against an emergency and the mooring warps laid out; my passport, address book and money needed to be unearthed from their forgotten hiding places; I washed and shaved; lastly, I filled the Optimus pressure lamp with kerosene, ready for warning steamers of my presence during the coming night.

It was as well that I made ready the lamp. I am informed that three hundred ships round the Cape of Good Hope each day. I could swear that at least that number threatened *Ice Bird* with destruction during that last night at sea. Two 5mgm tablets of amphetamine helped to keep me wide awake and all my alertness was needed, creeping between the freighters and the unlighted peninsula before a dying wind. Towards morning, by which time I had thankfully worked well inside the main steamer lanes, a bunch of 200-ton trawlers shattered my complacency by cutting close across our bows.

Daylight on 20 March found me mightily relieved to be alive – and becalmed off Cape Town's western suburbs! The engine started after a brief struggle and, still sporting her outlandish rig, *Ice Bird* rounded Cape Town's outer breakwater at nine o'clock and motored through the maze of docks towards the Royal Cape Yacht Club marina.

Now at last my dreary mood began to lift. As I looked afresh at the little ship, her ensign streaming, gallantly making port without assistance, for all her wounds, I felt a stirring of pride. Groups of sunbrowned men and girls on a score of beautifully kept yachts suddenly froze into immobility and stared unbelievingly as the small yellow ice-scarred veteran glided calmly into their midst and brought up alongside a vacant pontoon. *Ice Bird*'s voyage (so I thought, then) was ended.

Suddenly everyone exploded into activity, without so far a word having been spoken. Mooring warps were caught and made fast and a steaming cup of coffee was handed up to me. A yachtsman, who looked as if he could not quite credit what he was seeing, broke the silence.

'Wherever are you from, man?'

'Signy Base, in West Antarctica.'

Epilogue

The Road Goes Ever On

To my relief, Bob Hinings *was* in Cape Town and, from the moment he stumped into the yacht club lounge, profanely calling for me, I began to feel better. Hospitality surrounded me on every side but it was Bob and his daughter Annlee who really brought me back on to an even keel. To the kindness of those two people I owe more than I can say.

Things soon appeared in a truer perspective. *Ice Bird* had circumnavigated two-thirds of Antarctica during the whole of her ten thousand miles and more of voyaging and had been the very first vessel to convey a lone man to and from Antarctica. She had successfully breached the sea's last frontier.

Nor had the yacht's showing in her second Antarctic season been negligible. In the pack and the continental ice she had acquitted herself nobly. True, the 3,354 miles from Signy had taken her a full ten weeks, certainly no record, but three of those weeks had been spent among the crowded bergs and another three in sailing 814 miles under jury rig.

All in all, it seemed that the destiny of my personal dreaming had been pretty well fulfilled. And it is at this point that I, myself, retire from the stage. But the enterprise itself was bigger than me. It was not yet over.

I was racking my brains as to the best way of getting *Ice Bird* back to Australia, for my free interlude between jobs had been stretched to the uttermost. Could she be sailed home at some future date or, perhaps, shipped aboard a freighter?

At this point I was called to the telephone. It was my son Barry from Sydney. 'I hear you are flying back here. What are you going to do about *Ice Bird*, David?'

'I may ship her.'

'Have you thought of *my* sailing her back?'

'No, I hadn't. Would you like to?'

'Oh, *yes*.' The longing in the young man's voice came clearly across five thousand miles of space. A load lifted from my mind and I felt gratitude flood through me in the instant acceptance of this as the answer. Yes, the older generation had done all it could; here was the younger offering to take over the burden and the challenge.

'It would make me happier than anything I can think of to hand over to you, Barry,' I answered sincerely, and with simple truth.

Now, as I conclude this story in a different world – the cab of my Land-Rover at a desert rock hole (appropriately enough, an Old Man's Dreaming), with my Pintubi companions asleep by the campfire – Barry has been for two months in Cape Town, re-fitting *Ice Bird*. Her new mast, he writes, is an immensely strong one, specially stayed, and everything possible is being done to profit by previous lessons to ensure that the yacht is more sea-worthy than ever before. He will soon be setting sail for Sydney.

So, while the man who manned her has changed, the faithful *Ice Bird* is carrying on with her voyaging under the command of my successor. The adventure goes on. Tolkien eloquently ex-presses this universal continuity:

> The Road goes ever on and on
> Down from the door where it began,
> Now far ahead the road has gone,
>   And I must follow, if I can,
> Pursuing it with weary feet,
>   Until it joins some larger way,
> Where many paths and errands meet.
>   And whither then? I cannot say.

Barry Lewis at the helm of *Ice Bird* on his
arrival in Sydney after making the 6,000
mile passage from Cape Town single-
handed in 86 days.

Umari rock hole, Central Australia Aboriginal Reserve
August 1974

Appendix

Storm Handling

In certain respects only would I alter the procedures I adopted this year. I would again use an improvised sea anchor, made up and stowed ready for streaming from the stern, with no more preliminaries needed than a quick knife slash. But now I would fit a strut or a strop to keep it well clear of the self-steering gear.

An Aries self-steering gear (and no doubt, a number of other designs) can, in strong winds, exert far more force on the tiller than a man. It would seem logical, then, to keep it in operation all through a storm, but to substitute a stronger vane (? metal) for the standard thin plywood and, in any case, to carry several spare vanes. (I am thinking primarily of the lone seaman, since a gale is liable considerably to outlast his ability to hand steer.)

The most important change I would make, however, would be to set the tiny storm jib athwartships, the tack hanked to an off-set removable inner forestay and the clew bowsed down to a ringbolt on the other side of the deck. This would allow of the yacht's being run off more nearly, or directly, down-wind and to gybe or be thrown a-back with impunity. (It is hard to credit the shock of gybing even so minute a sail as a hard-sheeted thirty square-foot storm jib in a hurricane. The sail crashes across like a rifle shot, causing the tormented mast to whip and the whole boat to shudder.)

It is worth noting that capsizing, due to freak seas or storms of hurricane intensity, is not so very uncommon, especially in the Southern Ocean. In addition to the incidents mentioned in the book: Jean Gau's Tahiti ketch was capsized and dismasted off Cape Agulhas (the tip of Africa); Marcel Bardiaux turned over twice near Cape Horn; Bill Nance's *Cardinal Vertue* was flung on to her cabin top south of Cape Leeuwin (Western Australia); Bill King's *Galway Blazer* was hurled over upside down off South Africa; Chris Baronowski's *Polonaise* pitchpoled in the South Indian Ocean (Southern Ocean). This is nothing remotely like an exhaustive list – merely examples that happen to spring to mind, often because I know the protagonists. Nor are yachts altogether immune outside the Southern Ocean. It was in the tropical Mozambique channel that Bruce Dalling's *Vertue* was turned over, and off New South Wales that Roger Hopkin's *Gallivanter*, sister ship to *Ice Bird*, suffered the same mischance. While it is obviously desirable that a yacht venturing south of the forties should be self-righting and as strong above the water-line as below (preferably as nearly flush decked as possible), it is the mast that is the usual casualty in a capsize. Can anything be done to safeguard it? I would personally fit a short mast of about double the usual cross section, for in both my Southern Ocean dismastings the standing rigging remained intact while the mast itself broke. This is easy to understand. Normal sailing produces a compression loading on the mast; the rigging is designed accordingly and so gives little support to a mast subjected to the predominantly lateral stress of a capsize. A single or double pair of jumper struts, jutting out laterally on each side of the mast below the spreaders, should give the spar the required lateral support.

Exposure to Wet Cold

At +10°C. a wind of 40 km/hr (25 m.p.h.), which is only a *strong breeze*, produces by convection the same heat loss from the un-protected skin as would be lost in windless conditions at −30°C. Wet skin, because of greatly increased evaporation, loses heat much faster than dry (*Death by Exposure*, 1972). (See Appendix References p.218 for full details of books quoted herein.) The problem of finding suitable clothing for polar yachtsmen is not easy, since it must insulate against the wind-chill of gales and also offer protection against wetting from sleet and snow, spray and solid water – all in sub-zero temperatures.

Clothing insulates mainly by virtue of air trapped in the interstices of its layers. The more layers, the more air pockets and the greater the possibilities for moisture due to sweating to dissipate or be evaporated. Even in Arctic conditions the amount of water a man loses each day through 'insensible perspiration' is far from negligible, being of the order of 500 ml (0.9 pint) in resting conditions, and its evaporation accounting for a quarter of his daily heat loss. (Adam and Goldsmith, 1965, p. 253.) Excess sweating multiplies the loss of fluid and heat. The significance of this perspiration is, (1) If the water vapour cannot escape outward, underwear becomes moist and, in extreme conditions, may freeze. However, even moist clothing retains some insulating properties and, provided it is enclosed by an outer impervious layer, heat loss will be stabilized at a low level – at the cost of a little discomfort – the 'wet suit principle' discussed at the beginning of the Life Raft section. (2) In survival conditions at sea, *any* loss of body water is disadvantageous.

Modern synthetic materials are light, provide a high degree of thermal insulation and, at the same time, can transmit water vapour while themselves being water repellent. I was immeasurably better equipped with clothes and sleeping bags and infinitely more comfortable this season than last. I usually wore a skivvy or string vest and nylon briefs next to the skin. Acrilan pile or similar underwear would have been better in anything approaching polar winter conditions (Whittington, 1965, 157–8). Next came two woollen jerseys, quilted Teijin under-jacket and under-trousers, thick Teijin trousers and fur-trimmed Teijin parka. Waterproof overtrousers (Marlin) usually had to be worn over the quilted Teijin ones on deck in the open sea. The Teijin parka was very warm and spray-proof but not waterproof. It was too bulky to fit under my waterproof Marlin Ocean Master jacket so, when the weather dictated the need for the Marlin, a thinner quilted Terylene anorak had first to be substituted for the parka.

For small boats in sub-Antarctic waters (though not for mountaineering and sledging parties), *down*-filled quilted garments are

inferior to *synthetic*-filled ones, because the former readily become
wet and soggy and are extremely difficult to dry.

It was often necessary, aboard *Ice Bird* in periods of bad weather,
to wear the fully waterproof Marlin overgarments for days and
nights on end. This caused considerable condensation next to the
skin, so that the innermost layers of clothing became and remained wet for long periods, but the next layers out were merely
damp and the outermost impervious coverings prevented much
heat from escaping and were windproof when I was on deck.
In other words, evaporation and condensation were both effectively controlled (the wet suit principle again). Whenever possible,
however, I removed, or at least loosened, the waterproofs in the
cabin, when my own body heat would in time dry out the under-
garments.

Insulated Arctic rubber boots, of the same basic type, but with
more efficient insulation and better fitting than those I was loaned
the first season, were available to me this year (the makes were
American). Worn with very thin socks they were an absolute boon.
Usually conditions allowed me to remove them before getting
into my sleeping bag at night or, at the very least, to loose the
laces for a while. This was in welcome contrast to the constant
wet feet that had earlier been dictated by the inability of my frostbitten fingers to loosen laces.

The amount of heat that can be lost from the unprotected head
has often been underestimated. In fact it has been shown that, at
$-4°C.$, heat loss from the head can account for half a man's
resting heat production (Edwards and Burton, 1960, cited by
Whittington, 1965, p. 158). I found that my Japanese fur hat,
with ear flaps and strings to tie under the chin, was a godsend –
even if it did so often fall down over my eyes. A Balaclava helmet
proved much inferior.

Readers cannot fail to be aware of the overriding importance
of protecting the hands. As a rule everything on deck was soaking
wet; in the cabin general dampness was the rule. The solution, as
Arthur Owens showed me at Palmer, was to wear heavy fleece-
lined industrial rubber gloves over finely knitted woollen ones.
Even so, at least half a dozen pairs of each should be carried on a
long polar voyage for, within two months, both my pairs of

rubber gloves were punctured and my best woollen ones were in shreds. Standard Arctic fur-lined mitts were welcome wear during the hours spent in the companion-way on the lookout or steering. Sometimes I wore them when sitting below. Their main disadvantage was that they were not waterproof and I had no means of drying them once they got wet. Moreover, they were too bulky and clumsy for a variety of tasks.

To sum up: during the voyage's second season my clothing and sleeping bag came very close to the ideal. I could suggest no improvement. (The value of a wet suit will be considered under 'Life Rafts'.)

Apart from the *personal* insulation we have been considering, the yacht's enclosed cabin protected me from the convection heat loss of wind-chill and, by keeping out snow and salt water and restricting the escape of relatively warm air from the cabin, reduced heat loss from evaporation. This function would have been better subserved had the whole interior been lined with half an inch or so of a modern insulating material (instead of the roof only being lined).

A coke or diesel stove would have increased comfort and provided welcome clothes-drying facilities. In a boat of *Ice Bird*'s size, however, the problem of carrying sufficient fuel for a long passage would be difficult. Indeed, given clothing of the standard available this season, cabin heating would be more luxury than real need.

Health and Medical Kit for Long Cold Voyages

I do not propose to consider minor ailments that clear up spontaneously, but will concentrate on conditions requiring effective prevention and treatment. Before going into details two generalizations are worth noting:

First generalization: in stress situations *individual determination* is probably the greatest single survival factor. Thus Dr David Jones, who made a detailed study of the biochemical indices of fitness of his companions on a particularly arduous ascent of Annapurna, noted that one particular climber fulfilled his role, reaching a level of 24,000 feet, though 'he proved to be the *least fit* of the summit group' (Jones, pers. comm., 1974. My italics).

Similarly, Eric Lee sums up his vast experience as secretary of the Naval Lifesaving Committee, when he states: 'Men with a minimum of equipment, but with a strong will to live, have survived for long periods, whereas other men with ample equipment have succumbed in less' (E. C. B. and K. Lee, 1971, p. 161).

Second generalization: *Exhaustion begets errors of judgement.* This was demonstrated only too well by my extraordinary failure to recognize the onset of frostbite (see chapter 4, part 2). Studies conducted during single-handed transatlantic races have amply confirmed the correlation between tiredness and impairment of judgement (Bennet, 1973, pp. 7–10 and 17–18 and H. E. Lewis *et al*, 1964).

Since we are not concerned with 'First Aid' in the usual sense, which presupposes the availability of medical assistance within a matter of hours, but with individuals in total isolation, the remedies recommended will be powerful and effective. The list below is not exhaustive and equally useful alternatives exist to many of the examples suggested; also new drugs are constantly being developed. Not only must the circumstances of a particular voyage be taken into account but the personal medical needs of the individuals taking part. For this reason, the would-be voyager would be well advised to consult a doctor about any special requirements and to regard the recommendations that follow as general rather than specific. I have drawn on Chap. XIII of *Exploration Medicine* (Lewis, 1965) and the medical appendices of two of my earlier books (Lewis 1961 and 1967), as well as on E. C. B. and K. Lee, (1971, pp. 256–60). I am indebted to doctors K. Goulston and A. R. Shephard, both of Canberra, for bringing my pharmacology up to date. But I must stress, in fairness to them, that the final decisions on recommendations are my responsibility alone.

Maintenance of health

Crews of small craft usually remain healthy and injuries heal readily if left to themselves. The only deficiency condition to be considered is scurvy and this can readily be prevented, even in the absence of fresh or canned fruit, by taking one 50mgm tablet of ascorbic acid (vitamin C) daily.

A broad spectrum antibiotic

An ample supply of a drug of this class is an absolute 'must' for combating severe infections. In my opinion it is the most important single item in any ocean-going medical kit. *Tetracycline 250mgm capsules or tablets*, or one of its combinations – there are several brand names – would be my first choice. One or two capsules should be taken four times a day. Possibilities of over-dosage are negligible. Broad spectrum antibiotics are effective in such diverse conditions as *pneumonia* (a frequent sequel to the accident common to middle-aged yachtsmen – fractured ribs); infection following any *extensive burn*; *compound fractures*; *infections*, inflammations and abscesses in general; *appendicitis* (one Everest climber's appendicitis was controlled sufficiently by Tetracycline for him to climb the mountain and delay his operation until his return to India). The antibiotic's use in double doses saved my frostbitten fingers from permanent damage and performed a like service for *National Geographic* photographer Bill Curtsinger's shark bites six months later.

Pain relievers

I would place next on the list *Morphine* injected intramuscularly in 15mgm tubonic ampoules with needle attached, is the most potent (and incapacitating) agent for the agonizing pain of really severe burns, wounds, compound fractures and the like. It is of little use, however, for the single-hander, who must remain alert and mobile.

Pethidine, 50mgm tablets, one or two as required and *Methadone* (*Physeptone*), 5mgm tablets, one or two as required, are both very powerful pain relievers and far less incapacitating than morphine. Both are suitable for single-handers.

Dextrapropoxyphene napsylate (*Doloxene* – Lilly) in doses of 100mgm six-hourly is, despite its intimidating name, an extremely useful medium-strength pain reliever that does not cause dizziness.

The *Acetylsalicylic* (*aspirin*) group of compounds (except for the few people who are sensitive to them) are useful stand-bys for milder conditions.

Bowel infections and 'food poisoning'

Sulphadimidine or *Succinylsulphathiazole*, ½g. tablets, two to be taken four times a day, will usually be effective.

Eyes

Salt-reddened eyes are best bathed in fresh water. Actual infections, after bathing as above, will benefit from a little *Neomycin and Hydrocortisone eye ointment* (various brand names) squeezed into the corner of the eye.

To anaesthetize the eye for allowing the removal of foreign bodies (or to dull the agony if they are too deeply embedded), *Amethocaine hydrochloride* 0.5 per cent supplied as single-dose disposable units, e.g. *'Minims'* (Smith and nephew) may be used. An alternative (on individual prescription only) is *5 per cent Cocaine eye drops*.

Skin

Daily washing with fresh water, when available, is the ideal prophylactic.

An antiseptic cream like *Dibromopropamidine* 25g. tubes is excellent and does not produce allergic reactions. (A generous supply should be carried for use in possible burns.)

Protection from *sun glare* may be needed in heavy pack ice or ashore on glaciers. The impressively named *Isoamyl–pN,N–Dimethylamino-Benzoate in 70 per cent alcohol* comes under various trade names such as *'Block Out'*.

Seasickness

The malady affects many yachtsmen when they first put to sea. A minority fail to develop much immunity later. In survival situations, where water is scarce, particularly with the unaccustomed violent motion of a life raft in a gale, the wastage of fluid through vomiting may easily tip the scale.

Note: Seasickness remedies show great individual variation, both in their effectiveness in different individuals and in the degree of drowsiness they all tend to produce. Only practical trial can show which is best for a particular person.

Hyoscine Hydrobromide o.3mgm tablets, two tablets, up to an hour before or immediately on exposure and six-hourly thereafter if required, has come out particularly well in tests conducted by the Royal Navy (E. C. B. and K. Lee, 1971, p. 259).

Combinations of Hyoscine and antihistamines can also be very effective. Two examples are:

Benacine tablets (Parke Davis), containing *Diphenhydramine Hydrochloride* 25mgm and *Hyoscine Hydrobromide* o.33mgm. One tablet half an hour before exposure, then six-hourly if required.

Travcalm tablets (Hamilton), containing *Dimenhydrinate* 50mgm, *Hyoscine Hydrobromide* o.2mgm, and *Caffeine* 20mgm. One or two tablets half an hour before exposure, then six-hourly if required.

Prochlorperazine (*Stematil*, M. and B.), 5mgm tablets. One or two tablets, three times a day. This is a different type of chemical from the others. It can be useful, though sometimes incapacitating, in intractable cases of seasickness.

Stimulants to keep Single-Handers Awake

Only once, when approaching Cape Town during my second consecutive sleepless night, have I used stimulants. They kept me alert and wide awake and I regretted their lack during the approach to Palmer the year before.

It must be stressed that these are dangerous drugs, not to be used lightly. They require an individual prescription.

Dextoamphetamine Sulphate 5mgm tablets. One three times a day. This is an extremely powerful sleep antagonist.

Methylphenidate Hydrochloride, 10mgm tablets (*Ritalin*, Ciba), is a less drastic alternative. The dose is two tablets three times a day.

Note re Alcohol: it should be remembered that alcohol is a *depressant* not a stimulant and could impair wakefulness in situations like the above. It is quickly metabolized in conditions of intense cold, but it would be best reserved for less perilous circumstances, when its positive effect on morale may make it worthwhile. Individual preference and habit are the best guides.

Accidents

Fractures: inflatable splints, such as those manufactured by Protector Safety Products, are a great advance on anything previously available. All fractures demand pain relievers and, if major, especially compound (open wound down to bone), full doses of antibiotics, as well, to combat infection.

Fractured ribs: these should never be strapped up as this procedure restricts breathing and is a sure road to pneumonia. Pain relievers and antibiotics are all that are needed.

Fractured arms: after having been immobilized by splinting, broken arms at sea are best strapped or bandaged to the body. Otherwise, at any sudden lurch, the arm will instinctively shoot out to grasp the nearest object for support – with inevitable further injury.

Fractured legs: inflatable splints really come into their own here.

Extensive burns: the local antiseptic cream mentioned under 'Skin', *Dibromopropamidine*, should be applied liberally, after gentle cleansing of the burnt area – with fresh water if necessary – and covered with gauze dressing pads, cotton wool and crêpe bandages. Pain relievers and full doses of antibiotics are essential and the loss of fluid that occurs through the damaged skin should be made good, as far as possible, with frequent drinks.

Dressings suggested:

    Waterproof adhesive bandages (for minor injuries)
    Gauze dressing pads
    Cotton wool
    Crêpe bandages, three-inch
    A pair of blunt-pointed scissors
    N.B. No quantities are recommended as they will depend on the number of people at risk and the length of the voyage.

Radio

Conventional SSB radio transmitters designed for yachts and fishing boats have two major defects in small vessels on major ocean passages across stormy waters. Firstly, the saturated salt-laden air that fills the cabin, especially in high latitudes, penetrates the most carefully designed cases and soaks and corrodes the delicate wiring to an unbelievable extent. Secondly, keeping batteries fully charged is never easy in a sailing boat, even with a separate generator. This is probably because the wet, salty atmosphere impairs the conduction of leads and terminals. The generally rough and overcast weather of the Southern Ocean aggravates the problem.

I did not discover until much too late that there do exist at least two transceivers, both designed for polar use, that are in every way suitable for ocean yachtsmen. Both are weather-proof and have their own dry batteries. Even though their theoretical range is less than some run-of-the-mill sets, their absolute reliability and robustness make them ideal for such voyages as *Ice Bird*'s. They are:

The Racal Squadcal 5 Watt Transceiver. This has its own batteries, is impervious even to the driven snow of antarctic blizzards, and is standard British Antarctic Survey and ANARE (Australian) equipment. It is British made.

The Patrolphone. Model SC-120. This appears to be an American equivalent to the 'Squadcal'. It is manufactured by South Como. International of Escondido, California.

Though it is usually easy, either through the Admiralty List of Radio Signals or the publications of national governments, to ascertain the frequencies (and hence the required crystals) used in the countries to be visited, the Antarctic Peninsula is an exception. The 4067 KHz frequency, on which the British and American stations communicate each evening, does not appear to be listed anywhere.

An Inflatable Life raft for Self-help

The principle of the completely covered-in inflatable life raft (it should have a double floor in polar seas) is exactly the same as that of the wet suit. Convection heat loss is checked by the in-flated sides, floor and (preferably) roof, in the one case, and by the air cells in the Neoprene of the wet suit in the other.

Even if he has just climbed into the covered raft from icy water, the survivor's body heat production soon raises the tem-perature of the moist air inside the enclosure to a reasonable level (creates a fug); similarly, the thin water layer inside the wet suit warms rapidly to body temperature and thereafter is maintained by the insulation of the Neoprene. *The combination of a wet suit and covered inflatable life raft is, therefore, ideal for Arctic survival.*

The great snag with existing covered life rafts, however, is that they are designed to stay put, on the assumption that help, summoned by radio, will arrive within days. This is often the case in ocean races, which are generally run not too far offshore and are sometimes escorted. Such circumstances are in no way comparable with those of a lone craft in mid-ocean, probably out of radio range (even if the radio and batteries were not the most likely first casualties in a leaking vessel).

The ocean cruiser is on his own. (In fact, I am dubious of the morality of voluntarily setting out, allowing a situation to get out of hand and then demanding assistance.) He must think in terms of self-help – indeed, he should have been doing so all along.

But how *can* he help himself when even the most expensive circular covered-in inflatable that he can buy, though it may keep him alive for a long time in mid ocean, cannot be sailed or directed towards land? It is perhaps unreal to expect manufacturers to produce a *sailable*, *steerable*, covered-in inflatable for a miniscule market (though the passive rescue philosophy would often be inapplicable to service personnel in wartime), so the immediate problem is one of improvization. Several possible solutions present themselves.

One: Any of the larger models of inflatable boat (Avon, Zodiac, Gemini, etc.) could carry one of the very smallest of the circular (or preferably oval) covered-in rafts inside it. A tiny protective cabin would thus be provided.

Two: More satisfactory, would be the incorporation of an inflatable enclosed canopy in the manufacturing stage of an otherwise standard large sized inflatable boat. Obviously, some 'outside' space would have to be left for 'working ship'. This would be an excellent and not too expensive solution.

Three: Longitudinal cylindrical inflatable pontoons could be attached along either side of an inflatable life raft, so providing it with hulls of a sort, rather after the manner of a primitive catamaran. Again this modification would ideally be carried out during manufacture, but the contraption could be assembled when afloat (in Arctic waters by a wet-suited crew) at leisure, once the original storm had been ridden out.

Rigging a mast, sail and steering oar to any of the above would be a relatively simple matter, provided the necessary equipment had been collected beforehand.

Miscellaneous Survival Data

Immersion times in Cold Water

Survival times vary enormously according to a person's protective clothing, constitution and will. On the one hand, sudden death has been recorded from immersion in icy water; unconsciousness, due to the shock abruptly lowering the blood pressure, is followed by slowing, irregular action and finally stopping of the heart (Lee, E. C. B. and Lee, K., 1971, p. 51). At the other extreme we saw in Chap. 7, part 3, how Ian Smith struggled through sub-zero water for a remarkable one and three-quarter hours. Apart from his own build and courage, he undoubtedly owed his life to the fact that he was well insulated by about the best protective clothing, short of a wet suit, he could have had.

So while zero temperature water must never be taken lightly, the so-called 'maximum survival times' issued by some authorities for much warmer waters are so ludicrously short as to undermine a victim's most potent weapon, his determination to live. This is wholly mischievous. People should be told the physiological truth as far as we know it.

The case of Dr MacBain, whose ship was sunk on an Arctic convoy is probably as typical as any single incident could be. His description is all the more valuable for its clinical precision. The doctor was immersed, fully clothed, in water at 0°C. (32°F.) and was in the sea fifteen minutes before being able to board a wooden float. Skin anaesthesia was complete up to the neck, joint sense was impaired and his fingers and toes were white and dead. Massage and rowing restored sensation rapidly and painlessly except in the fingers, where sensation returned slowly over two months. It should be noted that his refuge was a simple float platform not a covered raft (Lee, E. C. B. and K. Lee, 1971, p. 53).

Water requirements

Usual issue: about 2.5 litres (one-half gallon) of water per man per day is generally allowed for total consumption as drink and in the preparation of food. Double this is ideally carried to cope with emergencies.

Note that the reconstitution of dehydrated food is not catered for in the half gallon daily estimate, nor is any but a bare minimum for washing. The amount suggested may be inadequate in the tropics. It is of interest that two gallons of water per man per day for all purposes is said to have been the allowance in Nelson's navy (Lewis, 1965, 340).

In this season's (1974) cruise, during the seven weeks in Antarctic and sub-Antarctic waters, between the South Orkneys and my last capsize (after which I used water *ad lib*), under a regime of provident conservation but without actual rationing, my average daily fluid intake was 1.1 litres (1.8 pints).

Emergency Water: it will be recalled that in 1973 I instituted strict fluid rationing for three weeks until it had become clear that there was a sufficient reserve in hand.

I followed the standard practice of drinking nothing at all for the first 24 hours to reduce the kidneys' output to a minimum and, thereafter, adjusted intake so that my urine remained dark (concentrated). While I was constantly conscious of thirst, and plagued by it after exercise, I remained in fluid balance on an average daily intake of 0.7 litres (700m.), or about 1¼ pints total liquids per day. This was actually a little under the 900ml. generally taken as the minimum to maintain fluid balance. Probably the difference was due to sub-Antarctic conditions, where reduction in sweating more than made up for streaming nasal mucus membranes.

As little as 500ml (⅘ pint) per day will maintain a person for a time. Eventually, however, he will deteriorate (Lewis, 1961, 153–4).

Emergency Life raft Supplies

A useful procedure is to attach to the life-raft with stout cords a number of plastic jerrycans filled (completely) with fresh water. When the raft is thrown over the side and inflates, the plastic cans are tossed after it. As they and their contents are lighter than sea water they will float. They may be pulled aboard the raft when convenient (Lewis, 1965, 345).

Life raft solid rations should consist *entirely* of carbohydrates (sugary and starchy foods) and include *no* protein or fat whatsoever. This is very important, because water must be withdrawn from the tissues to help eliminate the end products of the metabolism of protein or fat; whereas carbohydrates spare water, a small amount actually being converted into it in the tissues (Nicholl, 1960).

Appendix References

Adam, J. M., and Goldsmith, R. 1965, 'Cold Climates', chap. X in *Exploration Medicine*, (ed.) O. G. Edholm and A. L. Bacharach, Bristol, Wright, p. 253.

Bennet, G., 1973, 'Medical and Psychological Problems in the 1972 Singlehanded transatlantic yacht race', *The Lancet*, October 1973.

Death by Exposure, 1972, leaflet issued by the Federation of Victorian Walking Clubs, Melbourne.

Edwards, M., and Burton, A. C., 1960, *J. Appl. Physiol.*, 15, 209, cited by Whittington, P., 1965, in *Exploration Medicine*, p. 158.

Jones, D. P. M., M.D. Thesis, University of Wales 1974. Summary by courtesy of Dr Jones, personal communication.

Lee, E. C. B., and Lee, K., 1971, *Safety and Survival at Sea*, London, Giniger in association with Cassell.

Lewis, H. E., Harries, J. M., Lewis, D. H., de Monchaux, C., 1964, 'Voluntary Solitude', *The Lancet*, 1, p. 143.

Lewis, D. H., 1961, *The Ship Would Not Travel Due West*, Appendix, 'Polar Bear Bites and Sea Serpent Stings', London, Temple Press Books.

—, 1965, 'Small Boats at Sea', chap XII in *Exploration Medicine*, (ed.) O. G. Edholm and A. L. Bacharach, Bristol, Wright, pp. 338–47.

—, 1967, *Daughters of the Wind*, Medical appendix, London, Gollancz.

Nicholl, G. W. R., 1960, *Survival at Sea*. London, Adlard Coles in association with George Harrap and Co.

Whittingham, G., 1965, 'Problems of Survival', chap. VII in *Exploration Medicine*, (ed.) O. G. Edholm and A. L. Bacharach, Bristol, Wright.

Acknowledgements

People and Organizations

This list is necessarily incomplete because so very many people contributed to the venture that it would be impossible to thank them all;
a number of names and addresses were destroyed in the first capsize;
even more names and addresses are aboard *Ice Bird*, now at sea under
Barry's command and are hence unavailable to me. I hope the many
friends and helpers whose names must have been inadvertently omitted
will accept my sincere apologies.

Australia

I was helped beyond measure in my preparations by Jos Doel, Graham
Cox, Tim Curnow, Jack Muir, Sue Brierly, Dick Taylor (designer of
Ice Bird), Peter Cosgrove (former owner), John Goncz, Graeme Budd,
Heather Wain, Roger Hopkins, Lt-Cmdr Hall, Assistant Co-ordinator
Naval Safety, Chief Anderson, HMAS *Harman*, Dr Fowler, MO,
HMAS *Harman*, Brien Aylott, Naval liaison.

Truly princely gifts were the donation of food by Stan Fox, the gift
of a life raft by Jack Ingham and the gift of a Hasler self-steering gear
by Hope Costello.

I am greatly indebted to John Purnell of Canberra for gifts of a
sleeping bag, fleecy boots and snow goggles; Paddy Pallin of Sydney
for a Bogong sleeping bag and a rucksack; Marlin Co. for an Ocean
Master suit and a safety harness; Fesq and Co. for two cases of Red
Mill rum; Cantarella Bros. for a generous supply of wine; Protector
Safety Products for inflatable splints; International Red Hand for
paint; Racal Electronics for the loan of a transmitter; Air Vice Marshal
Cleary for his help in obtaining de-icing fluid; Civic Trading Centre
for discount goods; Les Cass for fishing gear; Fiona Lewis for my
invaluable Omega watch; Ruth Loveday for a fur coat; Jack Tranning
for a hand bearing compass (unfortunately I have lost the name of the
maker of my WWV radio); Nick and Julia Wilson, fleecy boots. Peter
Parsons painted my kiwi-kangaroo panel; Mr Phillpot of the Bureau
of Meteorology in Melbourne guided me through the mazes of sub-
Antarctic weather charts.

United Kingdom

Merton Naydler, to whom, as the reader will realize, I owe so much; Mrs Dean, secretary to Merton, who procured my second season's supplies; Michael Richey, Secretary Royal Institute of Navigation; Sir Vivian Fuchs and Mr D. R. Gipps of British Antarctic Survey; Dr G. de Q. Robin and Dr Charles Swithinbank of the Scott Polar Research Institute.

Thos. Walker and Sons (Mr Bishop) presented me with an anemometer; Clifford Snell (Mr Newman) provided an emergency transmitter; Kelvin Hughes Ltd. provided charts at cost price.

USA

The Secretary of the Department of the Navy, The National Science Foundation Office of Polar Programmes, especially Capt. Price Lewis and Mr Phil Smith.

The Editor and staff of the *National Geographic Magazine*. Any selection among so many must be invidious but I must mention Mel and Gil Grosvenor, Bill Garrett, Luis Marden, Joe Judge and Dave Arnold among a host of others. The magazine, apart from other assistance, provided me with an Aries self-steering gear.

Uniroyal Inc., N.Y. gave me a pair of insulated Oneida boots.

Japan

Dr Tetsuya Torii, Executive Secretary of the Japan Polar Research Association, personally arranged for the most generous gifts of a double Antarctic sleeping bag and a full set of Antarctic quilted clothing and accessories from the Teijin Co. and for a Seiko Diver's watch from the Hattori Watch Co. I am most indebted to these companies.

New Zealand

Pat Southern of Auckland. W. C. Crookshanks, Police Constable, Half Moon Bay, and Michael Gomes also of Half Moon Bay, as well as many others.

Chile

The Chilean Embassy in Canberra generously donated a full set of charts.

Aboard Lindblad Explorer

Anne Ryan. John Darby. A host of friends.

Aboard RRS *John Biscoe*

I can only express my appreciation to the Captain and crew and the FIDS (British Antarctic Survey personnel) for kindnesses too numerous to mention.

Palmer Antarctic Station

Jim Evans; Melvin Williamson (Willie); Kent Yates; Pat Smith; Charles Sandau (Sandy); Lloyd Jukkola; Paul Morgan; Al Giannini; Doc Spencer; Charles Thornhill; Phil Halley; Robert Houston; Jack Ames; Gary Cadle; Tom Kauffman; David Murrish; Arthur Owens; Erb Koenig and Dallas Smith.

The masters of the US ships *Marfak* and *Hero*.

Argentine Base Almirante Brown

The commander and entire personnel, especially Armando and Roberto (names of the base personnel are aboard *Ice Bird*).

Signy Base, South Orkney Islands

The commander and entire personnel, especially Ian Collinge, Ian Smith, Dave Weller. (As with Almirante Brown, the same circumstance applies.)

Cape Town

Bob Hinings and his daughter Annlee Hollard. Joan Fry, Secretary to the Yacht Club. The MacKays, Syndercombes and the rest of the helpful yachting community.

For Help in Preparing this Book

The heavy task of typing the various drafts was undertaken by Rosamund Walsh, Rose Wolfhope, Doug Munro and Mrs R. Spate.

The maps were the work of Mr Pancino of the Geography Department of the Australian National University.

Meredith Ardley and Danielle Bugnon made invaluable criticisms of early drafts of the manuscript.

I wish to thank the *National Geographic Magazine*, the artist Mr Noel Sickles and all those whose photographs appear (I hope, correctly attributed) for their extreme generosity in allowing me to reproduce their pictures.

Literary Sources

The opening quotation from T. E. Lawrence is from *The Seven Pillars of Wisdom*, by permission of Jonathan Cape Ltd., courtesy of the executors of the T. E. Lawrence estate.

The closing lines on p. 202 are from the poem 'The Road Goes Ever On' by J. R. R. Tolkien in the *Lord of the Rings*, by permission of George Allen and Unwin Ltd.

The quotations from the *Antarctic Pilot* are by permission of the Hydrographer of the Navy, Hydrographic Department, Ministry of Defence, Taunton, Somerset.

The verse by Louis MacNiece is from 'Bagpipe Music' in *The Earth Compels, Collected Poems of Louis MacNiece*, by permission of Faber and Faber Ltd.

The verse by Wilfred Noyce is from *Springs of Adventure*, by permission of John Murray. (Publishers) Ltd.

Data on the Antarctic Peninsula region are largely culled from the *Antarctic Pilot*, *Polar Record* (15 May 1971), Marie and John Darby, 1971, *Islands of the Scotia Arc and the Antarctic Peninsula*, Lindblad Travel, New York, *Soviet Geography*, *Atlas of Antarctica*, 1966 Moscow, 1967 New York, American Geographic Society.

Accounts of small boat voyages in the Southern Ocean are mainly abstracted from Capt. W. H. S. Jones, 1956, *The Cape Horn Breed*, London, Jarrolds Publishers Ltd., Charles Borden, 1967, *Sea Quest*, Philadelphia: Macrae Smith, H. W. Tilman, 1968, *Mischief Goes South*, Hollis & Carter, Ltd. and articles in *Modern Boating* and *Seacraft*.